Nutshell Series

of

WEST PUBLISHING COMPANY

P.O. Box 3526

St. Paul, Minnesota 55165

June, 1982

I

Community Property, 1982, 423 pages, by Robert L. Mennell, Professor of Law, Hamline University.

Comparative Legal Traditions, 1982, 402 pages, by Mary Ann Glendon, Professor of Law, Boston College, Michael Wallace Gordon, Professor of Law, University of Florida and Christopher Osakwe, Professor of Law, Tulane University.

Conflicts, 1982, 469 pages, by David D. Siegel, Professor of Law, Albany Law School, Union University.

Constitutional Analysis, 1979, 388 pages, by Jerre S. Williams, Professor of Law Emeritus, University of Texas.

Constitutional Power—Federal and State, 1974, 411 pages, by David E. Engdahl, Professor of Law, University of Puget Sound.

Consumer Law, 2nd Ed., 1981, 418 pages, by David G. Epstein, Professor of Law, University of Texas and Steve H. Nickles, Professor of Law, University of Arkansas.

Contracts, 1975, 307 pages, by Gordon D. Schaber, Dean and Professor of Law, McGeorge School of Law and Claude D. Rohwer, Professor of Law, McGeorge School of Law.

Contract Remedies, 1981, 323 pages, by Jane M. Friedman, Professor of Law, Wayne State University.

Corporations—Law of, 1980, 379 pages, by Robert W. Hamilton, Professor of Law, University of Texas.

Corrections and Prisoners' Rights—Law of, 1976, 353 pages, by Sheldon Krantz, Dean and Professor of Law, University of San Diego.

Criminal Law, 1975, 302 pages, by Arnold H. Loewy, Professor of Law, University of North Carolina.

Criminal Procedure—Constitutional Limitations, 3rd Ed., 1980, 438 pages, by Jerold H. Israel, Professor of Law, University of Michigan and Wayne R. LaFave, Professor of Law, University of Illinois.

7.95

Debtor-Creditor Law, 2nd Ed., 1980, 324 pages, by David G. Epstein, Professor of Law, University of Texas.

Employment Discrimination—Federal Law of, 2nd Ed., 1981, 402 pages, by Mack A. Player, Professor of Law, University of Georgia.

Energy Law, 1981, 338 pages, by Joseph P. Tomain, Professor of Law, Drake University.

Estate Planning—Introduction to, 2nd Ed., 1978, 378 pages, by Robert J. Lynn, Professor of Law, Ohio State University.

Evidence, Federal Rules of, 1981, 428 pages, by Michael H. Graham, Professor of Law, University of Illinois.

Evidence, State and Federal Rules, 2nd Ed., 1981, 514 pages, by Paul F. Rothstein, Professor of Law, Georgetown University.

Family Law, 1977, 400 pages, by Harry D. Krause, Professor of Law, University of Illinois.

Federal Estate and Gift Taxation, 2nd Ed., 1979, 488 pages, by John K. McNulty, Professor of Law, University of California, Berkeley.

Federal Income Taxation of Individuals, 2nd Ed., 1978, 422 pages, by John K. McNulty, Professor of Law, University of California, Berkeley.

Federal Income Taxation of Corporations and Stockholders, 2nd Ed., 1981, 362 pages, by Jonathan Sobeloff, Late Professor of Law, Georgetown University and Peter P. Weidenbruch, Jr., Professor of Law, Georgetown University.

Federal Jurisdiction, 2nd Ed., 1981, 258 pages, by David P. Currie, Professor of Law, University of Chicago.

Future Interests, 1981, 361 pages, by Lawrence W. Waggoner, Professor of Law, University of Michigan.

Government Contracts, 1979, 423 pages, by W. Noel Keyes, Professor of Law, Pepperdine University.

Historical Introduction to Anglo-American Law, 2nd Ed., 1973, 280 pages, by Frederick G. Kempin, Jr., Professor of Business Law, Wharton School of Finance and Commerce, University of Pennsylvania.

Injunctions, 1974, 264 pages, by John F. Dobbyn, Professor of Law, Villanova University.

Insurance Law, 1981, 281 pages, by John F. Dobbyn, Professor of Law, Villanova University.

International Business Transactions, 1981, 393 pages, by Donald T. Wilson, Professor of Law, Loyola University, Los Angeles.

Judicial Process, 1980, 292 pages, by William L. Reynolds, Professor of Law, University of Maryland.

Jurisdiction, 4th Ed., 1980, 232 pages, by Albert A. Ehrenzweig, Late Professor of Law, University of California, Berkeley, David W. Louisell, Late Professor of Law, University of California, Berkeley and Geoffrey C. Hazard, Jr., Professor of Law, Yale Law School.

Juvenile Courts, 2nd Ed., 1977, 275 pages, by Sanford J. Fox, Professor of Law, Boston College.

Labor Arbitration Law and Practice, 1979, 358 pages, by Dennis R. Nolan, Professor of Law, University of South Carolina.

Labor Law, 1979, 403 pages, by Douglas L. Leslie, Professor of Law, University of Virginia.

Land Use, 1978, 316 pages, by Robert R. Wright, Professor of Law, University of Arkansas, Little Rock and Susan Webber, Professor of Law, University of Arkansas, Little Rock.

Landlord and Tenant Law, 1979, 319 pages, by David S. Hill, Professor of Law, University of Colorado.

Law Study and Law Examinations—Introduction to, 1971, 389 pages, by Stanley V. Kinyon, Late Professor of Law, University of Minnesota.

Legal Interviewing and Counseling, 1976, 353 pages, by Thomas L. Shaffer, Professor of Law, Washington and Lee University.

Legal Research, 3rd Ed., 1978, 415 pages, by Morris L. Cohen, Professor of Law and Law Librarian, Yale University.

Legal Writing, 1982, 294 pages, by Dr. Lynn B. Squires, University of Washington School of Law and Marjorie Dick Rombauer, Professor of Law, University of Washington.

Legislative Law and Process, 1975, 279 pages, by Jack Davies, Professor of Law, William Mitchell College of Law.

Local Government Law, 1975, 386 pages, by David J. McCarthy, Jr., Dean and Professor of Law, Georgetown University.

Mass Communications Law, 1977, 431 pages, by Harvey L. Zuckman, Professor of Law, Catholic University and Martin J. Gaynes, Lecturer in Law, Temple University.

Medical Malpractice—The Law of, 1977, 340 pages, by Joseph H. King, Professor of Law, University of Tennessee.

Military Law, 1980, 378 pages, by Charles A. Shanor, Professor of Law, Emory University and Timothy P. Terrell, Professor of Law, Emory University.

Post-Conviction Remedies, 1978, 360 pages, by Robert Popper, Professor of Law, University of Missouri, Kansas City.

Presidential Power, 1977, 328 pages, by Arthur Selwyn Miller, Professor of Law Emeritus, George Washington University.

Procedure Before Trial, 1972, 258 pages, by Delmar Karlen, Professor of Law, College of William and Mary.

Titles—The Calculus of Interests, 1968, 277 pages, by Oval A. Phipps, Late Professor of Law, St. Louis University.

Torts—Injuries to Persons and Property, 1977, 434 pages, by Edward J. Kionka, Professor of Law, Southern Illinois University.

Torts—Injuries to Family, Social and Trade Relations, 1979, 358 pages, by Wex S. Malone, Professor of Law Emeritus, Louisiana State University.

Trial Advocacy, 1979, 402 pages, by Paul B. Bergman, Adjunct Professor of Law, University of California, Los Angeles.

Trial and Practice Skills, 1978, 346 pages, by Kenney F. Hegland, Professor of Law, University of Arizona.

Trial, The First—Where Do I Sit? What Do I Say?, 1982, 396 pages, by Steven H. Goldberg, Professor of Law, University of Minnesota.

Unfair Trade Practices, 1982, approx. 400 pages, by Charles R. McManis, Professor of Law, Washington University, St. Louis.

Uniform Commercial Code, 1975, 507 pages, by Bradford Stone, Professor of Law, Detroit College of Law.

Uniform Probate Code, 1978, 425 pages, by Lawrence H. Averill, Jr., Dean and Professor of Law, University of Arkansas, Little Rock.

Welfare Law—Structure and Entitlement, 1979, 455 pages, by Arthur B. LaFrance, Dean and Professor of Law, Lewis and Clark College, Northwestern School of Law.

Wills and Trusts, 1979, 392 pages, by Robert L. Mennell, Professor of Law, Hamline University.

Hornbook Series

and

Basic Legal Texts

of

WEST PUBLISHING COMPANY

P.O. Box 3526

St. Paul, Minnesota 55165

June, 1982

Administrative Law, Davis' Text on, 3rd Ed., 1972, 617 pages, by Kenneth Culp Davis, Professor of Law, University of San Diego.

Agency, Seavey's Hornbook on, 1964, 329 pages, by Warren A. Seavey, Late Professor of Law, Harvard University.

Agency and Partnership, Reuschlein & Gregory's Hornbook on the Law of, 1979 with 1981 Pocket Part, 625 pages, by Harold Gill Reuschlein, Professor of Law, St. Mary's University and William A. Gregory, Professor of Law, Southern Illinois University.

Antitrust, Sullivan's Hornbook on the Law of, 1977, 886 pages, by Lawrence A. Sullivan, Professor of Law, University of California, Berkeley.

Common Law Pleading, Koffler and Reppy's Hornbook on, 1969, 663 pages, by Joseph H. Koffler, Professor of Law, New York Law School and Alison Reppy, Late Dean and Professor of Law, New York Law School.

Common Law Pleading, Shipman's Hornbook on, 3rd Ed., 1923, 644 pages, by Henry W. Ballentine, Late Professor of Law, University of California, Berkeley.

Conflict of Laws, Scoles and Hay's Hornbook on, 1982, approx. 950 pages, by Eugene F. Scoles, Professor of Law, University of Illinois and Peter Hay, Dean and Professor of Law, University of Illinois.

Constitutional Law, Nowak, Rotunda and Young's Hornbook on, 1978 with 1982 Pocket Part, 974 pages, by John E. Nowak, Professor of Law, University of Illinois, Ronald D. Rotunda, Professor of Law, University of Illinois, and J. Nelson Young, Professor of Law, University of North Carolina.

Contracts, Calamari and Perillo's Hornbook on, 2nd Ed., 1977, 878 pages, by John D. Calamari, Professor of Law, Fordham University and Joseph M. Perillo, Professor of Law, Fordham University.

Contracts, Corbin's One Volume Student Ed., 1952, 1224 pages, by Arthur L. Corbin, Late Professor of Law, Yale University.

Contracts, Simpson's Hornbook on, 2nd Ed., 1965, 510 pages, by Laurence P. Simpson, Late Professor of Law, New York University.

Corporate Taxation, Kahn's Handbook on, 3rd Ed., Student Ed., Soft cover, 1981 with 1982 Supplement, 614 pages, by Douglas A. Kahn, Professor of Law, University of Michigan.

Corporations, Henn's Hornbook on, 2nd Ed., 1970, 956 pages, by Harry G. Henn, Professor of Law, Cornell University.

Criminal Law, LaFave and Scott's Hornbook on, 1972, 763 pages, by Wayne R. LaFave, Professor of Law, University of Illinois, and Austin Scott, Jr., Late Professor of Law, University of Colorado.

Damages, McCormick's Hornbook on, 1935, 811 pages, by Charles T. McCormick, Late Dean and Professor of Law, University of Texas.

Domestic Relations, Clark's Hornbook on, 1968, 754 pages, by Homer H. Clark, Jr., Professor of Law, University of Colorado.

Environmental Law, Rodgers' Hornbook on, 1977, 956 pages, by William H. Rodgers, Jr., Professor of Law, University of Washington.

Estate and Gift Taxes, Lowndes, Kramer and McCord's Hornbook on, 3rd Ed., 1974, 1099 pages, by Charles L. B. Lowndes, Late Professor of Law, Duke University, Robert Kramer, Professor of Law Emeritus, George Washington University, and John H. McCord, Professor of Law, University of Illinois.

Evidence, Lilly's Introduction to, 1978, 486 pages, by Graham C. Lilly, Professor of Law, University of Virginia.

Evidence, McCormick's Hornbook on, 2nd Ed., 1972 with 1978 Pocket Part, 938 pages, General Editor, Edward W. Cleary, Professor of Law Emeritus, Arizona State University.

Federal Courts, Wright's Hornbook on, 3rd Ed., 1976, 818 pages, including Federal Rules Appendix, by Charles Alan Wright, Professor of Law, University of Texas.

Future Interest, Simes' Hornbook on, 2nd Ed., 1966, 355 pages, by Lewis M. Simes, Late Professor of Law, University of Michigan.

Income Taxation, Chommie's Hornbook on, 2nd Ed., 1973, 1051 pages, by John C. Chommie, Late Professor of Law, University of Miami.

Insurance, Keeton's Basic Text on, 1971, 712 pages, by Robert E. Keeton, Professor of Law Emeritus, Harvard University.

Labor Law, Gorman's Basic Text on, 1976, 914 pages, by Robert A. Gorman, Professor of Law, University of Pennsylvania.

Law Problems, Ballentine's, 5th Ed., 1975, 767 pages, General Editor, William E. Burby, Professor of Law Emeritus, University of Southern California.

Legal Writing Style, Weihofen's, 2nd Ed., 1980, 332 pages, by Henry Weihofen, Professor of Law Emeritus, University of New Mexico.

Local Government Law, Reynolds' Hornbook on, 1982, 860 pages, by Osborne M. Reynolds, Professor of Law, University of Oklahoma.

New York Practice, Siegel's Hornbook on, 1978, with 1981–82 Pocket Part, 1011 pages, by David D. Siegel, Professor of Law, Albany Law School of Union University.

Oil and Gas, Hemingway's Hornbook on, 1971 with 1979 Pocket Part, 486 pages, by Richard W. Hemingway, Professor of Law, University of Oklahoma.

Poor, Law of the, LaFrance, Schroeder, Bennett and Boyd's Hornbook on, 1973, 558 pages, by Arthur B. La-France, Dean and Professor of Law, Lewis and Clark College, Northwestern School of Law, Milton R. Schroeder, Professor of Law, Arizona State University, Robert W. Bennett, Professor of Law, Northwestern University and William E. Boyd, Professor of Law, University of Arizona.

Property, Boyer's Survey of, 3rd Ed., 1981, 766 pages, by Ralph E. Boyer, Professor of Law, University of Miami.

Real Estate Finance Law, Osborne, Nelson and Whitman's Hornbook on, (successor to Hornbook on Mortgages), 1979, 885 pages, by George E. Osborne, Late Professor of Law, Stanford University, Grant S. Nelson, Professor of Law, University of Missouri, Columbia and Dale A. Whitman, Dean and Professor of Law, University of Missouri, Columbia.

Real Property, Burby's Hornbook on, 3rd Ed., 1965, 490 pages, by William E. Burby, Professor of Law Emeritus, University of Southern California.

Real Property, Moynihan's Introduction to, 1962, 254 pages, by Cornelius J. Moynihan, Professor of Law, Suffolk University.

Remedies, Dobb's Hornbook on, 1973, 1067 pages, by Dan B. Dobbs, Professor of Law, University of Arizona.

Sales, Nordstrom's Hornbook on, 1970, 600 pages, by Robert J. Nordstrom, former Professor of Law, Ohio State University.

· Secured Transactions under the U.C.C., Henson's Hornbook on, 2nd Ed., 1979, with 1979 Pocket Part, 504 pages, by Ray D. Henson, Professor of Law, University of California, Hastings College of the Law.

Torts, Prosser's Hornbook on, 4th Ed., 1971, 1208 pages, by William L. Prosser, Late Dean and Professor of Law, University of California, Berkeley.

Trial Advocacy, Jeans' Handbook on, Student Ed., Soft cover, 1975, by James W. Jeans, Professor of Law, University of Missouri, Kansas City.

Trusts, Bogert's Hornbook on, 5th Ed., 1973, 726 pages, by George G. Bogert, Late Professor of Law, University of Chicago and George T. Bogert, Attorney, Chicago, Illinois.

Urban Planning and Land Development Control, Hagman's Hornbook on, 1971, 706 pages, by Donald G. Hagman, Late Professor of Law, University of California, Los Angeles.

Uniform Commercial Code, White and Summers' Hornbook on, 2nd Ed., 1980, 1250 pages, by James J. White, Professor of Law, University of Michigan and Robert S. Summers, Professor of Law, Cornell University.

HORNBOOKS & BASIC TEXTS

Wills, Atkinson's Hornbook on, 2nd Ed., 1953, 975 pages, by Thomas E. Atkinson, Late Professor of Law, New York University.

Advisory Board

MASS
COMMUNICATIONS LAW
IN A NUTSHELL

By

HARVEY L. ZUCKMAN

Professor of Law, The Catholic University
of America
Director, Institute for Communications,
Law Studies, Washington, D.C.

and

MARTIN J. GAYNES, ESQ.

Washington, D.C.

SECOND EDITION

ST. PAUL, MINN.
WEST PUBLISHING CO.
1983

Library of Congress Cataloging in Publication Data

Zuckman, Harvey L.
    Mass communications law in a nutshell.

    (Nutshell series)
    Includes index.
    1.   Mass media—Law and legislation—United
States.   I. Gaynes, Martin J.   II. Title.

KF2750.Z9Z8   1982   343.73'099   82–20029

ISBN 0–314–69869–8   347.30399

To Charlotte and Barbara, who,
amazingly enough, have chosen to
remain married to the authors
through two editions of this book.

❉

PREFACE

All one need do to appreciate the interrelationship of law and mass communications is to look at a daily newspaper. There, one is likely to find news of important court decisions, perhaps even ones of concern to the newspaper itself, news of new legislation having great impact on the citizenry as well as news about the judiciary. Even on the sports page one may find as much news about law suits between team owners and players as about team performance. There has been a veritable explosion in media coverage of the law since the early 1960s. At the same time their increasing influence and complexity have resulted in increased legal problems for the mass media, particularly in the areas of first amendment protection and Federal Communication Commission regulation and deregulation of broadcasting and cable.

We have perceived a continuing need for a basic text that would be of value both to law students confronting their first course in communications law and to journalism and communication students who have a need to know, in general outline, the law governing their chosen profession in order to function effectively and to avoid some of the legal pitfalls along the path of mass communication.

We have been encouraged to think by the generous comments of students and educators who have used the first edition that this book is more or less meeting that need, and, therefore, we have avoided change for the sake of change in this second edition. There are only three major changes in structure. First, we have eliminated the chapter on copyright because of the availability of other more complete basic treatments of the subject. Second, we have moved the material on the copyright "fair use" defense and the material on judicial secrecy and courtroom closings to Chapter V "Freedom to Gather News and Information" because these subjects involve access questions. Finally, we have retitled the chapter on cable television to reflect the emerging communications technologies that promise to change our lives and have added sections to that chapter to describe the more important of these technologies and their legal ramifications.

We had expressed the hope in the first edition that this book and others like it would stimulate the development of more communications law courses in the journalism and communications schools and departments and the law schools. We are pleased to report that in recent months New York Law School has begun a masters degree program in media law; Boston University and Syracuse University have begun planning joint degree programs between their respective schools of communications and law schools; and Catholic University School of Law in Washington, D.C. has begun operation of its Institute for Communications Law Studies which offers numerous communications law courses and internships to law students seeking to specialize while seeking the J.D. degree.

We hope more of these programs will develop over time, including semester-long law programs for senior and graduate journalism and communications students.

The reader will note that the authors have made every effort to achieve sexually neutral exposition in the text. We believe the time has come to recognize the equality of opportunity and achievement of both sexes in the fields of law and communications. Our only regret is the need to resort to the awkward "he or she" and "him or her" pronoun construction in order to reflect that belief. We hope the reader will understand.

We wish to acknowledge our heavy debt to the following individuals and organizations in the preparation of this text: Professors Donald M. Gillmor and Jerome A. Barron, authors of the casebook, Mass Communication Law, for allowing their organizational scheme to be followed here; Professor Thomas I. Emerson, whose many writings greatly influenced our thinking on first amendment issues, and the editorial board of Law and Contemporary Problems for permitting us to reprint material from Professor Emerson's article "The Doctrine of Prior Restraint," appearing in a symposium on Obscenity and the Arts in Law and Contemporary Problems (Vol. 20, No. 4, Autumn, 1955), published by Duke University School of Law, Durham, North Carolina, copyright 1955, by Duke University; the late Dean William L. Prosser, author of the Handbook of the Law of Torts, whose works greatly shaped our thinking in Chapters 2 and 3 on the law of defamation and privacy; Professor Dan B. Dobbs, author of the Handbook of the Law of Remedies for his guidance on the law of damages in defamation actions; Earl W. Kintner, Esquire, author of "A Primer on the Law of Deceptive Practices," (copyright 1971 by Mr. Kintner, all rights reserved) whose thinking on the regulation of advertising greatly influenced the approach taken in Chapter 8; Professor Melville B. Nimmer without whose brilliant thinking on the law of copyright infringement and the "fair use" defense to infringement actions no rational discussion of those subjects could be presented; Professor William A. Kaplin, a colleague at Catholic University School of Law, whose perceptive suggestions concerning Chapter 1 greatly strengthened it; the editorial board of the Texas Law Review for permission to paraphrase portions of the article by Donna Murasky, Esquire, "The Journalist's Privilege: Branzburg and Its Aftermath," 52 Texas Law Review 829 (1974); the editorial board of the Washington Law Review for permission to paraphrase portions of the article by Professors Don R. Pember and Dwight L. Teeter, Jr., "Privacy and the Press Since Time, Inc. v. Hill," 50 Washington Law Review 57 (1974); Louis Snyder for his continuing technical assistance without which the drafting of this second edition would have been far more difficult; Charles B. Blackmar, distinguished Missouri trial lawyer and former teaching colleague and cherished friend of Professor Zuckman for his insights into first amendment problems engendered by lawyer advertising (he argued and won In re matter of R——— M. J.——— in the United States Supreme Court); our able student research assistant Robert Corn who took valuable time from his own moot court, law review and legal writing activities (his contemporaneous work Judicial Intervention for the Hearing Impaired: An Uneasy Partnership Between the FCC and the D.C. Circuit Court of Appeals" is published in 31 Cath.U.L.Rev. —— (1982)); our very efficient secretaries, Nancy Freil and Delores Wise for their cheerful assistance in the preparation of drafts. Special thanks must go to Catherine S. Neuren, Mr. Gaynes' paralegal assistant and former news producer at the CBS affiliate in Boston, WNAC–TV, and Kathleen M. Hanlon, another of Professor Zuckman's student research assistants who gave unstintingly of their time and energy to assure the accuracy of the material presented herein and to prepare the index to this edition.

HARVEY L. ZUCKMAN
MARTIN J. GAYNES

Washington, D.C.
November, 1982

*

OUTLINE

~ destroy the good reputation of :

OUTLINE

Zuckman & Gaynes Mass.Comm.2nd Ed. NS—2

OUTLINE

*

TABLE OF CASES

References are to Pages

TABLE OF CASES

TABLE OF CASES

TABLE OF CASES

MASS
COMMUNICATIONS LAW
IN A NUTSHELL

PART ONE

THE FIRST AMENDMENT AND MASS COMMUNICATIONS

CHAPTER I

THE FIRST AMENDMENT IN PERSPECTIVE

A. INTRODUCTION

The development of mass communications throughout the western world and particularly in the United States in the twentieth century is a product of both science and law. Science has given us the technology by which individuals may communicate information, ideas and images across time and space to other individuals. And for this we owe a debt of gratitude to scientists and inventors such as Edison, Bell, Marconi, DeForest, and Zworykin for their contributions.

But technology does not exist in a vacuum. It operates in organized societies governed by laws. These societies may be open ones in which the members are relatively free to express themselves and to communicate with others by whatever means available or they may be relatively closed, with the modes of communications tightly controlled by a very few persons. Gutenberg's invention of moveable type gave promise of spreading both literacy and ideas to the masses, but in Elizabethan England and beyond, licensing acts severely limited access to the printing press to a few printers considered "safe" by the ruling authorities. It was this legal restriction on the utilization of the first technology of mass communication that led the great poet John Milton to make his stirring call for a free press in "Areopagitica." In our own time the vast promise of cable television was retarded for years because of the complex of statutes and Federal Communications Commission regulations designed to reign in this new technology in order to protect existing economic interests.

Thus, while technology is the necessary antecedent to mass communication, a society's laws ultimately determine how the technology will be developed and how "mass" will be its reach.

In our country the fountainhead of the law governing mass communication is the First Amendment to the Constitution which says in spare but sweeping language "Congress shall make no law . . . abridging the freedom of speech or of the press; . . ." The way this mandate is carried out tells us much about the kind of society *we* have. For as that giant of electronic journalism Edward R. Murrow once noted, what distinguishes a truly free society from all others is an independent judiciary and a free press.

B. BACKGROUND, THEORIES AND DIRECTION OF THE FIRST AMENDMENT

1. Background

At the time Madison was directed by Congress to draft the amendment to the Constitution expressly protecting free speech and press from governmental encroachment, he and the other founders of the Republic were acutely aware of the long history of suppression in England and the Colonies of free expression, particularly that concerning the affairs of government. Even after Parliament refused to renew the last of the licensing acts in 1695, the Crown was largely able to retain its control over the press by the imposition of heavy taxes on periodicals in England, by the refusal to permit the introduction of printing presses in many of the American colonies and, most importantly, by vigorous enforcement of the criminal law of seditious libel everywhere.

Under that law printers and publishers who offended the government and its ministers could be severely punished even when their statements were true. The maxim at common law was "the greater the truth the greater the libel." The journalistic exposure of a Watergate or Teapot Dome style scandal would have been virtually impossible under that law. Worse yet for the defendant, it was the Crown's judges who determined whether the utterance or writing was defamatory to the government. Needless to say, the prosecutors won nearly all of their cases, including one against Daniel Defoe for a satirical essay "Shortest Way with Dissenters." For his efforts Defoe was fined, pilloried and imprisoned.

Much the same fate befell a number of colonial printers and publishers until the royal governor of New York, William Cosby, instituted a prosecution for seditious libel against a New York printer, John Peter Zenger. Zenger had had the temerity to criticize Cosby's administration of the colony in the pages of his Weekly Journal. In the face of the uncontested fact of publication by Zenger and the common law of libel previously described, the jury refused to convict and the seed of a free press was planted in America.

Doubtless, then, with this history in mind, the press guarantee of the First Amendment was aimed at the very least at the abuses of licensing, censorship and punishment of political expression. Indeed, when Alexander Hamilton raised the question what was meant by freedom of the press, Madison responded that it meant freedom from despotic control by the federal government. Beyond this, the drafters failed to hand down to us any clear theory of the amendment.

Only after the outbreak of World War I and the consequent increase in radical agitation in the country, did the Supreme Court and constitutional scholars begin to search for coherent theories to explain the allowance or suppression of expression in specific cases. This search for theory was further encouraged by the ruling in Gitlow v. New York, 268 U.S. 652, 45 S.Ct. 625, 69 L.Ed. 1138 (1925) that the constraints of the First Amendment applied to the states through the operation of the due process clause of the Fourteenth Amendment.

2. Theories and Tests of the First Amendment

Over the years a number of general theories have been espoused to justify the existence of the First Amendment guarantees of free speech and free press. The most famous of these is the "free trade of ideas" espoused by Justices Holmes and Brandeis in their dissenting opinion in Abrams v. United States, 250 U.S. 616, 630, 40 S.Ct. 17, 22, 63 L.Ed. 1173, 1180 (1919) and their concurring opinion in Whitney v. California, 274 U.S. 357, 375–77, 47 S.Ct. 641, 648–49, 71 L.Ed. 1095, 1105–06 (1927). By this theory the First Amendment stands as a protector of truth emerging from the public discussion of competing ideas. Other general theories include the encouragement of an informed citizenry to insure wise self-government, the somewhat cynical "safety valve" idea of permitting individual members and groups in society to "let off steam" without seriously affecting the status quo, and the more idealistic belief that free expression is a necessary aspect of individual development and growth.

[5]

a. The "Clear and Present Danger" Test

But these general theories and principles do not resolve hard cases. Thus, the quest has been for operative or functional tests permitting reasonably consistent decisions in the field of free expression. The first of these, reflective of the free trade of ideas approach, was the "clear and present danger" test. Proposed by Justice Holmes in Schenck v. United States, 249 U.S. 47, 39 S.Ct. 247, 63 L.Ed. 470 (1919), the test permitted the punishment of expression when "the words used are used in such circumstances and are of such a nature as to create a clear and present danger that they will bring about the substantive evils that Congress has a right to prevent. It is a question of proximity and degree." Id., at 52, 39 S.Ct. at 249, 63 L.Ed. at 473–474.

In Schenck, the expression was in the form of a leaflet authorized by the American Socialist Party attacking the Conscription Act of World War I and urging recent conscripts to resist serving in the armed forces by asserting their alleged rights under the Thirteenth Amendment. Defendant, an officer of the party, was indicted, inter alia, for conspiracy to violate the Espionage Act of 1917 by causing and attempting to cause insubordination in the military forces and obstruction of the recruiting and enlistment service during a period of war. In the circumstance of war time, Holmes, who had himself been an officer in the Union Army during the Civil War, found that the leaflet created a danger of disruption of the war effort of sufficient proximity and magnitude to permit punishment in the face of the sweeping guarantees of the First Amendment.

Aside from the problem that it frankly permits the Congress in certain circumstances to legislate punishment of expression, the test is vague and difficult to apply. As Brandeis and Holmes admitted in their concurring opinion in Whitney v. California, 274 U.S. at 374, 47 S.Ct. at 648, 71 L.Ed. at 1105 (1927), the Supreme Court had not yet "fixed the standard by which to determine when a danger shall be deemed clear; how remote the danger may be and yet be deemed present; and what degree of evil shall be deemed sufficiently substantial to justify resort to abridgement of free speech and assembly as the means of protection."

Moreover, even if there were a common understanding of the meaning of the test, the results of its application to challenged legislation directly or indirectly prohibitive of expression would vary according to extrinsic circumstances such as war or peace, cold war or detente, and prosperity or depression. Expression which might be afforded first amendment protection from legislative repression in one social context might be denied it in another, and the speaker or publisher would not know whether his particular expression was safeguarded until the courts passed upon it. Thus, the test might have the effect of discouraging borderline writings or utterances.

In recent years, doubts about the test by civil liberties oriented justices and constitutional scholars and the hostility of those more state security oriented, have sapped "clear and present danger" of its vitality as constitutional doctrine. For instance, Brandenburg v. Ohio, 395 U.S. 444, 89 S.Ct. 1827, 23 L.Ed.2d 430 (1969), involved a prosecution for violation by certain members of the Ku Klux Klan of the Ohio criminal syndicalism statute. While this prosecution was much like earlier prosecutions in which the "clear and present danger" test had been employed (compare Whitney v. California, 274 U.S. 357, 47 S.Ct. 641, 71 L.Ed. 1095 (1927) involving a similar state criminal syndicalism statute), the per curiam opinion of the Supreme Court striking down the state law as an infringement of the First Amendment did not mention the test. Rather, the Court simply drew a distinction between advocacy of forcible or illegal political action in the future and advocacy directed to inciting *imminent* lawless action and likely to produce just such action.

In the field of political speech akin to seditious libel, the test now appears to be inoperative. But it may retain vitality in the narrow area of criminal contempt of court. Beginning with Bridges v. California, 314 U.S. 252, 62 S.Ct. 190, 86 L.Ed. 192 (1941), the Supreme Court applied the test to determine whether out-of-court utterances or writings attempting to influence the outcome of pending judicial matters or to criticize or ridicule members of the judiciary for their conduct on the bench could be punished through contempt of court proceedings. The substantive evil to be guarded against by the judiciary's exercise of the contempt power in these cases was the subversion of the fair administration of justice. The question in each case then was whether the out of court expressions created a clear and present danger to the proper administration of justice. The Supreme Court held that under the circumstances of the cases the out of court attacks on the judiciary and their handling of pending matters did not pose the requisite danger and thus the contempt citations were violative of first amendment guarantees. See Bridges v. California, supra; Pennekamp v. Florida, 328 U.S. 331, 66 S.Ct. 1029, 90 L.Ed. 1295 (1946); Craig v. Harney, 331 U.S. 367, 67 S.Ct. 1249, 91 L.Ed. 1546 (1947); Wood v. Georgia, 370 U.S. 375, 82 S.Ct. 1364, 8 L.Ed.2d 569 (1962). An important theme in these cases is that judges are made of sturdy stuff and will not be affected by such expression. It must be borne in mind, however, that the last explicit application of the "clear and present danger" test in contempt cases was in 1962.

b. *Ad Hoc Balancing of Interests*

In Justice Frankfurter's dissent in Bridges is the seed of another general approach to first amendment cases. In his opinion Justice Frankfurter emphasized that other interests protected

[*9*]

by the Bill of Rights were also at stake—the interests of due process of law and fair trial. He would not give any special deference to the interests protected by the First Amendment. "Free speech is not so absolute or irrational a conception as to imply paralysis of the means for effective protection of all the freedoms secured by the Bill of Rights. . . . In the cases before us, the claims on behalf of freedom of speech and of the press encounter claims on behalf of liberties no less precious." Bridges v. California, 314 U.S. at 282, 62 S.Ct. at 203, 86 L.Ed. at 213.

Frankfurter would resolve competing claims by weighing their relative importance in each case. In Bridges, he came to the conclusion that the interest in the impartial administration of justice outweighed the competing interest in allowing the Los Angeles Times through its editorial pages to attempt to prevent a judge from granting a request for probation from several labor organizers convicted of strong arm tactics, or in allowing Harry Bridges, a Pacific Coast longshoremen's union leader, to proclaim in the newspapers his threat to tie up the entire Pacific Coast shipping business if a court order of which he disapproved was enforced.

Frankfurter's approach formed the basis for the ad hoc balancing of interests. This balancing of first amendment interests was embraced by a majority of the Court in American Communications Association v. Douds, 339 U.S. 382, 70 S.Ct. 674, 94 L.Ed. 925 (1950), in which certain labor unions attacked a provision of the Labor Management Relations Act barring unions from access to procedures important to the collective bargaining process unless their officers executed affidavits declaring, among other things, that they were not members of or affiliated with the Communist Party. The unions contended that the provision violated union leaders' fundamental rights guaranteed by the First Amendment such as the right to hold and express whatever political views they choose and to associate with whatever political groups they wish. In concluding that the section of the act was compatible with the First Amendment, Chief Justice Vinson weighed first amendment interests against the interest to be fostered by the statute in question, i.e., interstate commerce free from the disruption of political strikes.

Perhaps the most explicit statement of this approach was made by Justice Harlan in Konigsberg v. State Bar of Cal., 366 U.S. 36, 81 S.Ct. 997, 6 L.Ed.2d 105 (1961). There Konigsberg, a candidate for admission to the California Bar, was denied a license to practice law because he had refused to answer questions put to him by a bar committee (acting as a state agency) concerning his alleged membership in the Communist Party. Konigsberg challenged the state's action on several grounds including violation of protected rights of free speech and association. In rejecting this challenge Justice Harlan said, "Whenever . . . these constitutional protections are asserted against the exercise of valid governmental powers a reconciliation must be effected, and that perforce requires an appropriate weighing of the respective interests involved [citations omitted]. . . . With more particular reference to the present context of a state decision as to character qualifications, it is difficult, indeed, to imagine a view of the constitutional protections of speech and association which would automatically and without consideration of the extent of the deterrence of speech and association and of the importance of the state function, exclude all reference to prior speech or association on such issues [concerning bar membership] as character, purpose, credibility or intent." Id. at 51, 81 S.Ct. at 1007, 6 L.Ed.2d at 117. Following this standard, a majority of the Court found that the state's interest in safeguarding the bar from possible subversive influence outweighed interests protected by the First and Fourteenth Amendments.

The ad hoc balancing approach has the virtue of pragmatism. It recognizes the importance of first amendment interests but permits the making of pragmatic judgments as to when those interests should prevail over other and conflicting interests, often of a state security nature. But this virtue may also be a vice, for the protections afforded by the First Amendment are stated in absolute terms and the Amendment makes no provision for restricting freedom of speech and press when other interests are in conflict. This approach also suffers from vagueness. Because it is ad hoc, no consistent weight can be given to conflicting interests and the lower court judges are left on their own to determine when first amendment interests are outweighed. Under such an approach a judge's predilections either for state security or individual liberties may be easily rationalized and, as with the "clear and present danger" test, the individual can never have any advance notice whether his interest in freedom of expression will outweigh some competing interest of the state expressed in its legislation. See Frantz, "The First Amendment in the Balance," 71 Yale L.J. 1424, 1440–1443 (1962).

Militant exposition of this approach to problem solving under the First Amendment has waned in recent years with the passing of its two leading exponents, Justices Frankfurter and Harlan, and with the easing of the Cold War. But so long as individuals perceive a fundamental conflict between First Amendment protections and state security, ad hoc balancing remains viable and, indeed, its philosophy may underlie many of the Court's recent First Amendment decisions.

c. *Absolutist Approach*

In their respective opinions Frankfurter, Vinson, Harlan and others rejected the idea that the First Amendment provided a central core of protection for expression in all circumstances—the so called absolutist approach. While this approach has been characterized as holding that the "no law" injunction of the First Amendment *means* no law, the absolutist schools of thought are more complex than that.

The absolutists agree that the First Amendment does provide a central core of protection, but to determine whether particular expression is protected in the face of governmental efforts at regulation, the broad language of the First Amendment must be defined. What does "no law" mean? What constitutes abridgment? And what is the expression which is to be protected? "No law" is defined generally to include not only statutes but administrative regulations promulgated pursuant to statutes, municipal ordinances, executive orders and court orders. Insofar as abridgment is concerned, the absolutists would permit limitations on free expression incidental to reasonable regulation promulgated pursuant to a "law" directed solely to controlling the time, place and manner of expression. In determining whether a challenged regulation is reasonable, the absolutists would reject any regulation based on a law which does not contain appropriate safeguards to limit administrative discretion. If such safeguards are present the absolutists would then look to see whether the regulation has created a sufficient inroad on expression by its nature, degree and impact so as to constitute an "abridgment" of free expression.

The key to understanding the absolutist's view of abridgment is recognition that regulation must relate only to time, place and manner of the presentation of expression and that such regula-

tion must not be so restrictive as to interfere with
the *substance* of expression.   See, e.g., Saia v.
New York, 334 U.S. 558, 68 S.Ct. 1148, 92 L.Ed.
1574 (1948), in which Justice Douglas, an adherent of absolutism, while conceding that some narrow regulation of sound trucks to prevent abuses
would be constitutionally permissible, held unconstitutional a local ordinance which forbade the
use of sound amplification devices except with
the permission of the chief of police.   The grant
of such permission was placed in the chief's sole
discretion and thus under the ordinance he was in
a position to determine not only the time, location
and volume of operation but the kind of speech
which might be amplified and the particular
groups which might use amplification equipment.

The absolutists begin to disagree among
themselves when the issue is one of the definition
or scope of the words "speech" and "press" as
used in the First Amendment.   Some of them
would set up a clearly defined two-tier system,
separating expression into protected and unprotected categories.   An example of this is the approach to obscenity taken in Roth v. United
States, 354 U.S. 476, 483–485, 77 S.Ct. 1304,
1308–1309, 1 L.Ed.2d 1498, 1506–1507 (1957).
There, Justice Brennan, speaking for the Court,
held that only expression having social importance was constitutionally protected and that obscenity was without such importance.   Brennan
himself has since abandoned this approach as creating more problems than it solves.   See his dis-

[*15*]

sents in Miller v. California, 413 U.S. 15, 47, 93 S.Ct. 2607, 2627, 37 L.Ed.2d 419, 444 (1973) and Paris Adult Theatre I v. Slaton, 413 U.S. 49, 73, 93 S.Ct. 2628, 2642, 37 L.Ed.2d 446, 467 (1973). However, the majority in those cases continues to adhere to the two-tier approach.

A variation of the two-tier approach is the so-called Meiklejohn interpretation of the First Amendment. Named after its leading proponent, Professor Alexander Meiklejohn, this interpretation, broadly stated, holds that ours is a self-governing society and the First Amendment protects the freedom of thought and expression directed to the process by which we govern ourselves. Thus, it is concerned with the need for the citizenry to acquire such qualities of mind and spirit and such information as will make possible responsible self-governance. Implicit in this form of government is the idea that while the people delegate certain responsibility to their elected representatives, they reserve for themselves the means to oversee their government and that the elected representatives may not abridge the freedom of the people in maintaining this oversight. Thus, in the Meiklejohn view, the central meaning of the First Amendment is the protection it affords to the public power of the people collectively to govern themselves. See Meiklejohn, "The First Amendment is an Absolute," 1961 Sup.Ct.Rev. 245, 253–263.

Practically, what this thesis translates into is absolute protection for all thought, expression and communication which bears on the citizen's role of self-government. Major emphasis is placed on political expression; punishment for seditious libel becomes an impossibility. But Meiklejohn would also include within the coverage of the First Amendment all aspects of educational, philosophical, scientific, literary and artistic endeavors because sensitivity to humanistic values and rationality in judgment are dependent upon these pursuits. Other expression not directly or indirectly related to the process of self-government would be beyond the pale of the First Amendment, as perhaps horror comic books.

While no Supreme Court decision has completely accepted the Meiklejohn thesis, it has been embodied to some extent in New York Times Co. v. Sullivan, 376 U.S. 254, 84 S.Ct. 710, 11 L.Ed.2d 686 (1964). There, a civil rights group purchased a full page advertisement in the New York Times, entitled "Heed Their Rising Voices." The advertisement set out certain facts concerning private as well as governmental action in Alabama violative of the civil rights of black citizens and asked for contributions to continue the fight for racial justice in the South. Many of the statements asserted as fact were incorrect, including allegations concerning the police department of Montgomery, Alabama. The elected city commissioner of Montgomery, whose responsibility it was to supervise the operation of the police department, sued the New York Times Company and four individual signatories of the advertisement claiming that he had been libeled. The commissioner obtained a jury award of $500,000, the full amount sought, against the defendants. The Alabama Supreme Court affirmed the judgment under ordinary common law rules of defamation, rejecting the contention that the expression involved in the advertisement was protected by the First and Fourteenth Amendments. The Alabama court asserted that libelous publications were beyond the scope of such protection.

In reversing the judgment because the state's common law of libel was constitutionally deficient in failing to provide safeguards for freedom of speech and press in libel actions brought by public officials against critics of their official conduct, the United States Supreme Court drew support from the history of the controversy over the Sedition Act of 1798. That statute made it a crime punishable by a $5,000 fine and five years in prison for anyone to print or publish any false, scandalous and malicious writing against the government or certain of its officials with intent to defame. In declaring that the "central meaning" of the First Amendment was the protection of public discussion of government and its officials and that in the court of history the Sedition Act was unconstitutional, Justice Brennan, speaking for the Court, quoted James Madison's argument against its passage. "If we advert to the nature of Republican Government, we shall find that the censorial power is in the people over the Government, and not in the Government over the peo-

ple." Id. at 275, 84 S.Ct. at 723, 11 L.Ed.2d at
703. This idea is, of course, at the heart of the
Meiklejohn interpretation. If the New York
Times case retains its vitality, the idea of seditious libel will have been relegated to the scrap
heap of history and "uninhibited, robust, and
wide-open" debate on the public issues will be encouraged. See also Near v. Minnesota, 283 U.S.
697, 713–718, 51 S.Ct. 625, 630–632, 75 L.Ed.
1357, 1366–1369 (1931) for an earlier Supreme
Court expression of the same idea.

Of the various absolutist views of the scope of
the First Amendment, perhaps the most celebrated is that held by the late Justice Hugo Black.
Justice Black was an adherent of the Holmes-
Brandeis view of the First Amendment as primarily a protector of the free market in ideas. But
he was wary of their "clear and present danger
test" because judges could hold that certain expression in certain circumstances failed the test
for first amendment protection. Rather, Justice
Black came to believe that all ideas and their expressions, including the libelous and the obscene,
are to be given absolute protection. This view of
the scope of the First Amendment is, of course,
more expansive than that taken by Meiklejohn
and has never commanded majority adherence on
the Court.

While Justice Black was an implacable foe of
any infringement of free expression except the
most incidental occasioned by reasonable "time,
place and manner" regulation, "speech" and

"press" were to him technical terms and only expression encompassed within those terms was to be protected. Justice Black normally defined "speech" and "press" more broadly than anyone else on the Court, but in the context of public demonstrations he defined "speech" very narrowly so as to exclude expression bound up with essentially physical conduct. For instance, in Adderley v. Florida, 385 U.S. 39, 87 S.Ct. 242, 17 L.Ed.2d 149 (1966), he spoke for the Court in upholding the convictions of 32 students who demonstrated in a nonviolent manner on a nonpublic jail driveway to protest the arrests of fellow students and local segregation policies. The 32 were among 200 students who had apparently blocked the driveway and had engaged in singing, clapping and dancing to protest what they believed to be an unjust situation. Among the dissenters in the Adderley case were Justice Black's usual allies in first amendment cases, Justices Douglas, Brennan and Chief Justice Warren.

At bottom, whatever their differences as to the reach of the First Amendment, the late Justice Black and the other absolutists are attempting to remove from the judiciary the power to balance the interest in free expression against the exigencies of the times. For them, the balance was struck once and for all in favor of freedom of speech and press by the drafters of the Bill of Rights and that balance may not be disturbed.

The preceding approaches or tests have not been consistently applied by their proponents to all first amendment problem areas and when they are applied the competing approaches do not always yield results in conflict with each other. But, again with the caveat that tests or theories cannot always be relied upon to predict the outcome of specific cases, an understanding of them is useful in predicting the direction of the Supreme Court in relation to the First Amendment.

3.   Present Direction of the Supreme Court

Enough time has passed since the demise of the Warren era and the advent of the Burger Court to make some tentative judgments about the direction of the current Supreme Court regarding First Amendment philosophy. First, absolutist philosophy reached its zenith in New York Times Co. v. Sullivan, 376 U.S. 254, 84 S.Ct. 710, 11 L.Ed.2d 686 (1964) and its progeny, concluding with the plurality opinion of Justice Brennan in Rosenbloom v. Metromedia, Inc., 403 U.S. 29, 91 S.Ct. 1811, 29 L.Ed.2d 296 (1971). That opinion, rejected in Gertz v. Robert Welch, Inc., 418 U.S. 323, 94 S.Ct. 2997, 41 L.Ed.2d 789 (1974), extended the protection of the New York Times Co. case to defendants defaming non-public individuals voluntarily or involuntarily caught up in matters of public interest.

Second, the ad hoc balancers on the Court, following the appointments of the Nixon and Reagan administrations, likely form a majority on the Court. Indeed, with the retirement of Justice Douglas there are many observers who doubt whether any true absolutists remain on the Court.

Third, as a consequence of this increased strength of the balancers, the absolutists' expansive view of first amendment protection will remain submerged. The main evidence of this is provided by the decision in Gertz v. Robert Welch, Inc., supra. There, Gertz, a reputable lawyer not generally known to the public and not then associated with any particular causes, was retained by the family of a youth killed by a police officer to bring a civil suit against the officer. Perceiving that the state's successful criminal prosecution for murder and the family's civil suit was part of a nationwide conspiracy to discredit local law enforcement agencies, the corporate defendant, publisher of the magazine, "American Opinion," commissioned one of the regular contributors to the periodical to write an article about the case. Under the title "FRAME-UP: Richard Nuccio And The War on Police," the published article asserted that the police had a huge file on Gertz. The article also claimed that he had been an official of the "Marxist League for Industrial Democracy," which advocated the violent seizure of the government, and that he was a "Leninist" and a "Communist-fronter." Finally, the article stated that Gertz had been an officer of the National Lawyers Guild, described as a Communist organization which "probably did more than any other outfit to plan the Communist attack on the Chicago police during the 1968

Democratic convention." These statements contained many serious inaccuracies, especially the implication that Gertz had a police record and the express assertions that he was a "Leninist" or a "Communist-fronter" and that he supported violence against duly constituted authority. The editor had made no effort to verify or substantiate the author's charges.

Gertz brought suit for libel against the corporation and obtained a jury verdict for $50,000. Following the verdict, the United States District Judge concluded that the privilege afforded by New York Times Co. v. Sullivan, supra, should be extended to cover discussion of any public issue without regard to the status of the person defamed. Accordingly, the court entered judgment for respondent notwithstanding the jury verdict and Gertz appealed. The United States Court of Appeals affirmed the judgment, citing Rosenbloom v. Metromedia, Inc., supra.

In a 5 to 4 decision, the Supreme Court, speaking through Justice Powell, reversed, limiting the New York Times Co. doctrine to cases involving defamation of public officials or public figures and rejecting the plurality opinion in Rosenbloom. Justice Powell's opinion took, in large measure, the classic balancing approach to the First Amendment. "The need to avoid self-censorship by the news media is . . . not the only societal value at issue. . . . [A]bsolute protection for the communications media requires a total sacrifice of the competing value served by the law of defamation. The legitimate state interest underlying the law of libel is the compensation of individuals for the harm inflicted on them by defamatory falsehood." 418 U.S. at 341, 94 S.Ct. at 3007–3008, 41 L.Ed.2d at 806.

Two parallel events during the 1981 term of the Supreme Court underline the transformation of the Court from one giving special protection to First Amendment interests of the news media during the Warren era to one in which ad hoc balancing often results in the subordination of such interests to other competing interests.

In Street v. NBC, 645 F.2d 1227 (6th Cir. 1981), defendant NBC successfully defended against a libel action in the United States District Court and in the United States Court of Appeals for the Sixth Circuit brought by the rape prosecutrix in the infamous "Scottsboro Boys" prosecution in Alabama in the 1930s. A central issue in the case was whether Mrs. Street remained a public figure for purposes of dramatizing the case more than thirty years later. The Sixth Circuit ruled that she remained a public figure, thus requiring the application of the higher New York Times Co. v. Sullivan standard in establishing libel. The Supreme Court granted Mrs. Street's petition to review that ruling. Rather than face the Court with the issue, NBC, which had prevailed below, paid Mrs. Street a substantial sum of money in and out of court settlement and the writ of certiorari (review) was dismissed.

Similarly, in Wilson v. Scripps-Howard Broadcasting Co., 642 F.2d 371 (6th Cir. 1981), the media defendant successfully defended against a libel suit in the District Court and the Sixth Circuit, in which a crucial question was which party bears the burden of establishing the truth of falsity of the defamatory expression complained of. Here again the Sixth Circuit ruled in favor of the media defendant, holding that the plaintiff bears the burden of proving the falsity of the allegedly defamatory expression. Again, the Supreme Court granted review and again the media defendant chose to settle out of court and have the case dismissed rather than have the Court decide the issue.

It appears that there now exists considerable reluctance upon the part of important segments of the media to chance litigation in the Supreme Court because of the Court's embrace of ad hoc balancing philosophy. This is in marked contrast to the media's zest for First Amendment combat in the Supreme Court during the Warren era when there was a tilt toward absolutism by the Court.

Fourth, the Court appears to be moving away from the previously accepted idea that time, place and manner restrictions on protected expression may not be influenced by the content of the expression except where captive or juvenile audiences are involved, i.e., the restrictions must be "content neutral." In Young v. American Mini Theatres, 427 U.S. 50, 96 S.Ct. 2440, 49 L.Ed.2d

310 (1976), a five-judge majority upheld a Detroit zoning ordinance that requires dispersal of "adult" bookstores and motion picture theatres but not other bookstores and theatres in order to protect established commercial and residential neighborhoods. This "place" restriction was justified on the basis of the type of books sold and the motion pictures exhibited. In other words, the majority "peeked" at the content of the expression here and, having peeked, upheld the place restriction embodied in the ordinance because of the content.

Fifth, and related to the immediately preceding conclusion, the Court, led by Justice Stevens, may be moving toward the position that protected expression is not monolithic but divisible into categories with the extent of first amendment protection dependent upon the intrinsic worth of the expression in each category. See Young v. American Mini Theatres, 427 U.S. at 50, 66–71, 96 S.Ct. at 2450–52, 49 L.Ed.2d at 323–26 (1976), Federal Communications Commission v. Pacifica Foundation, 438 U.S. 726, 744–47, 98 S.Ct. 3026, 3038–3039, 57 L.Ed.2d 1073, 1090–92 (1978) (opinion of Justice Stevens joined by Chief Justice Burger and Justice Rehnquist).

If accepted, this position raises some very thorny questions for the courts: what criteria should they use in categorizing protected speech; how will individual judges be able to cast aside their own personal value systems in determining objectively the comparative worth of particular expression; and finally, what degree of first amendment protection will be afforded each of the categories of expression.

Sixth, the Court, perhaps to conserve judicial energy, occasionally avoids the philosophical struggle over the proper approach to the First Amendment by nullifying statutes, ordinances and governmental regulations infringing free expression simply on the basis of their "vagueness" or "overbreadth." See, e.g., Erznoznik v. City of Jacksonville, 422 U.S. 205, 95 S.Ct. 2268, 45 L.Ed. 2d 125 (1975) (ordinance making it a public nuisance and a criminal offense for a drive-in movie theater to exhibit any film containing nudity if the screen is visible from the street held overbroad and struck down as violative of the First Amendment); Gooding v. Wilson, 405 U.S. 518, 92 S.Ct. 1103, 31 L.Ed.2d 408 (1972) (statute providing that persons who, without provocation, direct "opprobrious words" or "abusive language" toward another, tending to cause a breach of the peace shall be guilty of a misdemeanor, held unconstitutionally vague and overbroad on its face). But the Court does not consistently utilize or apply the "vagueness" and "overbreadth" devices. Compare, e.g., Young v. American Mini Theatres, 427 U.S. 50, 96 S.Ct. 2440, 49 L.Ed.2d 310 (1976) (all opinions).

C. THE DICHOTOMY BETWEEN PRIOR RESTRAINT AND SUBSEQUENT PUNISHMENT OF EXPRESSION

On one point adherents of all schools of thought appear to agree. At a minimum the First Amendment was adopted to prevent the federal government—and later the state governments through the Fourteenth Amendment—from instituting a general system of prior restraint on speech or press similar to that employed in England and the Colonies in the seventeenth and eighteenth centuries, i.e., licensing of the press and censorship of expression.

There were those, including Blackstone in his Commentaries on the Laws of England, who believed that freedom of the press consisted only in proscribing prior restraints upon publication and that once publication was made the publisher had to accept the consequences which might be imposed upon him by an offended government or individual. That first amendment protection extended also to attempts by government to punish completed utterances and publications through imposition of criminal sanctions was not fully settled until the formulation of the "clear and present danger" test in Schenck v. United States, 249 U.S. 47, 39 S.Ct. 247, 63 L.Ed. 470 (1919). And that the amendment further provided the publisher or speaker some protection against subsequent defamation actions was not recognized until New York Times Co. v. Sullivan, supra.

Despite the fact that the threat of subsequent criminal punishment and civil judgments for damages may have a substantial deterrent effect upon free expression, the Supreme Court has not, as indicated in the preceding sections, achieved anywhere near the consistency of doctrine that it has regarding the condemnation of administrative and judicial prior restraints.

There are many reasons besides the historical for the Court's hostility toward governmental action smacking of prior restraint. Professor Emerson in his classic article "The Doctrine of Prior Restraint," 20 Law and Contemporary Problems 648 (1955) provides us with a modern catalogue of these reasons. A system of prior restraint is broader in its coverage, more uniform in its effect and more easily and effectively enforced than subsequent punishment. Everything which is published or publicly uttered would be subject to scrutiny. Then, too, expression which is banned never sees the light of day and that which is not banned may be so delayed in the administrative mill that it becomes superfluous or obsolete when it is "cleared." The procedural safeguards of the criminal judicial process, including public scrutiny, are not present to the same degree in the administrative censorial process. Finally, the entire process is geared toward suppression and the censor will be impelled to find things to suppress. Id. at 656–59.

The landmark case recognizing the dangers of prior restraint is Near v. Minnesota, 283 U.S. 697,

51 S.Ct. 625, 75 L.Ed. 1357 (1931). There, a state statute provided for the abatement as a public nuisance of "malicious, scandalous, and defamatory" publications. The statute further provided that all persons guilty of such a nuisance could be permanently enjoined from further publication of malicious, scandalous and defamatory matter. A county attorney brought an action under the statute to enjoin The Saturday Press on the ground that it accused law enforcement agencies and officials of the city of Minneapolis with failing to stop vice and racketeering activities allegedly controlled by a "Jewish Gangster." In the face of the publisher's claim that his activities were protected by the First and Fourteenth Amendments, the trial court perpetually enjoined him from conducting a public nuisance under the name of The Saturday Press or any other name. The state supreme court affirmed the injunctive order. The United States Supreme Court reversed. Cutting through the peculiar procedures of the statute, the Court indicated that its object and effect was to suppress further publication. This they equated to prior restraint of the press. Moreover, if the person enjoined were so bold as to resume his or her publishing activities, he or she would have to submit the material to the appropriate judicial officer for clearance prior to publication in order to avoid being held in contempt of court for violation of the injunctive order. To the Court this constituted effective cen-

sorship prohibited by the due process clauses of the First and Fourteenth Amendments.

This decision stands out for many reasons. It was the Court's first definitive statement concerning the constitutionality of prior restraint on expression. More than this, it made clear that what was important was not the form governmental action took but its effect on speech and press. And because it indicated that the constitutional ban on prior restraints was not absolute and did permit certain narrow exceptions, it opened up the question of the precise limits of the First Amendment in this area. Finally, it made the point very clearly that while expression was generally protected from prior restraint, it might subsequently be punished if it were determined that the expression was unlawful. This dichotomy drawn by the Court in Near persists today. It was relied upon expressly by four of the Justices in their separate opinions in New York Times Co. v. United States, 403 U.S. 713, 91 S.Ct. 2140, 29 L.Ed.2d 822 (1971) (the "Pentagon Papers" case). See also Vance v. Universal Amusement Co., 445 U.S. 308, 100 S.Ct. 1156, 63 L.Ed.2d 413 (1980).

———

In the chapters which follow, the First Amendment will be considered in several specific contexts. These include the permissible scope of defamation and invasion of privacy actions in tort, the efforts of government to suppress pornography, the possible conflict between protection of a free press and the Fifth and Sixth Amendment guarantees of a fair and impartial trial, the existence, or non-existence of a newsperson's privilege not to reveal his or her sources of information when compelled to do so, and the permissible limits of governmental regulation of advertising.

Traditionally, these First Amendment problem areas have involved questions concerning the limitation on the power of government or its agencies to act in certain ways, e.g., the power of courts to enter judgments in defamation actions. But we will also advert to a new theory largely developed by Dean Jerome A. Barron that the First Amendment actually compels the government to act affirmatively to insure freedom of expression by requiring citizen access to the mass media. While this theory has been rejected by the Supreme Court with regard to the print media, it has been instrumental in forcing a wide ranging re-examination of the nature of the First Amendment in the late twentieth century.

CHAPTER II

DEFAMATION AND MASS COMMUNICATION

A. INTERESTS IN CONFLICT

One of the interests which has competed with the interest in freedom of expression down through the centuries is that of reputation, both personal and proprietary. The importance of this interest should not be minimized. As Justice Stewart said in his concurring opinion in Rosenblatt v. Baer, 383 U.S. 75, 92, 86 S.Ct. 669, 679, 15 L.Ed.2d 597, 609 (1966), "The right of a man to the protection of his own reputation from unjustified invasion and wrongful hurt reflects no more than our basic concept of the essential dignity and worth of every human being—a concept at the root of any decent system of ordered liberty."

The early common law courts considered reputation to be an interest deserving of protection by recognizing an action for money damages to compensate for injury resulting from defamatory communications. This action has evolved into the complex (some would say "confused and confusing") twin tort actions of libel and slander. There is no doubt that the ever present fear that one may have to respond in damages for what one publishes has a limiting effect on the work of the modern journalist or public speaker. It has been reported that one of the reasons for the demise of Pulitzer's New York World was the drain on its resources from numerous libel actions brought against the paper.

The thrust of the recent significant cases in the field of defamation has been the recognition of the unavoidable conflict between these two interests and the attempt to provide a measure of legal protection for both.

B. COMMON LAW DEFAMATION

1. Definition and Elements

Defamation has been defined as the injury to reputation by words which tend to expose one to public hatred, shame, contempt or disgrace, or to induce an evil opinion of one in the minds of right-thinking persons and to deprive one of their confidence and friendly intercourse in society. Kimmerle v. New York Evening Journal, 262 N.Y. 99, 102, 186 N.E. 217, 218 (1933). While this definition provides a good starting place for understanding the nature of defamation, it fails to place any emphasis on loss of reputation in one's business or profession. Moreover, the loss of reputation need only be with regard to a small but significant segment of the community, whether "right-thinking" or not. Finally, as the late Dean William L. Prosser pointed out, one may be defamed by imputations of insanity or poverty, which would instead arouse pity or sympathy—feelings, however, that diminish esteem and respect. Prosser, Handbook of the Law of Torts 739 (4th Ed. 1971). An example of this would be a false statement that an individual was a hopeless alcoholic.

In the past, defamation actions have been either criminal or civil in nature. But in recent years, with the notable exception of the state's prosecution of New Orleans district attorney James Garrison for his verbal attacks on certain sitting criminal court judges (Garrison v. Louisiana, 379 U.S. 64, 85 S.Ct. 209, 13 L.Ed.2d 125 (1964)), the criminal action has largely fallen into disuse. Perhaps this is because of its odious historical association with prosecutions for political sedition. In any event, the focus of this chapter will be the modern civil actions of libel and slander.

The essential elements common to both libel and slander actions are (1) the making by the defendant of a defamatory statement; (2) the publication to one other than the plaintiff of that statement; and (3) the identification in some way of the plaintiff as the person defamed.

a. The Defamatory Statement

The words complained of must be such as will injure the reputation of a living person or existing organization because only the injured party may sue for defamation. Some words such as "thief," "cheat," "murderer" or "whore" are almost universally understood to affect adversely the person referred to. Other words may have that effect in relation to the times and the victim's position. Falsely labeling one a communist during the World War II period of United States-Soviet cooperation was not actionable. But the same false label was considered defamatory after the commencement of the "Cold War."

The plaintiff's situation in life may also give a damaging effect to otherwise innocent words. The selling of pork is normally a respectable occupation, but suggesting that a kosher butcher sells bacon has been considered defamatory, for clearly it would cause religiously oriented customers to think less of the butcher and to take their business elsewhere. See Braun v. Armour & Co., 254 N.Y. 514, 173 N.E. 845 (1930).

Defamatory words can be presented in numerous ways. One need not attack with a verbal axe. The stiletto of ridicule may suffice. The communication complained of, however presented, must be understood by those hearing or seeing it as having a defamatory meaning, regardless of whether they personally believe it to be true. Thus, it is incumbent on a plaintiff in a defamation action to establish that someone other than himself understood the words or image as an attack on his or her reputation. The defendant, on the other hand, may attempt to show that the communication had at least one nondefamatory meaning and others understand it in that sense or that the communication was made in jest and could not reasonably be taken seriously. But if only one person other than the plaintiff understands the communication to be defamatory and such understanding is reasonable, given its content and context, the improper nature of the communication is made out.

b. *Publication*

Publication is a legal term of art meaning that the defamatory communication, whatever its form, has been perceived by someone other than the person defamed. Publication in the sense of printing and distribution of printed matter is not required. For example, publication occurs if a patient makes a serious statement in a loud voice in a crowded waiting room directly to a licensed physician that he or she is a "quack" and the statement is overheard by one or more of the other patients.

In this situation, it is clear that the communicator either intends that others overhear his or her accusation or is so uncaring whether it is overheard as to be deemed reckless in his or her conduct. But where one does not intend the communication to be conveyed to anyone other than the target of his or her attack, and the means chosen to convey the communication will in the normal course prevent reception by third persons, there is no publication. For instance, Able writes his former business partner Baker a letter in which he accuses Baker of causing the downfall of their business by "stealing the company blind." Able places the letter in a sealed envelope, marks it "personal," addresses it to Baker and mails it to his house. Baker's son, curious about the letter from his father's former associate, opens and reads the letter prior to Baker and without authority. There is no publication here and, hence, no actionable defamation.

Moreover, since it is the *defamer* who must intentionally or recklessly promote publication, the requirement is not met by the victim himself or herself publicizing the communication to others. If in the above hypothetical, Baker opened the letter and then showed the letter to his son, the result would be the same—no publication. Where there is publication, however, repetition of the original defamation by persons other than the victim constitutes republication for which the original communicator will also be held liable provided the republication is foreseeable. Of course, the person who does the republishing may also be held liable.

A question of special significance to the print media is whether the distribution of each copy of a press run is a separate publication providing the basis for multiple defamation actions or whether the press run is to be viewed as constituting one publication. The early English cases suggested the first alternative but they were decided before the advent of high speed presses, large press runs and mass distribution. Shortly before World War II American courts began to move toward what has become known as the "single publication rule." The rule provides that only one cause of action for defamation arises when the product of a press run or printing is released by the publisher for distribution, no matter how many separate transactions may result. A corollary is that the statute of limitations for defamation commences to run from the moment of first release. See Gregoire v. G.P. Putnam's Sons, 298 N.Y. 119, 81 N.E.2d 45 (1948), the leading case for the single publication rule holding that a libel action based on the sale of a single copy of a book whose last printing was more than two years prior to the sale was barred by New York's one-year statute of limitation. Reinforcing this judicial trend is the Uniform Single Publication Act promulgated by the National Conference on Uniform State Laws in 1952. This model legislation extends the single publication concept to radio, television and motion pictures. The act has been adopted by the legislatures of seven states, including California, Illinois and Pennsylvania.

c. Identification

Published defamation is not actionable unless the complaining party can establish that it was he or she who was defamed. Very often the target of a defamatory communication is not clearly named therein and thus the identification of the complaining party with the communication becomes a problem of analyzing extrinsic circumstances. An example of this problem is the celebrated case of New York Times Co. v. Sullivan, 273 Ala. 656, 144 So.2d 25 (1962), reversed 376

U.S. 254, 84 S.Ct. 710, 11 L.Ed.2d 686 (1964). There, the defendants published a paid advertisement which made allegations, among others, that the police of Montgomery, Alabama had improperly "ringed" a black college campus to put down a peaceful demonstration for civil rights and that certain unnamed "southern violators" had bombed Martin Luther King's home, had physically assaulted him, arrested him seven times for "speeding," "loitering" and similar "offenses;" and finally charged him with "perjury." Some of these statements were erroneous in whole or part.

While no "southern violator" was named in the ad, L.B. Sullivan, the Commissioner of Public Affairs for Montgomery, Alabama, filed suit for libel. Sullivan persuaded the jury that he had been referred to in the advertisement because he was the city commissioner in charge of the police at all times in question and thus would have been responsible for the "ringing" of the campus and the multiple arrests of Dr. King for minor infractions as part of the alleged lawless campaign of harassment and intimidation. Sullivan also contended that being identified as a "southern violator" in conjunction with the arrests had resulted in his further identification in the public mind with the other lawless acts listed. Several Montgomery residents so testified. The United States Supreme Court reversed a judgment for Sullivan, holding, among other things, that the identification of Sullivan with the advertisement was inadequate.

Identification may also be difficult when a group is defamed. Generally, the courts will not entertain an action when the complainant is a member of a large group which has been defamed. In the case of defamation of small homogeneous groups, the courts will permit actions by the individual members of the group. And some courts will allow individual actions by certain members of small groups when the defamatory communication is directed to a segment of the group. Of course, in this last case the plaintiff must convince the finder of fact (normally the jury) that he or she was a member of the segment attacked. See Neiman-Marcus Co. v. Lait, 107 F.Supp. 96, 13 F.R.D. 311 (S.D.N.Y.1952) for an application of these rules regarding civil actions for group defamation.

d. *Economic Loss*

In addition to establishing the defamatory nature of the communication, its publication and the necessary identification, the plaintiff in certain cases must also plead and prove that he suffered actual pecuniary or economic loss (special damages). In determining when this additional requirement must be met, we are confronted with the herculean task of sorting out libel from slander, libel per se from libel per quod and slander per se from all other slander.

2. Libel and Slander

Broadly differentiated, the tort of libel includes defamatory communications of a more or less permanent sort such as printed material, photographs, paintings, motion pictures, signboards, effigies and even statuary, while slander includes more ephemeral communications such as the spoken word, gestures and sign language. The distinction arises out of the historical development of common law court jurisdiction. In wresting jurisdiction from the ecclesiastical courts of England, which heard cases of slander, and in succeeding to the jurisdiction of the notorious Star Chamber over printed defamation, the common law courts kept the two types of defamation separate. See Donnelly, "History of Defamation," 1949 Wis.L.Rev. 99.

While classification of communications as slander or libel might not have been too difficult in the late seventeenth century with the limited communications then available, it becomes troublesome in an electronic age with its dependence on telephones, radio, television and even computers for communication. Indeed, the courts have never agreed on the taxonomy of radio and television defamation. At least one court has classified defamation by radio as slander while a number of others have labeled it libel. Still others, seeking greater discrimination, classify it as libel if read from a script and slander if the remark is ad libbed. And finally, a few

[42]

courts try to avoid the classification problem by calling radio defamation a new tort.

What too many courts appear to do when they are confronted with defamation via a new medium is to fix their gaze on the medium rather than on the interest the law is trying to protect and the reasons supporting the libel-slander dichotomy. The interest is, of course, reputation and the sting of defamation is its injury to reputation. Initially, the main justification for labeling writings as libelous, with concomitantly more serious consequences, including fine or imprisonment, was the greater permanence of the defamation and the correspondingly greater potential for wider distribution and greater injury to the victim. Today, no medium surpasses radio and television in wide distributive power. The potential injury to reputation from electronic defamation is devastating and on principle justifies the libel classification whether the defamation is read from a script or made extemporaneously.

There is no real way to avoid the troublesome task of classifying defamation since the requirement of special damages rests upon that classification. Generally, if the defamatory communication is held to constitute libel, the complaining party is not required to plead and prove as part of his or her case actual pecuniary loss resulting from the libel. On the other hand, if the communication is categorized as a slander, the complaining party generally has to establish such loss. As a practical matter many slander suits are quashed in the law office when the angry prospective plaintiff is informed by his or her own attorney to forget a lawsuit because he or she has no out of pocket loss. There is, however, a qualification to the requirement of financial sting in slander actions.

a. The Special Cases of Slander

As another matter of jurisdictional development, the common law courts established three special categories of slander which were to be actionable without regard to the existence of special damages: (1) imputation of crimes recognized by the common law courts; (2) imputation of certain loathsome diseases (limited to venereal disease, leprosy and the black plague); and (3) imputations affecting the victim in his or her business, trade, profession or office. Later, by statute or common law decision a fourth category was created, i.e., the imputation of unchastity to a woman. These four categories of slander continue to be recognized by most courts as permitting a plaintiff to sue his or her slanderer without establishing special damages, though the fourth category will almost surely be modified under state equal rights amendments. The scope of the categories has not changed greatly over the years. However, the present day test for the imputation of criminal conduct is whether the conduct involves moral turpitude. Thus, today a false oral allegation to a third party that "X" embezzles from his employer, would be actionable in most

[44]

American jurisdictions without the need for "X" to establish pecuniary loss.

While from a plaintiff's perspective the existence of these special categories provides a liberalizing force in the law of slander, a somewhat parallel development in the law of libel has had the opposite effect.

b. *Libel Per Se and Per Quod*

As the tort of libel developed, the rule became fixed that in contrast to slander actions, special damages need not be pleaded and proven by the plaintiff in order for him or her to recover. An explanation often given for this distinction is that the written communication once had greater potential for mischief because of its more permanent form. Therefore, some injury to the victim could be conclusively presumed.

No distinction was drawn by the courts between those libelous communications plain upon their face (libel *per se*) such as "John Doe is a bastard" and those which require reference to extrinsic circumstances to give them the necessary defamatory meaning (libel *per quod*). The classic example of libel per quod is the erroneous newspaper story stating that Mary Doe of 1234 Shady Lane had just given birth to twins at a local hospital. The story was libelous because of the extrinsic fact that Mrs. Doe had been married only one month before and several persons reading the story knew this fact.

[45]

Originally, then, if the defamatory communication was broadly classified as libel, special damages were not essential to a successful action. This is still stated to be the majority rule by the American Law Institute's Restatement of the Law of Torts Second, Section 569. But the late Dean William L. Prosser stated flatly that some thirty-five American jurisdictions now draw a distinction between libel per se and per quod and hold that libel per quod is to be treated like slander, i.e., actionable only with the pleading and proving of special damages unless the libel falls within one or more of the four special categories associated with slander. W. Prosser, Handbook of the Law of Torts (4th ed. 1971) 763. A major reason for this apparent change in the law appears to be the reluctance of courts to hold newspapers and other media broadly liable for communications which they may not even be aware are defamatory.

To summarize:

1. Slander is actionable only with a showing of special damages . . .

2. . . . unless the slander imputes to the complaining party (1) criminal conduct recognized as involving moral turpitude; (2) infection with venereal disease, leprosy or the plague; (3) misconduct or mismanagement in business, trade, profession or office; or (4) unchastity (if the victim is a female).

3. Libels per se in all jurisdictions and libels per quod in a large number of jurisdictions (including New York) are actionable without the need for special damages.

4. Libels per quod in other jurisdictions are now actionable only with a showing of special damages unless they fall into one of the four special categories established originally for slander.

The above rules and the proper classification of defamation cases under them are extremely important since the establishment of special damages, i.e., pecuniary loss, as a result of the defamatory communication, is often very difficult for the plaintiff.

3. Theories of Liability

At common law, so long as the defendant intended to publish to a third person that which is ultimately adjudged to be defamatory toward the plaintiff, the defendant is strictly liable in tort, absent a valid defense. The plaintiff need only establish the intention of the defendant to publish and need not establish that the defendant intended the publication to be defamatory. Peck v. Tribune Co., 214 U.S. 185, 29 S.Ct. 554, 53 L.Ed. 960 (1909). Thus, a publisher under this rule "published at his own peril" and would be held liable for coincidences and honest errors as well as for intended defamatory attacks. Strict liability for the media was ended by the Supreme Court decisions in New York Times Co. v. Sullivan, 376

U.S. 254, 84 S.Ct. 710, 11 L.Ed.2d 686 (1964) and
Gertz v. Robert Welch, Inc., 418 U.S. 323, 94 S.Ct.
2997, 41 L.Ed.2d 789 (1974), discussed supra at
pp. 17–19, 22–24.

4. Remedies

Once the plaintiff has established his cause of
action and assuming the defendant has not inter-
posed any valid defense (see infra, pp. 51–61), the
focus of the defamation suit shifts from the question of liability to the question of remedies available to the defamed person. The major remedy
for injury to reputation is the award of monetary
damages.

a. Damages

We have already seen that in cases of libel per
quod in perhaps a majority of jurisdictions and in
cases of slander, excluding the four special categories, proof of special damages is necessary for
liability. Of course, such damages may be established in any defamation action. Such damages
require rather specific pleading and proof by the
plaintiff of pecuniary or economic loss actually
resulting from the defamatory communication
and reasonable foreseeability of the plaintiff's
loss by the defendant. Obvious cases are the loss
of one's employment, the loss of opportunity for
business profits and impaired credit rating because others are influenced by the defamation.

The existence of special damages may influence the jury's award of general damages.

These are damages awarded for actual losses to the plaintiff from the defamation and cover both proven and unproven pecuniary and nonpecuniary loss for such injuries as hurt feelings, embarrassment, mental and emotional distress and physical consequences. Unless the action is one which specifically requires the showing of special damages, such damages are not a prerequisite for the award of general damages.

Many factors may be considered by the jury in attempting to determine reasonable and appropriate general damages. These are catalogued by a leading authority as including (1) the nature of the defamation (e.g., irrational name calling or insinuation of serious wrongdoing); (2) the form and permanency of the publication (oral conversations between individuals or communication by the mass print or electronic media); (3) the degree of dissemination; (4) the degree to which the defamatory communication is believed; (5) the nature of the plaintiff's reputation; (6) in certain cases, the good faith of the defendant in publishing the defamatory matter and (7) the defendant's subsequent conduct in retracting the complained of communication or in making apology. D. Dobbs, Handbook on the Law of Remedies, 513–520 (1973).

In awarding these compensatory damages jurors are instructed that they are to consider both past injury suffered by the plaintiff and likely future injury. Prospective future injury is to be es-

[*49*]

timated and made an element of the total award of damages.

Occasionally, a jury may determine that a plaintiff has suffered no general damages either because his or her good reputation was left unimpaired by the defamation or because his or her reputation was worth little or nothing to begin with. In that event, unless the plaintiff has established special damages the jury will award only nominal damages, ordinarily six cents or one dollar, depending on the jurisdiction.

If actual malice in the form of spite, evil intent or reckless disregard for the truth is present, the jury will be instructed that it may, but need not, award the plaintiff punitive damages. As the term implies, such damages are designed to punish the defamer and are not compensatory in nature. The degree of actual malice involved will have an effect on the amount of the award. In addition, if such damages are to make the defendant "smart" for his or her indiscretion and deter him or her in the future, the jury must be entitled to know the defendant's net worth and to reduce it to where it hurts.

Punitive damages may have too great a deterrent effect. One lower court has suggested that when first amendment interests are balanced against the interests of the state in punishing defamers, the "chilling effect" of punitive damages on freedom of expression is too great a price for a free society to pay in attempting to rid itself of defamation. Maheu v. Hughes Tool Co., 384

F.Supp. 166 (C.D.Calif.1974). This suggestion was rejected, however, when the Ninth Circuit reviewed the case. Maheu v. Hughes Tool Co., 569 F.2d 459, 480 (9th Cir. 1977).

C. THE COMMON LAW DEFENSES

Once the plaintiff has provided sufficient evidence of the elements necessary to establish a prima facie case of defamation and the consequent award of damages, the defendant is put to his or her defense. He or she may, of course, deny one or more aspects of the plaintiff's case such as the defamatory nature of the communication or the publication of the offending communication. In addition or alternatively, he or she may attempt to establish one or more of the complete common law defenses of truth, privilege and fair comment in order to defeat liability or to attempt to establish certain incomplete defenses to reduce the award of damages. In resorting to these defenses, the defendant accepts the burden of pleading them in his or her answer and then proving them by a preponderance of the evidence at trial.

1. Truth or "Justification"

As we have seen in Chapter I, truth was not a defense to criminal libel prosecutions at common law. But in civil actions for defamation the rule was to the contrary. Truth was recognized as a complete bar to liability. This is the rule followed in a large majority of American jurisdictions.   Behind this rule are the ideas that one is not entitled to a greater reputation than he or she in fact merits and that the public is served by knowing as much as possible about those in their midst with whom they may deal.   Therefore the motives of the communicator are irrelevant to the availability of truth as a defense.   A minority of states legislatively qualified the common law defense of truth in civil actions by requiring that the defendant establish his or her good motives or the justifiable ends to be served or both.   As we shall see below, this requirement has been largely nullified by the Supreme Court.

Whether qualified or not the defense of truth is a risky one.   Knowing something to be true and proving it in a court of law are, of course, two different things.   In many situations only the plaintiff will have access to the necessary proof and, understandably, he or she will not make it easy for the defendant to establish the defense.

Moreover, the defense must be as broad in its reach as the communication complained of.   The defense will fail if only a portion of the allegation is verified.   For example, a newspaper charge that X is a habitual vice law offender is not justified by the paper establishing one conviction of X for a gambling violation.   And a statement that a reliable source has informed the communicator that X is guilty of tax evasion is not justified by establishing only that someone informed the defendant about X and that someone is indeed a reliable source.   The truth of the charge itself must be established even though the defendant was not the originator of the story. But this does not mean that the defendant will have to verify every detail of his communication. The defense is available if the substance of the communication can be established. An individual who publicly accuses his or her neighbor, the treasurer of the local homeowners association, of embezzling $1500 from the association, will escape liability by proving embezzlement of $150 and a news service report that volume beef sellers were ordered by a state court to make restitution to customers that could total $700,000 is not actionable when the actual amount of money obtained by the sellers as a result of unfair and deceptive practices was substantially less than $700,000.

2. Privilege

As with most intentional torts, the common law recognizes the defense of privilege in certain cases of defamation. Despite the fact that the plaintiff suffers harm to his or her reputation from the defamation, the defamer may be shielded from liability because the law accords supremacy to conflicting interests of the defendant in communicating the defamation or of third persons in receiving the communication or of the public generally in encouraging free expression of matters of general concern. The defense, which is relatively narrow in scope, is divided into two aspects: the absolute privilege to defame and the qualified privilege.

a.   Absolute Privilege

One who possesses an absolute privilege to defame or, perhaps more accurately, an absolute immunity from suit is not required to establish his or her good faith in making the defamatory communication.   Motivation is immaterial.

Only the most compelling interests of society justify this license to injure or destroy reputations, and it is properly conferred almost exclusively on those directly involved in the furtherance of the public's business.   So long as the defendant is so involved and the expression complained of is relevant to the public business at hand, he or she will, for the most part, be accorded the absolute privilege.   While earlier cases imposed strict evidentiary standards of relevancy, the modern trend is to protect any expression which is at all related to the public proceeding. This trend accords with one of the major purposes for granting absolute immunity, i.e., insuring the independence and fearlessness of those participating in the public's business.   If participants are forced to analyze their remarks for strict legal relevance and risk civil liability should they be in error, their fearlessness and independence may be impaired and their actions on the public's behalf inhibited.   The public proceedings in which the absolute privilege may be available are divided into the judicial, legislative, executive and administrative.

There are a few instances aside from governmental activity in which the absolute privilege obtains. These include communications between husband and wife, defamatory communications either expressly or impliedly invited by the party defamed and the carriage of communications required by law where the carrier is not permitted to control the content of the material. From a mass communications perspective the last situation is the important one.

The principle that absolute immunity attaches to those required by law to publish, without editorial control, communications which may be defamatory was established in Farmers Educational and Co-operative Union v. WDAY, Inc., 360 U.S. 525, 79 S.Ct. 1302, 3 L.Ed.2d 1407 (1959). There, a radio station licensee required by the so-called "equal time provision" of Section 315 of the Federal Communications Act of 1934 to carry a speech by a political candidate and barred by the same provision from controlling the content of the speech, was held absolutely immune from suit by those allegedly defamed by the speech.

b. Qualified Privilege

In contrast to the absolute privilege previously discussed, the qualified privilege to communicate defamatory matter is defeated by the plaintiff establishing actual malice on the part of the defendant. This entails proving a publication was motivated chiefly by some consideration other than furthering the interest for which the law accords the privilege in the first place. The law's recognition of this lesser privilege reflects the idea that some of the interests competing with that of reputation, while not as compelling as those which justify an absolute privilege or immunity for the publisher, are still sufficiently important to justify a lesser degree of protection.

In the case of the media, the interests supporting the existence of the qualified privilege in reporting the proceedings of government and some private institutions and organizations are those of public oversight of governmental activity and legitimate public desire for information about matters affecting the public generally or a substantial segment thereof. And even when the oversight function is not involved the public may have some legitimate interest in being informed of public proceedings of both governmental and private organizations in order to prepare for or guard against the consequences of those proceedings.

(1) Limitations on the Scope of the Privilege

The courts have placed certain limitations on the scope or availability of the privilege to the media in reporting public proceedings. A majority of courts, for instance, led by Massachusetts, takes the position that the privilege does not extend to reporting allegations or statements contained in complaints, affidavits or other pretrial papers unless and until such papers are brought before a judge or magistrate for official action. See, e.g., Sanford v. Boston Herald-Traveler

Corp., 318 Mass. 156, 61 N.E.2d 5 (1945). Thus the reporter must be alert to the law of his or her state and, if it follows the majority view, must be wary of the content of court papers filed with the clerk of court but not yet acted upon by a judicial officer vested with discretionary authority. The minority view, exemplified by the New York case of Campbell v. New York Evening Post, Inc., 245 N.Y. 320, 157 N.E. 153, 52 A.L.R. 1432 (1927), is that the report of the contents of papers properly filed and served on the required parties may be privileged since the filing and serving of pleadings or other papers authorized by the rules of court are public and official acts done in the course of judicial proceedings.

Then, too, reports of the activities of executive officers or administrative agencies are generally not privileged until the officer or agency has taken some definite final action, as a district attorney filing a criminal information or obtaining an indictment. The report of a district attorney's preliminary investigation would not in most jurisdictions be privileged. As Professors Nelson and Teeter point out, police proceedings are especially dangerous for the newsperson to report because of the significant variations from state to state regarding the point at which the privilege attaches. The status of the police blotter, the record of arrests and charges and the oral reports of police officers concerning their preliminary investigations varies according to the jurisdiction involved.

H. Nelson and D. Teeter, Jr., Law of Mass Communications 141 (3d ed. 1978).

With regard to the legislative process, so long as the particular proceeding reported upon is authorized, the report itself will be privileged, assuming conformity with the general requirements discussed below.

The proceedings subject to the privilege must normally be public in nature unless a statute provides otherwise. Thus, a report of secret grand jury deliberations would not be considered privileged though such deliberations are official proceedings. Exceptions to the "public proceeding" requirement are occasionally recognized such as in Coleman v. Newark Morning Ledger Co., 29 N.J. 357, 149 A.2d 193 (1959), where a fair and accurate report of Sen. Joseph McCarthy's press conference summarizing the secret proceedings of his subcommittee's investigation into alleged communist activity at Fort Monmouth, New Jersey, was held to be privileged despite the fact, pointed out in the dissenting opinion, that there was no verification of whether Sen. McCarthy's report of the secret legislative proceeding was itself fair and accurate. Such exceptions are rare and the reporter should not assume from them that there is legal justification for publishing reports of secret governmental proceedings.

(2) General Requirements of the Privilege

As indicated by the Coleman case, if the qualified privilege is to attach the report must be fair and accurate and motivated by a sense of duty to make disclosure to those receiving the report. The privilege will be unavailable if it is held to be either an unfair or inaccurate account of that portion of the proceeding covered. The report need not, of course, be verbatim, but its condensation, abridgment or paraphrasing must accurately and fairly reflect what transpired. An erroneous detail will not destroy the privilege so long as it does not affect the essential accuracy or fairness of the report. A report may, of course, be literally accurate so far as it goes and yet unfairly portray the proceedings and the complaining person's involvement in them because the report ends at a critical point or omits important facts favorable to that person.

Moreover, if the defamatory report is made chiefly for a purpose other than to inform those who have a "need to know," the publication will be considered malicious and the privilege will be destroyed. Malice is found when the main reason for the publication is not the proper one of informing those the law recognizes as having a legitimate interest in the contents of the report. A fair and accurate account of a proceeding containing defamatory matter given to a friend at a party to make idle cocktail conversation could be considered malicious because the proper motivation for making the account is missing. And the privilege will not obtain if the communication is motivated mainly by some selfish objective of the reporter or publisher such as enhancing their business interests at the expense of a competitor who is unfavorably referred to in the public proceeding reported.

3. Fair Comment

Because this most popular of the common law defenses, involved as it is with criticism of the public conduct of public persons, is made largely unnecessary by the holding in New York Times Co. v. Sullivan, 376 U.S. 254, 84 S.Ct. 710, 11 L.Ed.2d 686 (1964) and by dictum in Gertz v. Robert Welch, Inc., 418 U.S. 323, 94 S.Ct. 2997, 41 L.Ed.2d 789 (1974), the treatment here will be quite summary.

As traditionally viewed fair comment involved the honest expression of the communicator's opinion on a matter of public interest based upon facts correctly stated in the communication. Such expression had to be free of speculation as to the motivation of the person whose public conduct is criticized unless such discussion was warranted by the stated facts. See, e.g. Foley v. Press Publishing Co., 226 App.Div. 535, 235 N.Y.S. 340 (1929). Chief among the unique characteristics of this defense were (1) its emphasis upon opinion based upon fact rather than the reporting of the facts themselves and (2) its broader scope, permitting comment on all matters of public interest rather than simply proceedings of a public nature. It was these characteristics which made possible political and artistic criticism by the media prior to New York Times v. Sullivan.

The courts gave broad meaning to fair comment. Commentaries containing exaggeration, illogic, sarcasm, ridicule and even viciousness were protected if at all justified by the underlying facts.

Malice would negate the defense but it could not be inferred merely from the words chosen by the publisher or speaker. Malice could only be found from an examination of the communicator's motives in publishing. The defense was also negated in a majority of the jurisdictions if the comment or opinion were based on a major error of fact.

4. Incomplete Defenses

Certain defenses in defamation actions are labeled incomplete because they do not bar liability even if successful but only reduce the amount of damages recoverable by the plaintiff. Chief among them is that of retraction. If the defamer publishes a retraction of the defamatory communication punctually and with essentially the same prominence as he or she gave to the defamation, the danger of a punitive damages award will be negated and compensatory damages may be reduced.

The theory behind this mitigation of damages is that a true retraction of the defamation evidences the good faith of the communicator, thereby rebutting the existence of actual malice and likely reducing the actual damage done to the plaintiff's reputation. However, the retraction cannot erase the defamation entirely because the plaintiff's legally protected interest in his or her reputation has already been violated, the cause of action arising with the original publication. Therefore, at least nominal damages and special damages, if any, must be awarded if there is no complete defense available to the defendant.

It should be emphasized that the retraction must be complete and unequivocal. Less than full retraction or a veiled continuance of the defamation will not mitigate damages but, in fact, may increase them. It will not do to state that "John Doe hasn't the morals of a tom cat" and then be willing to "retract" by stating that "John Doe does have the morals of a tom cat." It should also be noted that the availability of the partial retraction defense, the effects of retraction and the consequences of a refusal to retract are governed in a number of states such as California by statute. The California retraction statute figured prominently in the celebrated libel suit by comedienne Carol Burnett against the National Enquirer. The statute by its terms applies to and provides partial protection for newspapers. In the Burnett case the trial court ruled that the National Enquirer was a magazine and thus, although it had published a retraction of the libelous material about Miss Burnett, it was not protected against the imposition of punitive damages.

Somewhat akin to retraction is the idea of allowing the defamed party the right to reply to personal attack. The voluntary agreement by the defamer to allow use of his facilities by the victim to reply to the attack does not necessarily establish the defamer's good faith and the award of punitive damages remains a possibility. But the actual injury to the defamed party may be reduced because of the opportunity afforded to reach and favorably influence those whose good opinion of him or her has been affected. However, any effort by government to mandate the right of reply insofar as the print media are concerned would appear to be violative of the First Amendment. See Miami Herald Publishing Co. v. Tornillo, 418 U.S. 241, 94 S.Ct. 2831, 41 L.Ed.2d 730 (1974). But as of this time, a distinction is made by the Supreme Court with regard to broadcasters, and they may be compelled to extend the right to reply, in certain narrow circumstances, to those personally attacked over their facilities. Red Lion Broadcasting Co. v. Federal Communications Commission, 395 U.S. 367, 89 S.Ct. 1794, 23 L.Ed.2d 371 (1969).

———

This completes the discussion of common law defamation, a law in many respects quite favorable to the defamed party's interest in reputation. Witness, for instance, its theory of strict liability. Conversely, this law imposes many restrictions upon and dangers for those who seek to exercise their right of free expression under the First Amendment.

No more graphic illustration of the dangers posed to a free press by the common law can be suggested than the decision of the Alabama Supreme Court in New York Times v. Sullivan, 273 Ala. 656, 144 So.2d 25 (1962), reversed 376 U.S. 254, 84 S.Ct. 710, 11 L.Ed.2d 686 (1964). That decision was, in almost all respects, in accord with accepted common law principles concerning the elements of libel, malice, compensatory and punitive damages and the recognized defenses.

The effect of that litigation in the state courts was to cause the New York Times Company to halt distribution of its newspaper in Alabama for a time and to saddle the company with a massive judgment for $500,000 damages which, if not reversed, would (along with a potential $2,500,000 more in damages claimed in other pending related suits) have caused a weakening of its financial position, with all the implications that that might have had for the Company's continued ability to adhere to its motto "all the news that's fit to print."

The common law principles which were applied by the Alabama courts and which have been considered at length in this chapter are still applied in whole to communications which do not involve public figures and matters of public interest and in part to communications which do. They are, therefore, worthy of continued discussion. But the very serious question posed to the Supreme Court by the New York Times case was whether the application of all aspects of the common law of defamation to newspapers and other media is consistent with the guarantees of the First Amendment. The answer to that important question and its qualifications is the subject of the next section of this chapter.

D. THE NEW CONSTITUTIONAL LAW OF DEFAMATION

1. New York Times v. Sullivan

The facts of New York Times v. Sullivan are set out in detail in Chapter I at pp. 17–19. It is sufficient to say here that the paid advertisement in question in the case did contain erroneous information which if satisfactorily identified with the plaintiff police official would be considered defamatory toward him at common law. However, the United States Supreme Court held that there was not adequate proof of identification of the plaintiff to support liability of the defendants for defamation and reversed the state court judgment for the plaintiff.

It also seemed clear to the Court that, at most, the defendant newspaper was guilty of negligence in publishing the advertisement without checking the facts alleged therein against its own news files to verify the accuracy of the advertisement. Money judgments against newspapers and other media for honest mistake or negligence in publication of defamatory material concerning public officials would, in the Court's view, interfere with "a profound national commitment to the principle that debate on public issues should be uninhibited, robust, and wide-open. . . ." 376 U.S. at 270, 84 S.Ct. at 721, 11 L.Ed. 2d at 701. In the Court's understanding, the encouragement of such debate was part of the central meaning of the First Amendment. The court therefore laid down the rule that a public official may not recover damages for a defamatory falsehood relating to his official conduct unless he proves with "convincing clarity" that the statement is made with actual malice. "Actual malice" was defined by the Court as publication with knowledge that the statement in question is false or with "reckless disregard" of whether or not it is false.

Thus, for the first time in the long history of this country, certain false and defamatory communications were accorded constitutional protection if not maliciously made. This historic ruling represents a corollary to Barr v. Matteo, 360 U.S. 564, 79 S.Ct. 1335, 3 L.Ed.2d 1434 (1959), in which the Court accorded government officers an absolute privilege to make defamatory communications within the bounds of their offices. Critics of official conduct are given an equivalent privilege in order to encourage public oversight of these same officers.

2. Effects of the New York Times Case

The effects of the New York Times case on common law defamation are many and wide-sweeping. Briefly summarized they include the following:

1. The idea of "fair comment" is broadened to include facts and to permit the communication of erroneous facts, and is raised to a constitutional privilege when the comment concerns conduct of public officials relating to their office.

2. Strict liability for the making of defamatory communications concerning public officials is eliminated and a new fault standard of intentional or reckless conduct is substituted.

3. The definition of actual malice to mean evil motive, spite or ill will is rejected and a new definition of knowing falsehood or reckless disregard for the truth is substituted when public officials are complaining parties.

4. Under common law the defense of privilege, including lack of actual malice, was for the defendant to establish; after New York Times the plaintiff public official has the burden of negating the defendant's constitutional privilege by proving that the defendant acted with actual malice in publishing the false and defamatory material, i.e., intentionally or recklessly. Implicit in

this is the shifting of the burden of proof on the issue of truth to the plaintiff. He or she must now establish falsity as part of his or her prima facie case.

5. The plaintiff's proof of malice and his or her identification as the party defamed must now be made with convincing clarity; at common law the normal standard of proof for defamation is mere preponderance of the evidence.

Another important effect is somewhat more indirect. As a practical matter, plaintiff public officials have had, since the New York Times Co. case was decided, a very hard time in making out their defamation cases against media defendants because of the difficulty of establishing actual malice under the convincing clarity standard. Responsible media organizations rarely traffic in known falsehoods or act recklessly in disseminating news or information. Very often then when there is no real dispute as to the material facts, defendants are able to obtain summary judgments on the basis of preliminary papers, documents and affidavits showing no actual malice and thus do not have to defend themselves at trial. However, as we shall see, subsequent Supreme Court decisions have decreased the availability to news organizations of the constitutional privilege afforded by New York Times v. Sullivan with a consequent reduction in the availability of summary judgments.

3. The New York Times Progeny

As great a charter as the New York Times case is for the mass media, it raised more questions than it answered, and only the existence of two decades of subsequent court decisions permits an assessment of the true boundaries and impact of that case. One of the questions raised was as to the meaning of "reckless disregard." In the New York Times case itself the facts pointed so strongly to honest mistake in publication, that no real clue was given as to the boundaries of the concept.

Considerable light is cast on this issue in St. Amant v. Thompson, 390 U.S. 727, 88 S.Ct. 1323, 20 L.Ed.2d 262 (1968). There, the defendant, a candidate for office, made a television speech in the course of which he read questions which he had put to a local Teamsters Union member and the member's responses. The member's answers falsely charged the plaintiff, a local deputy sheriff, with corruption and the deputy sued. The defendant had no personal knowledge of the deputy's alleged corrupt activities, had relied solely on what the Teamster told him though the candidate had no apparent reason to accept his informant's veracity, had failed to make his own investigation of the charge, had given no heed to the seriousness of the charge and had rather cavalierly assumed that he had no responsibility for his conduct because he was merely quoting someone else. In reversing the Louisiana Supreme Court's affirmance of the trial court's judgment for the deputy sheriff, the Supreme Court held that the facts proved fell short of proving the candidate's reckless disregard for the accuracy of the quotations. Analyzing cases following New York Times Co. v. Sullivan, supra, the Court concluded that reckless conduct is not measured by whether a reasonable person would have investigated before publishing. Rather, the Court generalized, "[t]here must be sufficient evidence to permit the conclusion that the defendant in fact entertained serious doubts as to the truth of his publication." 390 U.S. at 731, 88 S.Ct. at 1325, 20 L.Ed.2d at 267. See also Herbert v. Lando, 441 U.S. 153, 156, 99 S.Ct. 1635, 1639, 60 L.Ed.2d 115, 122 (1979). This comes very close to requiring the public official to prove knowing publication of falsehood and appears to protect those publishers who deliberately avoid discovering the truth.

Another question expressly left open in New York Times Co. is the meaning of "official conduct." This concept now appears to parallel closely the boundaries of an executive or administrative officer's duties and responsibilities in office set forth in Barr v. Matteo, supra. As long as the defamatory material is published within the constitutional and statutory bounds of his or her office, the public official would be bound by the New York Times Co. rule. Cf. Butz v. Economou, 438 U.S. 478, 98 S.Ct. 2894, 57 L.Ed.2d 895 (1978). In addition, erroneous charges of criminal conduct on the part of public officials and candidates for public office, no matter how remote in time or place, are protected by the constitutional privilege because such charges are always relevant to the question of fitness to hold or seek office. Monitor Patriot Co. v. Roy, 401 U.S. 265, 91 S.Ct. 621, 28 L.Ed.2d 35 (1971); Ocala Star-Banner Co. v. Damron, 401 U.S. 295, 91 S.Ct. 628, 28 L.Ed.2d 57 (1971). On the other hand, even public officials are entitled to private lives and false and defamatory communications relating thereto would not be protected by the privilege established in the New York Times case. For instance, a defendant who publishes a negligently erroneous accusation that a county assessor owns an extensive collection of pornographic films would not be entitled to such protection since possession does not constitute a crime and is hardly relevant to the conduct of his or her office.

The Court in New York Times v. Sullivan also declined to provide a general definition of "public official." The cases that followed New York Times have established that "public official" includes at least those in governmental hierarchies who have or appear to have substantial responsibility for the conduct of government business, including judges (Garrison v. Louisiana, 379 U.S. 64, 85 S.Ct. 209, 13 L.Ed.2d 125 (1964)); county clerks (Beckley Newspapers Corp. v. Hanks, 389 U.S. 81, 88 S.Ct. 197, 19 L.Ed.2d 248 (1967)); chiefs and deputy chiefs of police (Henry v. Collins, 380 U.S. 356, 85 S.Ct. 992, 13 L.Ed.2d 892 (1965); Time, Inc. v. Pape, 401 U.S. 279, 91 S.Ct. 633, 28 L.Ed.2d 45 (1971)); mayors (Ocala Star-

Banner Co. v. Damron, 401 U.S. 295, 91 S.Ct. 628, 28 L.Ed.2d 57 (1971)); and even deputy sheriffs (St. Amant v. Thompson, 390 U.S. 727, 88 S.Ct. 1323, 20 L.Ed.2d 262 (1968)). The term also included former office holders who exercised substantial responsibility while in office and who are attacked for their past official conduct (Rosenblatt v. Baer, 383 U.S. 75, 86 S.Ct. 669, 15 L.Ed.2d 597 (1966)).

While the term "public official" is thus an expansive one, it covers only a small percentage of public personages. Recognizing this, the Court subsequently extended the reach of the New York Times Co. decision to public figures and their non-official but public acts, such as famous college athletic directors and football coaches and resigned Army generals who, by their public conduct, thrust themselves into the limelight (Curtis Publishing Co. v. Butts, 388 U.S. 130, 87 S.Ct. 1975, 18 L.Ed.2d 1094 (1967); Associated Press v. Walker, 388 U.S. 130, 87 S.Ct. 1975, 18 L.Ed.2d 1094 (1967)); a prominent real estate developer involved in a land dispute with a local city council (Greenbelt Cooperative Publishing Association v. Bresler, 398 U.S. 6, 90 S.Ct. 1537, 26 L.Ed.2d 6 (1970)); and candidates for public office (Monitor Patriot Co. v. Roy, 401 U.S. 265, 91 S.Ct. 621, 28 L.Ed.2d 35 (1971)).

But what of persons who are neither public officials nor public figures but who are caught up in matters of public interest? Should the media have the same constitutional privilege regarding

communications about private persons who may
be less able to defend themselves against false
and defamatory allegations because of less access
to the corrective mechanisms of the mass media?
In other words, should the focus be shifted from
public persons to matters of public interest, regardless of the status of the participants involved? These are extremely important questions. Affirmative answers might so alter the
balance between the interest in free speech and
press and the interest in individual reputation as
to destroy the latter. Whomever the media
deemed newsworthy might be regarded by the
courts as being bound by the New York Times
rule when they sought legal redress.

Initially, a plurality of the Supreme Court in
Rosenbloom v. Metromedia, Inc., 403 U.S. 29, 91
S.Ct. 1811, 29 L.Ed.2d 296 (1971), answered this
question in the affirmative, deeming the distinction between public and private individuals to be
artificial in relationship to the public's interest in
a broad range of issues, including, in that case,
the arrest of an obscure distributor of nudist
magazines on obscenity charges and the confiscation of his magazines as pornographic.

4. The Basic Public Figure–Private Person Distinction of Gertz v. Welch

Strong dissent was registered in Rosenbloom
to this extension of the constitutional privilege,
and in Gertz v. Robert Welch, Inc., 418 U.S. 323,
94 S.Ct. 2997, 41 L.Ed.2d 789 (1974), a majority of

the Court rejected that plurality decision, holding that the privilege recognized in New York Times Co. v. Sullivan was applicable only to cases involving defamation of public officials and public figures. The facts of the Gertz case are set out in detail in Chapter I at pp. 22–24. It is only necessary to note here that the trial judge had applied the constitutional privilege even though he was convinced that Gertz, a prominent lawyer, was neither a public official nor a public figure. The judge did this because of Gertz's involvement as an attorney in litigation of some public interest. The trial court's judgment denying Gertz recovery for libel was affirmed by the Court of Appeals on the authority of Rosenbloom.

In reversing that judgment and rejecting the Rosenbloom approach, the Supreme Court drew a sharp distinction between the private person who is defamed and the public one. According to the majority in Gertz the private person is more in need of judicial redress and the state has a greater interest in providing it because he or she has not voluntarily invited public comment, thus choosing to put his or her reputation at risk. Moreover, the private person will normally have less access to the channels of effective communication (the media) to correct the record than will the public person. Therefore, while the media's first amendment interest in matters of public or general concern is a constant factor regardless of the plaintiff's status, the plaintiff's interest in achieving legal redress for injury to his or her reputation varies according to whether he or she is a private person. By its decision the majority in Gertz was attempting to restore the balance between protection of expression and protection of reputation which it perceived had been upset in New York Times Co.

The Court's reasoning was vigorously criticized by Justice Brennan in his dissenting opinion. He suggested that the social interaction in a society which places primary value on freedom of speech and press necessarily exposes all of its members to some degree of public exposure. As for the assumption that public persons have greater access to the media for non-judicial redress Brennan argued that empirically this is often not the case. The main concern expressed by Brennan, the author of the plurality opinion in Rosenbloom, is that anything less than the constitutional privilege will result in self censorship by the media in handling matters of public concern when the participants are not clearly public persons.

This concern was recognized by the majority and, aware of the dangers of leaving the media subject to the unreconstructed common law in suits by private persons, they directly modified the common law in two fundamental respects. First, they abolished strict liability for the publication of defamatory material and left to the individual states the determination of the appropriate fault standard of liability. This means that while the states may no longer impose liability on the media where there is no fault in the communication of defamatory material, they may impose it on one of the following bases (listed in ascending order of protection for the media): unreasonable publication (negligence), extremely unreasonable publication (gross negligence) or knowingly false or reckless publication (New York Times standard).

Second, when liability is imposed on the basis of a lower standard of fault than that of New York Times Co., i.e., negligence or gross negligence, recovery is to be limited to compensation for proved actual injury caused by the defamation. The Court thus ruled out presumed general damages and punitive damages in states choosing to adopt a lower standard of liability such as negligence. But apparently in defamation actions against the media tried pursuant to the New York Times Co. standard, presumed and punitive damages might still be awarded.

This modification of the common law system of damages is clearly designed to protect the media from massive judgments based on the jury's imagination, its ideas of punishment and deterrence and its prejudices. An example of such a judgment is the $725,000 punitive damages originally awarded by the jury in Gertz against the defendant publisher of an unpopular right wing periodical.

Whether this modification provides sufficient protection to the media to discourage self censorship and undue timidity in their handling of news and information remains to be seen. Actual injury may still encompass such things as impairment of reputation, personal humiliation and mental and emotional distress, none of which may be reduced to precise monetary figures. Therefore, once the plaintiff proves the existence of these injuries, the jury, of necessity, must be given some latitude in fixing their value.

5. The Progeny of Gertz and the Public Figure—Private Person Distinction

a. The Narrowing of the Public Figure Classification

In righting the perceived imbalance in constitutional protection between expression and reputation it was important for the Gertz majority to reduce the range of applicability of New York Times Co. This could be accomplished by defining narrowly who was a public figure and thus who was governed for purpose of defamation actions by the stringent New York Times Co. standards.

Gertz, of course, created the dichotomy between public figures and private persons and set out the basic tests for determining a public figure: (1) the general fame or notoriety of the plaintiff in the community; or (2) the plaintiff's thrusting himself or herself voluntarily into the middle of the specific public controversy involved in the suit.

But it was left to the progeny of Gertz to establish the truly restrictive nature of the public figure category. In Time Inc. v. Firestone, 424 U.S. 448, 96 S.Ct. 958, 47 L.Ed.2d 154 (1976), Mrs. Firestone brought suit for separate maintenance and her husband counterclaimed for complete divorce on grounds of extreme cruelty and adultery. Mrs. Firestone was a socially prominent hostess in Palm Beach, Florida and her husband was an heir to the Firestone tire empire. After a lengthy and spicy public trial the judge granted the husband's request for a complete divorce but without clearly setting out the ground or grounds therefor and granted Mrs. Firestone $3000 per month alimony. Time Magazine published the following item in its "Milestones" section: "Divorced by Russell A. Firestone, Jr., 41, heir to the tire fortune: Mary Alice Sullivan Firestone, 32 . . . on grounds of extreme cruelty and adultery . . . ." After her request for a printed retraction was rejected, Mrs. Firestone sued for libel in Palm Beach. The material in Time's Milestones section was defamatory and untrue because an adulterous wife could not, under Florida law, receive alimony and, of course, the Florida trial court had made a substantial award of alimony to her.

Time however claimed that Mrs. Firestone was a public figure by reason of her celebrity in Palm Beach Society and the public nature of the trial and divorce, not to mention her impromptu press conferences on the courthouse stairs and her hiring of a press agent. Thus according to Time, she was required to show that the magazine was guilty of publishing a known falsehood or recklessly disregarding the truth.

In rejecting Time's contention the Supreme Court said that local social prominence is not enough to categorize a plaintiff as a public figure. More importantly, involvement in a public trial does not necessarily make one a public figure. Marriage dissolution is not the sort of "public controversy" referred to in Gertz. It is essentially a private matter which the state requires to be resolved in a public forum. The Court did not even mention Mrs. Firestone's open air press conferences or her hiring of a press agent designed to get out to the public her side of the divorce story.

Firestone considerably narrows the public figure category, given Mrs. Firestone's notoriety. The category was further narrowed by two cases decided by the Supreme Court on the same day in its 1978–1979 term.

In Wolston v. Reader's Digest Association, Inc., 443 U.S. 157, 99 S.Ct. 2701, 61 L.Ed.2d 450 (1979) defendant published a book about Soviet intelligence agents in the United States and listed Wolston as one of them. Sixteen years earlier Wolston had been subpoenaed to testify before a federal grand jury investigating the activity of Soviet agents in this country. Because of claimed poor health he did not comply with the subpoena and he was cited for contempt. His trial on the contempt charge was attended with great publicity but following the conclusion of the criminal proceedings at which he was sentenced to a one-year suspended jail term, Wolston sank back into anonymity.

Wolston denied any connection to the Soviet intelligence apparatus and sued the Reader's Digest Association for libel. The trial court granted the Association summary judgment on the basis that petitioner was a public figure and that the papers supporting and opposing summary judgment did not show knowing untruthfulness or reckless disregard for the truth on the part of the defendant. The United States Court of Appeals affirmed the summary judgment.

The Supreme Court reversed, ruling that Wolston was not a public figure. According to the Court, Wolston's failure to answer the subpoena was not of itself a voluntary thrusting of himself into the middle of the public controversy regarding Soviet espionage even though such failure was sure to generate publicity. Only if the failure had been designed as a protest against the investigation and to influence public opinion would Wolston have become a limited public figure in relationship to the Soviet spy controversy.

This holding restricts limited issue public figures to those who draw attention to themselves in order to advocate a particular view on a public matter and to affect public opinion. Thus, as in Firestone, mere involvement in a matter of public interest is not enough.

This same restrictive view of limited-issue public figures lead the Court to reject the Association's other contention that any person who engages in criminal conduct automatically becomes a public figure regarding his trial and conviction. As in the Firestone case, one involved in a public trial (here a criminal one) does not necessarily become a public figure.

In the companion case of Hutchinson v. Proxmire, 443 U.S. 111, 99 S.Ct. 2675, 61 L.Ed.2d 411 (1979), Senator William Proxmire awarded his uncoveted "Golden Fleece of the Month" awards to NASA and the Office of Naval Research for spending almost a half-million dollars to fund Dr. Hutchinson's research on the aggressiveness of animals, particularly monkeys, for the purpose of finding ways to reduce aggressiveness in humans thrown together in close quarters for extended periods of time. In his speech making the award as well as in a related news release Proxmire described Hutchinson's research as transparently worthless and called for an end to his making "a monkey out of the American taxpayer" and putting the "bite" on the taxpayer's resources. Dr. Hutchinson sued the Senator and his administrative assistant for libel. As in Wolston, summary judgment was granted by the trial court because the plaintiff was a public figure. Public figure status was conferred on him, according to the trial court, because of his long involvement with publicly funded research, solicitation of such funds, local press coverage of his research and

[*81*]

the public interest in the expenditure of public funds for such research. Applying the New York Times Co. standard the trial court could find no issue of malice in the pretrial papers. The United States Court of Appeals affirmed the summary judgment.

On the "public figure" issue the Supreme Court reversed rejecting the view that the plaintiff's successful application for federal funds, local newspaper reports regarding the grants and his research and his technical publications made him a limited-issue public figure. In so ruling the Court made these points:

1. Dr. Hutchinson's media celebrity or notoriety occurred only as a consequence of the defamatory Proxmire award; clearly those charged with defamation cannot create their own defense by themselves making the victim a public figure;

2. Merely receiving or benefitting from publicly funded research grants does not make one a public figure;

3. The access to the media required by Gertz is a regular and continuing one and not merely that made available to rebut a specific defamatory attack.

As to this last point, the Court appears to have shrunk the public figure category significantly because, as originally conceived in Gertz, the purpose of the media-access test for public figure status appeared to be the availability of self-defense to the victim of defamation, with a consequent lesser need for judicial remedy in the form of money damages. Here, Hutchinson had been given media access to defend himself. Consider how many (or few) persons in this country have regular and continuing access to the mass media.

In summary, the public figure category has been narrowed by the Gertz progeny in these important respects:

1. Simply appearing in the newspapers in connection with some newsworthy story or stories does not make one a public figure;

2. Social, professional or business prominence does not by itself make one a public figure;

3. Forced involvement in a public trial, either civil or criminal, does not by itself make one a public figure;

4. Those charged with defamation cannot by their own conduct in making their victims notorious thereby create their own defense;

5. Merely applying for, receiving or benefiting from public research grants does not make one a public figure;

6. In order to meet the Gertz test of thrusting oneself into the forefront of a public issue or controversy, the issue or controversy must be a real dispute, the outcome of which affects the general public or some segment of it in an appreciable way and

one's conduct must be calculated or clearly be expected to invite public comment respecting that issue or controversy, e.g., the value and conduct of a federal investigation into KGB activity in the United States during the McCarthy era.

7. In order to meet the Gertz test of access to the media the access must be regular and continuing.

All in all, following the Firestone, Wolston and Proxmire decisions, the category of public figures for purposes of New York Times v. Sullivan protection is much smaller than could have been imagined when Gertz was decided. For an extended discussion of the public figure-private person dichotomy see Note, 30 Cath.U.L.Rev. 307 (1981).

b. The Effect of Time Passage on Public Figure Status

Wolston v. Reader's Digest Association was marked by an interesting concurring opinion by Justice Blackmun in which he assumed for purposes of argument that Wolston had become a public figure in 1958. But, Blackmun argued, by Wolston's return to anonymity and the passage of time until the offending book was published some sixteen years later, he no longer had "significantly greater access to the channels of communication" to defend himself and had no longer knowingly chosen to run the risk of public scrutiny. Consequently, he had lost his public figure status. Justice Blackmun recognized that such analysis implies that a person may be a public figure for purposes of contemporaneous reporting of his activities but not a public figure for purposes of historical commentary on the same activities and events.

Because Justice Blackmun's approach provides less protection for the historical commentator than it does for the contemporaneous journalist, it has been rejected by at least one lower court. See Street v. National Broadcasting Co., 645 F.2d 1227 (6th Cir. 1981); and compare Brewer v. Memphis Publishing Co., Inc., 626 F.2d 1238 (5th Cir. 1980). Despite these lower court decisions the popular or scholarly historical commentator should be wary for the Supreme Court majority did not reject Justice Blackmun's analysis as a corollary means of narrowing the media's constitutional privilege. Thus, special care should be taken to achieve factual accuracy in the preparation of the "where are they now"—type features concerning formerly famous or notorious people.

6. The Broad Meaning of Gertz

The case of Gertz v. Robert Welch, Inc. sets, of course, the boundaries of the constitutional privilege established in New York Times Co. v. Sullivan. From here on the privilege of the media negligently to make false and defamatory communications may be limited by the states when it is determined that the complaining party is not a public person. But beyond this, Gertz puts an end, at least temporarily, to the expansion of the absolutist interpretation of the First Amendment which gives primacy to the societal interests in free expression.

As a result the media will have to be more concerned about what they communicate relative to the "unknowns" of our society and will have to review and strengthen verification procedures to avoid the charge of negligence in news gathering, interpretation and dissemination. The other side of the new coin minted in Gertz is the greater recognition of the individual's personal worth and dignity.

7. Specific Problems for the Media Created by Gertz

The media may find it difficult to come to terms with the system made possible by Gertz. Aside from the pervasive specter of self censorship raised by it, Gertz presents a number of very specific problems.

Distinguishing between public persons and private ones may not be easy for the media, particularly under the pressure of deadlines. Even the United States District Court and the United States Court of Appeals were at odds over the status of Gertz, an author and prominent attorney long active in community and professional affairs. The Supreme Court's guidelines here are, at best, difficult to apply. They present two

standards for the characterization of a public figure: (1) general fame or notoriety of the plaintiff
in the community, which makes the protection of
the constitutional privilege general; or (2) the
plaintiff's thrusting himself or herself voluntarily
into the vortex of the specific public issue involved, in which event the media's protection is
limited to communications concerning that issue.
The Supreme Court stressed the fact in Gertz
that the plaintiff had not achieved any general
fame in the community—the jurors had never
heard of him. Moreover, the Court did not think
that simply because he was counsel in the civil litigation in question that he had "thrust himself into the vortex." But can a newspaper, for instance, make these fine judgments in advance of
publication?

Another determination which the media may
be required to make in advance of publication, depending on the standard of liability embodied in
the relevant state law, is the reasonableness of
its publishing procedures in every given case.
But even if the particular publisher satisfies itself that its procedures are reasonable (non-negli-
gent), the jury will have the last word on this
question. Factors to be considered in making an
assessment of reasonableness of publication include the apparent risk of defamation as perceived by a reasonable person in the publisher's
position and the gravity of the injury to the victim if the risk is realized. These factors have to
be balanced against the reasons for the publica-

tion, the deadline pressures on the publisher, the means actually used in verifying and interpreting the information, the alternative means of verification and interpretation available to the publisher which were not utilized, and, of course, the costs involved in using such alternative means. Since some of these factors which the jury must consider are qualitative and subjective, prudent communicators will be very cautious in what and how they publish and will be left to hope that juries will overcome any prejudices they may have against the media. One thing does seem clear even in this early stage of the Gertz era. The head in the sand approach to verification taken by the defendant in St. Amant v. Thompson, supra, will almost certainly be deemed negligent or even grossly negligent by juries.

Because of the great uncertainties involved in determining the reasonableness of the publisher's conduct prior to trial, the media can also expect many less favorable determinations on motions for summary judgment against private plaintiffs. Unless the publisher's conduct can be held by the trial judge to be reasonable beyond question, a trial will have to be conducted to permit the jury to decide this issue. Thus, more protracted litigation can be expected with increasing pressure on media defendants to settle even nuisance claims.

Finally, the problem of large damage awards discussed previously will remain a very real concern of the media and may add to the pressure for out of court settlements that can only weaken the financial structure of media organizations.

8. Questions Remaining After Gertz

Gertz raises important questions about the existence and operation of common law defenses. Who now has the burden of establishing the truth or falsity of the alleged defamatory communications? While technically the defense of truth may still be available, as a practical matter the plaintiff will be unable to prove fault in publication without establishing why it was faulty, i.e., that the communicated material was false and the defendant would have discovered it to be so had it acted reasonably or non-recklessly. See Wilson v. Scripps-Howard Broadcasting Co., 642 F.2d 371 (6th Cir. 1981). Until the matter of allocation of the burden of proof on this issue is finally resolved, one can expect media defendants to continue pleading truth as a defense. But Gertz does appear by necessary implication to invalidate the requirement in a majority of jurisdictions that the truth be accompanied by good motives. Publication of truthful information no matter how damaging is inconsistent with concepts of negligence and gross negligence.

The dictum in Gertz that under the First Amendment there is no such thing as a false idea or opinion raises questions as to the continued need of fair comment as a defense. That common law defense is, after all, designed to protect comment and opinion so long as they are based on correct facts. If the defense has vanished, the media has lost little or nothing, for now comment, opinion and ideas (as distinguished from supporting fact) are constitutionally protected from defamation actions.

Finally, the question remains what the states have done following Gertz. They had at least three fault standards of liability to choose from (see p. 76, supra). The earliest returns indicated a preference for the New York Times Co. standard. See Walker v. Colorado Springs Sun, Inc., 538 P.2d 450 (Colo.1975); AAFCO Heating and Air Conditioning Co. v. Northwest Publications, Inc., 321 N.E.2d 580 (Ind.App.1974). In neither case, however, was the adoption of that standard of fault unanimous and subsequently the highest courts of most other states considering the question have opted for a simple negligence test. See e.g., Phillips v. Evening Star Newspaper Co., 424 A.2d 78, 87, 94 n. 10 (D.C.1980) (all state holdings on this issue collected); Stone v. Essex County Newspapers, Inc., 367 Mass. 849, 330 N.E.2d 161 (1975); Troman v. Wood, 62 Ill.2d 184, 340 N.E.2d 292 (1975); and Martin v. Griffin Television, Inc., 549 P.2d 85 (Okl.1976). But New York has chosen to impose liability for defamation only if the defendant "acted in a grossly irresponsible manner without due consideration for the standards of information gathering and dissemination ordinarily followed by responsible parties," (Robart v. Post-Standard, 52 N.Y.2d 843, 845, 418 N.E.2d 664, 437 N.Y.S.2d 71 (1981), an intermediate stan-

dard between that of New York Times Co. and
ordinary negligence.

9. Miscellaneous Constitutional Privileges Claimed by Journalists in Defamation Cases

a. Nondisclosure of the Editorial Decision Making Process

In Herbert v. Lando, 441 U.S. 153, 99 S.Ct.
1635, 60 L.Ed.2d 115 (1979), a CBS news producer
involved in the production and broadcast of "Sixty Minutes" claimed a First Amendment right not
to divulge his state of mind in the preparation of
a segment about Army Col. Anthony Herbert and
his conduct during the Vietnam War. Col. Herbert, who did not contest his status as a public
figure, claimed that the material in the segment
was defamatory and was put together in a knowingly untruthful way or with reckless disregard
of the truth. He attempted to establish this necessary element of malice in the course of a pretrial deposition of CBS News producer Lando. The
United States District Court rejected Lando's
claim of privilege and ordered him to answer Herbert's questions, but a divided United States
Court of Appeals reversed.

The United States Supreme Court reversed
the Court of Appeals and ruled that no First
Amendment privilege existed to protect newspersons from testifying as to the editorial process
when such testimony is material to the proof of a

critical element of the plaintiff's action, here defendant's malice, i.e., knowing untruthfulness or
reckless disregard of the truth.

In public figure cases, the plaintiff's inquiry
into the editorial process may therefore include:

1. the reporter's or editor's conclusions during research and investigation regarding
   people or leads to be pursued or not pursued;

2. the reporter's or editor's conclusions about
   facts imparted by interviewees and his or
   her state of mind with respect to the veracity of the persons interviewed;

3. the basis for the reporter's or editor's conclusions as to the veracity of persons or information.

4. conversations with journalistic colleagues
   and others concerning the manner in which
   a story should be approached, handled and
   published, particularly discussions as to
   the inclusion and exclusion of material;

5. the reporter's or editor's intentions as manifested by his decisions to include or exclude particular material.

While it is now clear after the Herbert case
that no privilege exists under the First Amendment for newspersons to refuse to reveal the information listed above, at least one state reporter
"shield" law has been construed as protecting
newspersons from testifying as to editorial
processes on the ground that forced revelations

in this area would have a chilling effect on the free exchange of ideas between journalistic colleagues. Maressa v. New Jersey Monthly, 89 N.J. 176, 445 A.2d 376 (1982).

b. Neutral Reportage

An official of the National Audubon Society gave a reporter for the New York Times a list of five scientists whom the Society believed were being paid by the chemical industry to lie about the impact of DDT on the bird population. The story concerning the bird count with the names of the five scientists was subsequently published by the Times and three of the named scientists filed libel actions against the Society, Society officials and the Times.

In reversing the jury award and judgment against the Times, the United States Court of Appeals for the Second Circuit held that the First Amendment protects the accurate and disinterested reporting of charges by a responsible and prominent person or organization, regardless of the reporter's private views regarding their accuracy. Such protection of journalists from tort liability for defamation was characterized by the Second Circuit as "neutral reportage." Edwards v. National Audubon Society, 556 F.2d 113 (2d Cir. 1977), cert. denied 434 U.S. 1002, 98 S.Ct. 647, 54 L.Ed.2d 498. In a subsequent case the Second Circuit made clear that the repetition of defamatory charges in a piece of advocacy journalism espousing and concurring in such charges did not constitute neutral reportage and was not constitutionally protected. Cianci v. New York Times Publishing Co., 639 F.2d 54 (2d Cir. 1980).

Ultimate recognition of such a First Amendment privilege by the Supreme Court is highly doubtful because, at least in part, it flies in the face of St. Amant v. Thompson, 390 U.S. 727, 88 S.Ct. 1323, 20 L.Ed.2d 262 (1968), which would deny First Amendment protection under New York Times v. Sullivan to those who would publish defamatory material while entertaining serious doubts as to the truth of the publication. See Dickey v. CBS, Inc., 583 F.2d 1221 (3d Cir. 1978) rejecting the neutral reportage privilege for this reason.

It seems unlikely that the Supreme Court would deny the constitutional privilege recognized in New York Times Co. to one who publishes a damaging charge he or she strongly suspects to be untrue but then substitute another constitutional privilege to protect one who, with reckless disregard for the truth, publishes the charge simply because it came from a reputable and prominent source. And if the publisher does not suspect the story is untrue, he or she will be protected under the New York Times Co. privilege if the target of the charges is a public figure in relation to the controversy without regard to "neutral reportage".

Newspersons, therefore, may find the neutral reportage privilege to be a very weak reed to rely on when publishing questionable charges made by even responsible sources.

CHAPTER III

PRIVACY AND THE MASS MEDIA

A. INTRODUCTION

The invasion of personal privacy by government, private organizations and the mass media
has reached monumental proportions in the last
decades of the twentieth century. This invasion
is almost inevitable given our crowded society
and the development of sophisticated electronic
devices such as directional microphones, powerful
miniature listening devices, telephoto lenses and
the all-pervasive computer with its power to store
and retrieve the minutiae of our lives. The problem is exacerbated by the power of the mass media to disseminate widely information about individuals, including their physical images.

The difficulty that confronts the law is to control this invasion without, at the same time, crip-
pling a free society's ability to obtain the information necessary for its proper operation. Thus
far, the common law has not been very effective
in harmonizing the competing private and societal
interests. Perhaps this is because the competing
interests are so fundamental yet so difficult of
definition. It has been said that the right to be
let alone and to withdraw from the "madding
crowd" is the essence of individualism and that

[*96*]

privacy is the first interest to go in a totalitarian
state. Nevertheless, the individual lives in a society which may, from time to time, have curiosity
about him or her. And the mass media may become the instrument for satisfying that curiosity.
As difficult as the task is, it is for the law to determine when public interest concerning an individual fulfills a legitimate need of a democratic
society and when it does not.

B. COMMON LAW DEVELOPMENT

1. History

As common law torts go, invasion of privacy
is of relatively recent vintage. Its development is
traceable to an article in the Harvard Law Review for December 15, 1890 by Samuel D. Warren and his then law partner Louis D. Brandeis.
In it they argued that accepted tort doctrine confirmed the existence of a right to privacy, the violation of which was actionable. 4 Harv.L.Rev.
193 (1890). The article was apparently precipitat-
ed by the Boston newspapers' coverage of Warren's private social affairs. It should be
remembered that this was the era of vicious circulation battles and sensational and often fraudulent press coverage to win readership—the age of
"yellow journalism."

The article created great interest in the legal
profession but the first test of the theory was unsuccessful. In Roberson v. Rochester Folding
Box Co., 171 N.Y. 538, 64 N.E. 442 (1902) a flour

mill ordered a woman's portrait lithographed on its boxes without her consent. The woman, who did not relish being referred to as the "Flour of the Family" brought suit for damages for invasion of privacy. In a four to three ruling, the New York Court of Appeals held, contrary to Warren and Brandeis' contention, no right of privacy existed at common law. If interests in privacy were to be protected, the legislatures would have to do it. The New York legislature did just that the following year by enacting a civil rights statute making it both a crime and a tort to appropriate the name or likeness of any person for "trade purposes" without that person's consent.

The first judicial acceptance of the existence of a right to privacy came in Pavesich v. New England Life Insurance Co., 122 Ga. 190, 50 S.E. 68, 69 L.R.A. 101 (1905), a case very much like Roberson in which a newspaper advertisement for an insurance company contained a photograph of the plaintiff and attributed to him certain words encouraging the purchase of the company's life insurance. He had not consented to such depiction and sued the company. Contrary to the New York court the Georgia Supreme Court found a right of privacy in the common law and reversed the trial court's order dismissing Pavesich's complaint.

2. The Common Law Today

As of 1982 a right of privacy of some dimension was recognized in 48 states and the District of Columbia. Of the jurisdictions accepting the concept at least five have done so by statute: California, New York, Oklahoma, Utah and Virginia. Pember and Teeter, "Privacy and the Press Since Time, Inc. v. Hill," 50 Wash.L.Rev. 57, 58 (1974). The right that is accorded varies to some extent in definition and scope from jurisdiction to jurisdiction, reflecting the immaturity of the tort and its imperfect development to date.

The imperfect development extends to the lack of any articulated theory of liability. While the tort in several of its forms is suggestive of an intentional civil wrong, it is possible that some aspects of it permit strict liability. The uncertainty as to the theory of liability may arise from the fact that the tort has four distinct branches:

appropriation of another's name or likeness;

unreasonable intrusion upon another's seclusion;

publicity which unreasonably places another in a false light before the public; and

unreasonable publicity given to another's private life.

See Cox Broadcasting Corp. v. Cohn, 420 U.S. 469, 493–94, 95 S.Ct. 1029, 1045–1046, 43 L.Ed.2d 328, 348–49 (1975); Restatement of Torts 2d 652A–652E; W. Prosser, Handbook of the Law of Torts, 804–14 (4th ed. 1971).

a. Appropriation

We have already come across this aspect of the right of privacy in relation to the Roberson and Pavesich cases and the New York statute. What is protected here is the individual's concern for the uses to which his or her name, personality and image are put. The law gives the individual the option to prevent others from trading on his or her name or likeness or to permit such trading for a price. In this respect the tort appears to protect something akin to a property right in one's own personality and image—a right of publicity.

The media are rarely sued for appropriation type invasions. It has long been settled that while the media normally disseminate news about individuals in the hope, overall, of obtaining a profit for their operations from circulation and advertising, this is not such appropriation as would justify the award of damages.

When such suits are brought they are usually in connection with a medium's self promotion in which a news or feature story involving the plaintiff is republished to evidence the medium's self proclaimed excellence in informing the public. For instance, in Booth v. Curtis Publishing Co., 15 App.Div.2d 343, 223 N.Y.S.2d 737 (1962), affirmed 11 N.Y.2d 907, 228 N.Y.S.2d 468, 182 N.E.2d 812, the actress Shirley Booth, whose photograph had appeared by consent in Holiday Magazine in connection with an article about a prominent resort in Jamaica where she had been a guest sued the magazine's publisher when it reproduced her photograph in full page promotional advertisements for the magazine published in two other periodicals. Both advertisements presented the striking photograph of Miss Booth in a large straw hat and up to her neck in water as a sample of the contents of Holiday. Beneath the photograph were the words "Shirley Booth and chapeau, from a recent issue of Holiday." But even here, the court refused to award damages under the New York privacy statute because such advertising was only "incidental" to the sale and dissemination of news. The decision turned on the court's construction of the statute and it is uncertain that a similar case would have the same resolution in jurisdictions recognizing a common law right of privacy. Prudence therefore dictates that when a medium advertises itself by use of antecedent news and feature stories and photographs it obtain the permission for republication from the individuals involved.

b. Intrusion

This tort consists of the unconsented to violation of one's legally protected physical sphere of privacy. The intrusion may or may not also constitute the tort of trespass. Often the intrusion itself is not physical but consists of eavesdropping with telephoto lenses or electronic listening devices in areas private to the aggrieved individual such as his or her home or office. When the individual is in a public zone, however, he or she

[*101*]

may be photographed or otherwise recorded without fear of legal action so long as the recordation is reasonable.

This particular aspect of invasion of privacy is different in nature from the other three in that no publication regarding the victim need be involved. This distinction is important when through an intrusion a news medium learns of matters of public interest and publishes them. In that situation, while the publication itself may be privileged on the basis of newsworthiness (see pp. 114–115 infra), the intrusion that made the story possible is not.

An excellent and fortunately rare example of media intrusion is Dietemann v. Time, Inc., 449 F.2d 245 (9th Cir. 1971). There, a male and female employee of Life Magazine, went to the home of Dietemann, a plumber who practiced healing with clay, minerals and herbs. Through misrepresentations of fact they gained entry to the plaintiffs home. Once inside, the female employee complained to Dietemann of a lump in her breast. While examining the breast, with an assortment of gadgets, Dietemann was secretly photographed by Life's male employee using a hidden camera. In addition, the conversation between the woman and Dietemann was transmitted by a radio transmitter hidden in the woman's purse to a tape recorder in a parked car occupied by another Life employee and officials from the local district attorney's office and the California Department of Health. The whole affair was a cooperative venture of Life and the public officals to aid in the crackdown on quackery in Southern California and to allow the magazine to write about it. Life published its story and pictures following Dietemann's plea of nolo contendere to criminal misdemeanor charges.

Dietemann thereafter sued for invasion of privacy and won a trial court judgment for $1,000. In contending on appeal that the judgment should be reversed, Time, Inc. took the position that the First Amendment immunized it from liability for its intrusion because its employees were using the secret devices to gather news. In answer Judge Hufstedler pointed out that the First Amendment has never been construed to accord newspersons immunity from the consequences of torts or crimes committed in the process of newsgathering. In affirming the judgment for Dietemann, Judge Hufstedler clearly distinguished between the intrusion and the subsequent publication of the story and photographs. A privilege might exist for the publication but it does not extend to the antecedent intrusion.

Dietemann is a troubling case not so much because of its denial of any privilege to intrude in the course of bona fide newsgathering but because it raises questions as to the extent to which newsgatherers, especially investigative reporters may go before they are liable for intrusion. As media lawyer Floyd Abrams has said, "It is one thing to say that as a general matter one's home is sacrosanct from invasion by outsiders and that journalists are as responsible as the rest of us for illegal or improper eavesdropping . . . .

"It is quite another to conclude that when a person passes himself off as a doctor and uses his home as his office, journalists may not act as prospective patients and record the illegal activities that occur there." Abrams, "The Press, Privacy and the Constitution," N. Y. Times Magazine, Aug. 21, 1977, p. 68.

There is great uncertainty as to the line between legality and intrusion regarding admission to private property. But as a result of recent cases we do know that:

(1) outright misrepresentation by newsgatherers to gain initial entry to private or even public property is a very risky business and should not be resorted to except in extremis;

(2) unauthorized entry by newsgatherers onto private or public property constitutes intrusion as to individuals present and trespass as to the property, and that goes for private places of public accommodation as well;

(3) permission of relevant public officials provides the necessary license to gather news in public buildings;

(4) permission by police or fire officials to news gatherers to accompany the officials onto private property while they conduct official business in the absence of the own-

er will insulate newsgatherers against tort
liability in Florida and very probably elsewhere (see Florida Publishing Co. v.
Fletcher, 340 So.2d 914 (Fla.1976), cert. denied, 431 U.S. 930, 97 S.Ct. 2634, 53 L.Ed.
2d 245 (1977).

While Dietemann and other recent cases make
clear the danger of intrusive behavior by representatives of the media, they are limited to situations in which media representatives are directly
involved. In situations in which the media simply
publicize the fruits of another's intrusion the
courts have usually rejected the idea of liability
on the part of the media. For instance in Pearson v. Dodd, 133 U.S.App.D.C. 279, 410 F.2d 701
(1969) employees of Senator Dodd rifled his files,
made copies of some allegedly incriminating documents and turned the copies over to defendant
Jack Anderson, who was aware of the manner in
which they were obtained, and who subsequently
published excerpts from them. The United
States Court of Appeals held that the defendants
had not themselves been guilty of any intrusion.
See also Liberty Lobby, Inc. v. Pearson, 129 U.S.
App.D.C. 74, 390 F.2d 489 (1968). But compare
Barber v. Time, Inc., 348 Mo. 1199, 159 S.W.2d
291 (1942), wherein Time, Inc. was held liable for
publishing an unconsented to photograph of a woman in a hospital bed suffering from an exotic
disease. The photograph had been taken by an
International News Service photographer and
subsequently sold to Time Magazine.

The position taken in the Dodd case makes considerable sense. If the media were required to consider the means by which news is obtained by independent sources out of fear for tort liability, the newsgathering process would be severely hampered. But it should be kept in mind that if media representatives actually encourage or aid and abet others in acts of intrusion, it is reasonably certain that they and their corporate employers will be held liable for such conduct under ordinary principles of tort law.

While outright intrusion by the media into the privacy of individuals is rare, an analogous problem is becoming increasingly frequent. Property owners may refuse to cooperate with newspersons, particularly television crews, seeking news on their premises. This raises the question whether media representatives have the right under the First Amendment to go without authorization upon private property or otherwise to utilize such property in the interest of obtaining news. The issue often comes up in connection with private property which is open to the public for business purposes. For example, a large new hotel in an eastern metropolitan area recently experienced a fire in which one of the hotel employees lost her life. A local television station sent a camera crew over to the hotel to film the after effects of the fire. The hotel management refused to permit the camera crew to enter the premises. The station news director told the crew to get into the hotel by subterfuge if necessary in order to get the story. The camera crew, sensing a serious legal problem, refused to follow orders and came away without the desired film.

The basic position of media executives in this kind of situation is that their representatives ought to be able to enter privately owned places of public accommodation along with the rest of the public and that if they are not allowed to enter, the flow of news will be constricted in violation of the First Amendment.

These arguments are doubtful for reasons suggested in the analogous case of Lloyd Corp., Ltd. v. Tanner, 407 U.S. 551, 92 S.Ct. 2219, 33 L.Ed.2d 131 (1972), involving the distribution of handbills protesting the draft and the Vietnam War in a privately owned mall-type shopping complex. First, the public's license to enter a private business establishment is limited to engaging in activities directly related to that business and does not normally extend to the pursuit of unrelated business, e.g., newsgathering or propagandizing customers. Cf. Hudgens v. NLRB, 424 U.S. 507, 96 S.Ct. 1029, 47 L.Ed.2d 196 (1976), permitting a shopping mall owner to bar on his premises union picketing of a particular store involved in a labor contract dispute. Second, it is generally difficult to find state action when the ordinary property owner bars media representatives from using his or her property. The purpose of the First and Fourteenth Amendments is to protect freedom of expression from governmental encroachment only. Finally, even accepting the applicability of the First Amendment, the media's position assumes that first amendment rights are always superior to common law property rights and statutory criminal trespass provisions. But given the current disposition of the Supreme Court and the revitalization of the balancing approach to the First Amendment this assumption is not necessarily correct.

c.   *"False Light"*

(1) Nature and Limitations

Creating a false image for an individual or placing him or her in a false light through publication may be actionable as an invasion of privacy whether or not such falsity involves defamation. One form of this invasion is to ascribe to individuals political or other views which they do not in fact hold or falsely to attribute to them authorship of certain writings or remarks. Another dangerous practice is to use an individual's photograph out of context. For example, in Leverton v. Curtis Publishing Co., 192 F.2d 974 (3d Cir. 1951), a photograph of the plaintiff, a child who had been struck down on a public street by a careless motorist, was properly published in a local newspaper because of its newsworthiness. But when the same news photograph was published several months later in the Saturday Evening Post to illustrate an article entitled "They Ask to Be Killed" dealing with childhood carelessness, the defendant publisher was found liable for placing the child in the false light of being a careless pedestrian.

Still another dangerous enterprise is the intentional fictionalization of activities or events involving actual identifiable persons. One book publisher discovered to its sorrow the cost of such venture when it published a fictionalized biography of the great baseball pitcher Warren Spahn. The book dramatized and fictionalized such matters as Spahn's relationship to his father, his war record, his courtship with his wife and even his thoughts while on the pitching mound. The author even invented long dialogues between Spahn and those with whom he associated. While the New York trial court in Spahn v. Julian Messner, Inc., 43 Misc.2d 219, 250 N.Y.S. 2d 529 (1964) cast its decision for Spahn in terms of the New York privacy statute, i.e., appropriation of Spahn's image and personality by the defendant for commercial advantage, the decree to enjoin further publication and distribution of the book and to award substantial damages was ultimately upheld by the New York Court of Appeals on a theory consistent with that underlying the United States Supreme Court's first decision in the area of invasion of privacy by the media— Time, Inc. v. Hill, 385 U.S. 374, 87 S.Ct. 534, 17 L.Ed.2d 456 (1967).

The importance of the element of intention in false light cases was underlined by the Supreme Court in the Hill case. There, the complaining parties, James J. Hill and his wife and five children, had become the involuntary subjects of a front page news story after being held hostage by three escaped convicts in their home for 19 hours in the late summer of 1952. The family was released unharmed and Hill stressed to newspersons at the time that the convicts had treated the family courteously and had neither molested anyone nor acted violently. After the incident Hill discouraged all media efforts to keep the family in the public spotlight. Less than a year later Joseph Hayes' novel, "The Desperate Hours," was published depicting the experience of a family of four held hostage by three escaped convicts in the family's home. But, unlike the Hill family's experience, the fictional family suffered violence at the hands of the convicts; the father and son were beaten and the daughter subjected to verbal sexual insult.

At this point a lawsuit by Hill against Hayes and his publisher for invasion of privacy would have been doubtful because of the difficulty of identifying the fictional family of four with the Hill family of seven. That difficulty was removed when in conjunction with the production of a play based upon the book, Life magazine published an article indicating that the play "The Desperate Hours," actually mirrored the Hill family's experience. The article was accompanied by staged photographs taken in the house in which the Hill family had been held captive. The photographs dramatized supposed incidents during the family's ordeal.

Though there was no doubt that the Life article and photographs had placed Hill and his family in a false light, a closely divided Supreme Court reversed a lower court judgment awarding compensatory damages to Hill because the trial court's instructions to the jury failed to require that the plaintiff establish that the defendant either knew the facts creating the false light were untrue or that it acted in reckless disregard of the truth. Innocent mistake or negligence in creating the false light were held to be improper bases for liability under the First and Fourteenth Amendments. This ruling is obviously parallel to that in New York Times Co. v. Sullivan, 376 U.S. 254, 84 S.Ct. 710, 11 L.Ed.2d 686 (1964), discussed supra, at pp. 65–66.

Thus, only intentional or reckless falsification by the media is presently actionable in the false light area. Although successful actions will be less frequent as a result of the Hill case, there is little doubt that this branch of the tort still lives. Certainly, a knowing use of a photograph out of context as in Leverton would be actionable as would a fabricated biography like that in the Spahn case. Indeed, the Supreme Court has upheld a properly instructed jury's award of damages in a false light case, Cantrell v. Forest City Publishing Co., 419 U.S. 245, 95 S.Ct. 465, 42 L.Ed.2d 419 (1974).

(2) Relationship to Defamation

While not every false light case involves untruths that injure reputation, e.g., the Hill case, every act of defamation will, while injuring reputation, also place the victim in a false light in the public's mind. Indeed, many actions for defamation are accompanied by actions for invasion of privacy. This raises the intriguing question whether the defamation action might not eventually fall into disuse because of the comparatively greater ease in establishing false light. The defamatory character of false communication need not be shown and many technical requirements of defamation actions may be bypassed. But unless and until defamation actions fade away, both invasion of privacy and defamation should be pleaded in appropriate cases.

d. *Public Disclosure of Private Facts*

(1) Nature and Limitations

Of the four common law branches of the invasion of privacy tort the most troublesome is the unreasonable publication of private facts of an embarrassing and objectionable nature. It is not always easy for reporters and editors to determine when publicity is unreasonable or even when facts must be viewed as private. There is the further problem of determining when private facts will be viewed by a reasonable person of ordinary sensibilities as offensive and objectionable, thus making public disclosure actionable. Then, too, in contrast to false light, truth will not shield the disclosing medium since the gravamen of the tort is the publication of private *facts* which the law deems worthy of protection.

Illustrative of this type of case is Sidis v. F–R Publishing Corp., 113 F.2d 806 (2d Cir. 1940). William James Sidis was a child prodigy in the field of mathematics and graduated from Harvard College at the age of sixteen amid considerable public attention. A shy and retiring person, Sidis attempted to live down his fame and succeeded quite well until the New Yorker magazine for August 14, 1937, published a brief biographical sketch of Sidis under the title "Where Are They Now?" The sketch recounted Sidis' unusual background, traced his attempts to conceal his identity through the years, described his menial employment far from the field of mathematics and detailed certain bizarre conduct such as his collecting old street car transfers. The facts stated in the article were not alleged to be untrue. Rather, Sidis sued for the destruction of the obscurity he had so laboriously constructed for himself. His suit was unsuccessful because, among other things, the facts disclosed were held not of such nature as to be offensive and objectionable to persons of ordinary sensibilities.

The Sidis case is fairly typical of the result reached in cases brought in this area of invasion of privacy. While such cases are troublesome, only a handful of plaintiffs have met with success in the years since publication of Warren and

[*113*]

Brandeis' article. The reason for this is the recognition by the courts of a very broad defense peculiar to this branch of the tort.

(2) The Newsworthiness Privilege

By this commonlaw defense the media are protected in publishing truthful matters of public interest. By and large, the courts have deferred to the media in determining what is of public interest. The motto of the judiciary here might be, "If they publish it, it must be a matter of public interest." This approach has two major virtues, according to Professors Don R. Pember and Dwight L. Teeter, Jr. First, it provides a wide range of freedom of expression and second, it is easy to administer because the judge does not have to act as a social censor, determining what is of public interest and what is not. Pember and Teeter, "Privacy and the Press Since Time, Inc. v. Hill," 50 Wash.L.Rev. 57, 77 (1974).

Given such deference, the media would be protected in the exercise of news judgment in publishing almost anything true about individuals which has any colorable claim to the public's interest, including the repetition, for instance, of years-old sensational stories about ex-convicts and other formerly unsavory characters. Certainly the content of public records, which, almost by definition, involve matters of public interest, may be publicized under this privilege. There are limits to judicial tolerance, however, such as the publication without consent of a photograph showing the plaintiff emerging from a fun house with her dress blown above her waist by a jet of air (Daily Times Democrat v. Graham, 276 Ala. 380, 162 So.2d 474 (1964)) or publication of the intimate details of a hospitalized woman's exotic and embarrassing disease together with a picture of her in her hospital bed taken without consent (Barber v. Time, Inc., 348 Mo. 1199, 159 S.W.2d 291 (1942)). But normal judicial deference to media news judgment explains the general lack of success of plaintiffs in this area.

The major exception here is California whose courts refuse to defer to the media on the issue of newsworthiness and, since Melvin v. Reid, 112 Cal.App. 285, 297 P. 91 (1931), have balanced the social value in publicity against the interests of the individual in maintaining privacy. This balancing is not unlike that engaged in by the Supreme Court in the area of defamation. In Melvin a prostitute charged with murder and subsequently acquitted in a sensational trial had abandoned her former life, married and assumed a place of respectability in society. Seven years after the trial a motion picture entitled "The Red Kimono" was produced and distributed, truthfully depicting the unsavory facts of the woman's earlier life and using her true maiden name. Mrs. Melvin sued for invasion of privacy. The California court ruled that while presentation of the events of the plaintiff's past was permissible since they were matters of public record, the producer had no right to identify the plaintiff with these events because she had abandoned her former ways and had rehabilitated herself. To like effect is Briscoe v. Reader's Digest Association, 4 Cal.3d 529, 93 Cal.Rptr. 866, 483 P.2d 34 (1971) (exposure of a rehabilitated man's crime of truck hijacking eleven years after its commission).

Obviously relevant to such judicial balancing is the social value of the information published, the lapse of time between the matter in question and its publication, the manner and context in which it is publicized and the effect on the individual of the unwanted publicity. The latter factor seems to have weighed heavily in the Melvin and Briscoe cases because of the judicial fear that publicity might seriously affect efforts at rehabilitation.

Eventually, the time lapse factor may be the one that has the most impact on the availability of the newsworthiness privilege. Journalists often publish accounts of past events embarrassing to the participants in "where are they now" and other type feature stories or columns. While the original stories may be defended as being newsworthy because of their contemporaneousness, doubt has been expressed about the availability of the privilege when the stories have lost their immediacy. This doubt is increased by Justice Blackmun's concurring opinion in Wolston v. Reader's Digest Association, Inc., 443 U.S. 157, 99 S.Ct. 2701, 61 L.Ed.2d 450 (1979), discussed in greater detail at pp. 79–81, supra. There, Blackmun presented a legal theory in a defamation case that may have relevance to the time lapse factor. He argued that the substantial passage of time can change a former limited issue public figure into a private one. If that is so then a parallel case can be made for the erosion of the newsworthiness privilege in a given case with the passage of time and the consequently greater protection for the individual newsmaker's right of privacy as the embarrassing news event fades into the past.

Even if authorities who take the position that the press is generally protected against liability when it publishes accounts of past news events are correct (see, e.g., Pember, The Burgeoning Scope of "Access Privacy" and the Portent for a Free Press, 64 Iowa L.Rev. 1155, 1185–1186 (1979)), such republication is a fertile ground for litigation and the expenditure by the media of considerable time, energy and money.

Until first amendment protection is accorded the media in cases like Sidis, Barber, Melvin and the time lapse cases, journalists should approach the intimate and embarrassing facts of an individual's past or even present life with caution and exercise discretion in publishing such material. In this area good taste is the watchword.

e. Common Characteristics of the Branches

While it is useful to an understanding of the tort of invasion of privacy to recognize the existence of its four branches, it must also be recognized that these branches often overlap each other or are bound up together. For instance, the same act of appropriating a woman's name and photograph for an advertisement endorsing a particular brand of whiskey may also place her in a false light as a serious drinker of alcoholic beverages. And an act of intrusion such as in the Dietemann case may be followed by publication of private information.

Moreover, the similarities between the branches *of tort* probably outweigh the differences. The tort is a personal one in all of its manifestations and dies with the complaining party. The only apparent qualification is a deceased person's image becoming so desirable for commercial exploitation that a transferable property right in the image may be held to have been created as in the case of the actor Bela Lugosi's image as Count Dracula or the Marx Brothers' show business persona.

Whatever the invasion the damages recoverable to the plaintiff are the same: (1) general damages; (2) special damages, though in contrast to slander or libel per quod they are not required; and (3) punitive damages, upon a showing of malice in the form of ill will, spite or improper motive.

Finally, there are certain defenses common to all four branches. The most obvious is consent. If the plaintiff can be found to have consented to the alleged invasion, the defendant's conduct is not actionable. Rarely in these cases will the

[*118*]

plaintiff's alleged consent be express and unequivocal. With this defense the question for the
trier of fact is normally whether the plaintiff's
words or deeds implied consent to the defendant's
appropriation, intrusion, false characterization or
publication of private information.

The other common defense is that of privilege.
It is generally accepted that the privileges recognized in the law of defamation are included in the
law of privacy. If the circumstances would protect the publication of false and defamatory material, then the publication of truthful material is
also protected. In rare cases a privilege may
even extend to the intrusion on another's privacy
where as already noted publication is not even involved.

C. THE CONSTITUTION AND PRIVACY

1. Applicability of First Amendment Theory to Appropriation and Intrusion Cases

It is now clear after the Supreme Court's decision in Zacchini v. Scripps-Howard Broadcasting
Co., 433 U.S. 562, 97 S.Ct. 2849, 53 L.Ed.2d 965
(1977) that no First Amendment protection is afforded newsgathering organizations which appropriate the name, image, persona or unique presence of an individual, thus invading the
individual's so-called right of publicity. Zacchini
performs a "human cannonball" act in which he
is shot into a safety net 200 feet away. Over his
objection his act, presented at a local county fair,

[*119*]

was videotaped by a reporter for the defendant's television station and was shown on a news program later the same day. Zacchini sued the broadcasting company for unlawful appropriation of his professional property.

While Zacchini was unsuccessful in the trial court, the United States Supreme Court ultimately upheld Zacchini's right to seek damages against the defendant. The Court held that the defendant's conduct invaded both Zacchini's right to earn a living as an entertainer and society's interest in encouraging creative activity. The First and Fourteenth Amendments were not designed to protect conduct of a news gatherer which interferes with an individual's right to earn money by publicizing himself.

The rationale of the Court in refusing First Amendment protection to the newsgatherer who violates an individual's right of publicity is that news and information will not be denied the public in this type of situation because the individual will make it available to the public but for a price which he or she has a legally protected right to exact.

As for intrusion, since it involves no publication in and of itself, the First Amendment is not directly implicated. And as Judge Hufstedler said in Dietemann v. Time, Inc., 449 F.2d 245, 249 (9th Cir. 1971), "The First Amendment is not a license to trespass, to steal, or to intrude by electronic means into the precincts of another's home or office" simply because such means are used by media representatives in the course of news-gathering.

2. Applicability of First Amendment Theory to False Light Cases

In marked contrast to the appropriation and intrusion branches, the Constitution does place limits on the reach of the false light tort because of its potential to interfere with publication and restrict the flow of news and information to the public. The analogy with defamation impelled a narrow majority of the Supreme Court in Time, Inc. v. Hill, 385 U.S. 374, 87 S.Ct. 534, 17 L.Ed.2d 456 (1967) to limit recovery in false light cases to those situations in which the falsity was known to the defendant or the communication was made by him or her in reckless disregard for the truth. The concern of the majority was to provide a margin for error for the media in gathering and reporting the news.

While the Hill case was narrowly decided after oral arguments in two successive terms of the Court, its basic first amendment thrust was confirmed by a broad majority of the Court in Cantrell v. Forest City Publishing Co., 419 U.S. 245, 95 S.Ct. 465, 42 L.Ed.2d 419 (1974). Yet the Court in Cantrell did raise, without deciding, the question whether, parallel to Gertz v. Robert Welch, Inc., 418 U.S. 323, 94 S.Ct. 2997, 41 L.Ed. 2d 789 (1974), a state might constitutionally limit Hill by applying a more relaxed standard of liability, i.e., negligence, for the communication of false light type statements injurious to private persons. The very act of questioning the scope of the ruling in Hill suggests that the Court may be disposed to limit the protection afforded the media in this area in much the same way it did with the protection originally afforded in the New York Times Co.-Rosenbloom line of defamation cases (see Chapter II, supra).

Because of the essential element of falsity involved in the Hill and Cantrell cases the constitutional doctrine formulated therein seems clearly confined to false light theory and should have little impact on the evolving constitutional law relevant to invasion of privacy involving publication of private matters. But for a different view see Nimmer, "The Right to Speak from *Times* to *Time:* First Amendment Theory Applied to Libel and Misapplied to Privacy," 56 Cal.L.Rev. 935 (1968).

3. Applicability of First Amendment Theory to Public Disclosure of Private Facts

The applicability of first amendment protection to the invasion of privacy tort seems most compelling in the case of communications involving truthful matters of a private and embarrassing or harmful nature. Without broad constitutional protection here the media can be required under existing tort law to respond in damages for truthfully informing the public about certain matters which individual plaintiffs consider private. As with false light the potential threat of damages could have a chilling effect on the enterprise of the media in gathering and disseminating news about individuals.

The issue here is whether the First and Fourteenth Amendments mandate the recognition of truth as an absolute defense in invasion of privacy cases. This broad issue was raised though not decided in Cox Broadcasting Corp. v. Cohn, 420 U.S. 469, 95 S.Ct. 1029, 43 L.Ed.2d 328 (1975). There, a reporter for an Atlanta television station learned the name of a 17-year-old gang rape victim during the course of the proceedings against the rapists by examining the indictments, which had been made available by the clerk of the court. Later the same day the reporter broadcast a news report concerning the court proceedings and named the deceased victim of the crime. Shortly after the broadcast the father of the victim brought a civil action for damages against the reporter and his company, relying on a Georgia statute which prohibited the media from communicating the name or identity of any female who is raped and made such communication a misdemeanor. The trial court rejected the broadcasters' claim that their report was constitutionally privileged and entered summary judgment for the plaintiff father, who claimed his own privacy had been invaded by the broadcast.

The Georgia Supreme Court initially held that the statute did not create a civil cause of action but that the plaintiff had stated a cause of action under the common law of invasion of privacy.

Holding also that summary judgment was improper the Georgia court remanded the case for trial.   Consistent with this latter holding the court ruled that the First and Fourteenth Amendments did not require that truth be a complete defense in every invasion of privacy action.   On motion for rehearing the broadcasters argued that they were privileged to publish the victim's name because it was a matter of public interest.   In countering this argument the court upheld the statutory prohibition as a legitimate limitation on the right of freedom of expression contained in the First Amendment.

On appeal to the United States Supreme Court the defendant broadcasters sought a broad holding that the press may not be made criminally or civilly liable for publishing information that is absolutely accurate, however damaging or embarrassing it may be to individual sensibilities. While gaining a reversal the broadcasters lost their bid for a sweeping privilege for the media when the Court refused to go beyond ruling that both the common law and the First and Fourteenth Amendments protected mass dissemination of truthful matters contained in public records open to public inspection, including indictments and other judicial papers.

The effect of the Supreme Court's narrow decision in Cox Broadcasting Corp. is to leave uncertain the constitutionality of the Georgia statute and similar statutes in Florida, South Carolina and Wisconsin insofar as they make punishable the identification of rape victims when such identification is not a matter of public record. Similarly, the common law rules permitting recovery of damages for the publication of truthful but embarrassing or harmful private information are left in doubt.

Obviously, the issue whether the Constitution mandates truth to be a complete defense in these cases will have to be faced by the Supreme Court eventually. At that time the Court could defer to the media and hold that whatever is accurately published about anyone is constitutionally privileged. Such approach is akin to the Black-Douglas absolutist view of the First Amendment. Or the Court might adopt Professor Meiklejohn's approach and ask if the particular truthful communication is important to the process of self-government. If the answer were "yes" then first amendment protection would be afforded. If the answer were "no," the states would be free to recognize a cause of action and permit the award of damages. Under this approach there will always be a degree of uncertainty prior to litigation concerning the legality of truthful communications.

Even greater uncertainty for the media would be engendered by the Court balancing competing interests on an ad hoc basis. Under this approach the communication of truthful but embarrassing matters of public interest could result in judgments against the media if it were found that the competing interest in individual privacy in particular cases outweighed the media's interest in free expression. Who could say in advance of litigation whether the media's interest in communicating the details of a rape, including the victim's identification, would outweigh her interest in avoiding further pain and embarrassment through public disclosure?

Such balancing was engaged in by the United States Court of Appeals for the Ninth Circuit. In Virgil v. Time, Inc., 527 F.2d 1122 (9th Cir. 1975), cert. denied 425 U.S. 998, 96 S.Ct. 2215, 48 L.Ed. 2d 823 (1976), the plaintiff had been interviewed by a reporter for an article on body surfers practicing their sport at a California beach reputed to be the most dangerous site for body surfing in the world. When the plaintiff learned that the article to be published in Sports Illustrated would involve his lifestyle as well as his sport, he expressly revoked his consent to being mentioned in the article. The magazine published the article anyway and the publisher sought summary judgment when the surfer sued, in part on the ground that the facts detailed about him were true. In upholding the trial court's denial of summary judgment, the Ninth Circuit rejected the idea that truth is always a complete defense when private facts about an individual are published. Only if those facts are newsworthy and not merely the subject of the public's idle curiosity would the defense obtain. While recognizing that its decision posed serious judgmental problems for the news media, the Court said, "Where competing values are involved . . . unless one competitor is to be sacrificed outright . . . [the press] must accept that risks are inherent and the problem lies in attempting to minimize them to the extent that the conflict permits." 527 F.2d at 1129–1130.

Given the balancing approach taken by the Supreme Court in recent years, the availability of very respectable direct authority for a balancing approach found in the California cases, beginning with Melvin v. Reid, supra, and the recent decision of the Ninth Circuit, we would conclude that such approach is the one most likely to be embraced by the High Court should the issue present itself in the foreseeable future.

CHAPTER IV

SIGNIFICANT AREAS OF RESTRAINT OF EXPRESSION

A. RESTRAINT OF OBSCENITY

1. The Definitional Problem

Western societies generally seem to have a preoccupation with suppression of explicit public discussion or depiction of sexual matters. And English speaking societies are no exception. Censorship and confiscation of sexually obscene materials and even prison sentences may be the lot of the professional or amateur pornographer. There are those in positions of authority who would characterize all public expression concerning sex as obscene and suppress or punish it, but the prevailing view in this country is to the contrary and clearly not all sexual expression is condemned.

This view has within it the seeds of confusion because it requires a definition of what is obscene. And because obscenity, like beauty, is in the mind of the beholder, a precise definition seems beyond the reach of the law. It may be that the only honest test for obscenity is the one authored by retired Supreme Court Justice Stewart, "I know it when I see it." Jacobellis v. Ohio, 378 U.S. 184, 197, 84 S.Ct. 1676, 1683, 12 L.Ed.2d

793, 804 (1964). Because the First Amendment requires more than instinctual reaction to suppress and punish obscene expression, the Supreme Court has spent the last twenty or more years attempting to separate the chaff of obscenity from the wheat of protected sexual expression.

2. Background

Attempts at suppressing the dissemination of obscenity were sporadic in both England and the United States until shortly after the end of the American Civil War. At that time the English judiciary crystallized a standard for suppression which was by and large accepted in the United States. Contemporaneously, the Congress enacted certain statutes advocated by the notorious bluenose Anthony Comstock prohibiting, with criminal penalties, the importation or mailing of materials characterized as obscene (now 18 United States Code, Sections 1461–1463). Many of the states followed suit with their own criminal obscenity statutes.

The standard set down in the English case of Regina v. Hicklin, L.R. 3 Q.B. 360 (1868) was a very broad one: suspect material was to be judged by the effect of isolated passages upon persons particularly susceptible to prurient appeal or lustful thoughts. The combination of the Comstock laws and the Hicklin test provided much work for the censors and the prosecutors. Occasionally, lower federal courts inveighed against the Hicklin test but it remained influential well into the twentieth century.

3. Modern Doctrinal Development

Until 1957 the Supreme Court, while assuming the constitutionality of attempts to suppress obscene expression in Near v. Minnesota, 283 U.S. 697, 716, 51 S.Ct. 625, 631, 75 L.Ed. 1357, 1367 (1931), had never definitively held that obscenity was beyond the pale of First and Fourteenth Amendment protection. In that year in Roth v. United States, 354 U.S. 476, 77 S.Ct. 1304, 1 L.Ed. 2d 1498 (1957) the Court so ruled, over the strong dissent of Justices Black and Douglas. The Court then considered the appropriate standard for separating protected expression from unprotected obscene expression. In affirming the conviction of Roth for sending obscene matter through the mails, the Court rejected the Hicklin standard because its concern for isolated passages and particularly susceptible individuals would result in the condemnation of much material legitimately and seriously dealing with sexual matters that ought to be protected by the First and Fourteenth Amendments. In its place the Court adopted the test whether to the *average* person, applying contemporary community standards, the dominant theme of the material taken as a *whole* appealed to prurient interest.

While this test or definition of obscenity is clearly narrower than Hicklin and has had some liberating influence regarding serious expression concerning sex, it still permits censorship and criminal punishment for mere incitation to impure sexual thoughts not shown to be related to overt antisocial conduct. In the years since the decision in Roth, shifting majorities and pluralities of the Court have had difficulty and shown dissatisfaction with the test laid down there because of the uncertainty in (1) gauging the psychic effect of specific material on mythical "average" persons; (2) measuring the dominance of particular obscene themes in large unified works in books or motion pictures or collections of materials as in magazines; (3) determining the relevant community to be referred to in judging the suspect material, i.e., local, state or national; and (4) because of the continuing danger that some serious expression might still be condemned as obscene.

New tests were formulated and coupled with the Roth standard in an effort to meet these problems until in the celebrated "Fanny Hill" case, A Book Named "John Cleland's Memoirs of a Woman of Pleasure" v. Attorney General of Commonwealth of Massachusetts, 383 U.S. 413, 86 S.Ct. 975, 16 L.Ed.2d 1 (1966), a plurality of the Court announced a basic threefold formulation to isolate obscenity: (1) a restatement of the Roth standard; (2) a test that the material be patently offensive because it affronts contemporary community standards relating to the description or representation of sexual matters; and (3) a test that the material be utterly without redeeming social value. Because the tests were stated in the conjunctive a censor or prosecutor was required to establish that the expression in question met all three.

The "utterly without redeeming social value" test was particularly frustrating to the anti-obscenity forces because a defendant could almost always produce expert testimony that his or her material possessed some redeeming social value. After Fanny Hill, prosecutions and censorship attempts dwindled and successful efforts at suppression became rarer while the flow of pornographic material increased. Under this scheme of things, the pornographer had little to worry about so long as he or she did not pander to the public and encourage the belief that his or her product was obscene (see Ginzburg v. United States, 383 U.S. 463, 86 S.Ct. 942, 16 L.Ed.2d 31 (1966)) or engage in commerce with minors (see Ginsberg v. State of New York, 390 U.S. 629, 88 S.Ct. 1274, 20 L.Ed.2d 195 (1968)). By the same token the serious communicator was to a very great extent freed of the fear of criminal prosecution for describing life as he or she saw it, no matter how raw his or her view might be.

The question inevitably arises in a free society whether almost unrestricted publication, distribution and exhibition of obscenity is too high a price to pay for the protection of serious expression concerning sex. This is a political question as well as a legal one and a large portion of the electorate appeared to answer the question in the affirmative in the election of 1968 when they elected as President Richard M. Nixon, a man who had publicly pledged to clean up the spreading pornography traffic. But his pledge could only be redeemed by changing the direction of the Supreme Court and this in turn would require new faces on the Court.

4. The Last Word on Obscenity (for the Moment)

By 1973, Nixon had made four appointments to the Supreme Court and in that year the Court signaled a change in attitude toward attempts to suppress obscenity. In Miller v. California, 413 U.S. 15, 93 S.Ct. 2607, 37 L.Ed.2d 419 (1973) and Paris Adult Theatre I v. Slaton, 413 U.S. 49, 93 S.Ct. 2628, 37 L.Ed.2d 446 (1973) a five person majority made up of the Nixon appointees, Chief Justice Burger, and Justices Blackmun, Powell and Rehnquist together with Justice White, a Kennedy appointee, laid down new and tougher legal standards for dealing with the problem of obscenity and made clear that even "consenting adults" might not be exposed to "hard core" pornography. The following term the same five person majority elaborated on these rulings in the important case of Jenkins v. Georgia, 418 U.S. 153, 94 S.Ct. 2750, 41 L.Ed.2d 642 (1974). For a fuller understanding of the Court's new position these three decisions are considered together.

In Miller, the petitioner had been convicted of mailing unsolicited sexually explicit material to persons in Orange County, California in violation of a California statute that approximately incorporated the tests for obscenity formulated in the Fanny Hill decision. The trial judge gave these tests to the jury and instructed them to evaluate the materials in light of the contemporary community standards of the state of California. The new Supreme Court majority affirmed Miller's conviction and did the following:

1. reaffirmed the holding in Roth that obscenity is not protected by the First and Fourteenth Amendments;

2. rejected important aspects of the tests set out in Fanny Hill, especially the "utterly without redeeming social value" standard and substituted its own conjunctive three-fold test to guide the trier of fact (normally the jury):

    (a) whether the average person, applying contemporary community standards, would find the material taken as a whole, appeals to prurient interest (a restatement of the Roth test);

    (b) whether the work depicts or describes, in a patently offensive way, sexual conduct specifically defined by the applicable state law; and

    (c) whether the work, taken as a whole, lacks serious literary, artistic, political or scientific value;

3. indicated that only "hard core" pornography might be condemned under these tests

and included in that classification for the guidance of legislative draftspersons patently offensive representations or descriptions of ultimate sexual acts, normal or perverted, actual or simulated and patently offensive representations or descriptions of masturbation, excretory functions and lewd exhibition of the genitals; and

4. held that hard core pornography is to be determined by reference to local or state community standards and not national standards.

In the companion case Paris Adult Theatre, decided the same day, the Court upheld the right of states to enjoin the exhibition of motion pictures which are hardcore pornography under the Miller standards even when the exhibitor makes every effort to limit the audience to consenting adults. In so ruling, the majority recognized that the states, and, by necessary extension, the United States, have a legitimate interest not only in shielding the young and the unwilling from the obscene but the consenting adult as well. This legitimate interest encompasses the elevation of the quality of life and the environment in the community, the tone of commerce in the cities and, arguably, the public safety itself. In this connection the majority refused to extend the individual constitutional right of privacy in personal heterosexual intimacies of the home (see Griswold v. Connecticut, 381 U.S. 479, 85 S.Ct. 1678, 14 L.Ed.2d 510 (1965)) to the viewing of pornography in a place of public adult accommodation. By this refusal, the Court avoided the necessity of balancing the state's recognized interest in preventing the exhibition of pornographic films against any individual privacy interest in viewing them.

Paris Adult Theatre is also significant for its holding that the censor or prosecutor need not produce expert evidence of the obscenity of the materials complained of when the materials are placed in evidence. This substantially lightens the burden on the anti-obscenity forces and encourages increased attempts at censorship and criminal prosecutions.

In Miller, the Chief Justice said all he could, given the limitations of the English language, to prevent local suppression of serious expressions concerning sex. This did not inhibit the State of Georgia from convicting Billy Jenkins, the manager of a movie theater in Albany, Georgia for exhibiting the film "Carnal Knowledge," produced by a recognized group of serious movie makers, including director Mike Nichols and actor Jack Nicholson. Jenkins' conviction was affirmed by a divided Georgia Supreme Court which concluded that the judgment accorded with the standards laid down in Miller.

The Supreme Court, in holding "Carnal Knowledge" not obscene and reversing the conviction, was forced to confront the paradox of differing community standards delimiting the protection afforded by a national constitution. The

Court first made clear its commitment to local community standards though indicating its willingness to accept statewide community standards if the states should decide to use them instead.

The Court then turned to the state's contention that under Miller, the obscenity of the film was a question for the jury and that the jury having resolved the question against Jenkins under the evidence and pursuant to local community standards, the conviction should be affirmed. In other words, the state was arguing that appellate review of the constitutionality of the conviction was precluded so long as the jury was properly instructed pursuant to the three-fold test laid down in Miller. Here the Court simply held that the scope of protection afforded by the First and Fourteenth Amendments was ultimately for it to decide and substituted its own judgment regarding the nature of the film for that of the local jury. In the final analysis, then, it is the Supreme Court, sitting in urban Washington, D. C., which decides whether the application by juries of local community standards comports with the national constitution. Of necessity, the Court does this by applying the standards of five or more essentially urbane men of relatively sophisticated tastes and not by presuming to apply the standards of Albany, Georgia.

The three decisions have had considerable effect on the administration of state and federal obscenity statutes and free expression. The most important effect is to encourage prosecutors and censors to renew the fight against obscenity. In the Atlanta, Georgia area, for instance, one zealous prosecutor managed to close down all of the "adult" movie houses.

The very fact that convictions were affirmed in two of the three cases should hearten the anti-obscenity forces. Moreover, the Court has relaxed the evidentiary burden on the public officials charged with suppressing obscene expression. The material is now allowed to speak for itself and expert testimony as to its obscene nature is not required. In addition, proof that the material is utterly devoid of redeeming social value is no longer necessary. Now the prosecutor will be required to show only that it is patently offensive and lacks serious value.

Conversely, the burden on the defendant to rebut the claim of obscenity is increased because evidence that the material in question is acceptable by national standards is no longer relevant. The defendant must make out his or her case with expert testimony that it is acceptable locally or, as in Miller, statewide. The sanctioning of local standards also encourages the anti-obscenity forces to shop for the most unsophisticated and intolerant localities within which to seek criminal or civil suppression of material. Of course, the Supreme Court, as it demonstrated in Jenkins, stands ready to correct the worst abuses arising out of the application of local standards but not all abuses are likely to be corrected.

Another effect is to narrow the theoretical boundaries of unprotected expression set by the majority in Roth. After Roth, even serious material could be condemned if, taken as a whole, it appealed to the prurient interest of the average person. After Miller, this is theoretically impossible because one of the three tests laid down there requires the prosecutor or censor to establish that the material taken as a whole lacks serious literary, artistic, political or scientific value. Of course, more practically, the Court has now made it easier than it once was to prove lack of serious value.

The other test in Miller which could have the effect of narrowing the area of unprotected expression is that of patent offensiveness. The Court equates this to hard core pornography and gives some reasonably explicit examples of what it means by hard core expression. If the state legislatures and the Congress were to amend existing general obscenity statutes in conformity with Miller by including concrete statements of sexual conduct which could not be publicly expressed, the target area for the anti-obscenity forces ought to be constricted. Of course, the statutes might verge on the obscene themselves but this is a price the public must pay for constitutionally permissible anti-obscenity statutes.

The Paris Adult Theatre decision has the effect of limiting the area of the consenting adult's constitutional right of privacy to view pornographic material to one's own home. It seems clear that the majority did this to insure the primacy of the state's interest in maintaining and elevating the quality and tone of life and environment particularly in the large urban centers where commercial pornography often flourishes.

Finally, the Court's encouragement of local efforts at suppression will almost surely result in the disruption of the national distribution of sexual films, books, magazines and other materials. Rather than risk confiscation or prosecution in localities like Albany, Georgia, film makers and publishers may pass up these markets and distribute their wares only in more sophisticated urban population centers, if that is economically feasible. If it is not, the film maker or publisher's work may not see the light of day.

5. Difficulties with the New Approach

The Court's new approach perpetuates certain myths regarding obscenity control. The majority assert that beyond "knowing it when they see it," they can define obscenity with sufficient precision to give fair advance warning as to what is forbidden. But clearly the "serious value" test is highly subjective and in the final analysis only a majority of five justices can say, after the fact of publication, what is serious expression and what is not. And even the patent offensiveness-hard core pornography test will allow for subjectivity unless the legislatures are willing to define in obscene detail the sexual conduct to be suppressed. So far there has been no great trend in that direction, perhaps because the Court is permitting the state and federal courts to construe the existing more general "obscene, lewd, lascivious, filthy" type statutes in light of the Miller decision.

The other major myth fostered by the Court is that obscenity can be constitutionally controlled at the local level using local standards. But as the Court was forced to admit in Jenkins, First and Fourteenth Amendment rights and protections are uniform and do not vary depending on the nature of the jurisdiction in which the attempt is made to suppress allegedly obscene expression. Try as it might, the Supreme Court, under the present approach, cannot escape the need to impose national standards to measure national rights and protections and, in the end, to act as a national censorship board.

6. Supplemental Obscenity Standards

Certain other standards have been developed by the Supreme Court to permit suppression and punishment of expression which does not meet the basic obscenity test directed to the average adult laid down in Miller and earlier in Roth and Fanny Hill. These supplemental tests are designed to prevent pandering of borderline material as the real thing, to suppress expression directed to the prurient interest of sexually deviant adults and to shield minors from "adult" materials such as "girlie" magazines and from exploitation and abuse in the production of sexually explicit material.

In Ginzburg v. United States, 383 U.S. 463, 86 S.Ct. 942, 16 L.Ed.2d 31 (1966), the defendant publisher of a purported sexual autobiography, a hard-cover sex magazine and a sex newsletter, was convicted of sending obscene matter through the mail. His conviction for violation of Title 18, Section 1461 of the United States Code was affirmed at least in part because of his open advertising representations and other suggestions that the materials would appeal to the recipient's prurient interest. A majority of the Court ruled that where the purveyor's sole emphasis is on the sexually provocative aspects of his or her publications, that fact may be decisive in determining whether the material is obscene. Otherwise stated, in a close case, one who panders material as obscene will be taken at his or her word.

Since audiences vary as to age and sexual preferences, the Court has also held that the standards for suppression may also vary as to these audiences. In Mishkin v. State of New York, 383 U.S. 502, 86 S.Ct. 958, 16 L.Ed.2d 56 (1966), the Court rejected the argument of a publisher and seller of sex books for sadists, masochists, fetishists and homosexuals that his materials were not obscene because they would not appeal to the prurient interest of average persons but rather would disgust and sicken them. The Court held that where material is designed for and primarily disseminated to a clearly defined deviant group, the prurient appeal test of Roth is satisfied if the dominant theme of the material taken as a whole appeals to the prurient interest in sex of members of that group. And in Ginsberg v. State of New York, 390 U.S. 629, 88 S.Ct. 1274, 20 L.Ed.2d 195 (1968) the defendant, an operator of a stationery store and luncheonette, was convicted of violating a New York penal statute which prohibited the knowing sale to minors under the age of 17 of any picture which depicts nudity. Ginsberg sold two "girlie" magazines to a sixteen-year-old male. While conceding that the magazines were not obscene for adults, the Court affirmed the conviction because of its belief that obscenity varies with the age of the audience and that the state has the constitutional power more greatly to restrict minors in their access to sex materials. See also New York v. Ferber, ____ U.S. ____, 102 S.Ct. 3348, 73 L.Ed.2d 1113 (1982), the so-called "Kiddie porn" case in which the court held that states may, consistent with the First Amendment, utilize more relaxed standards than those in Miller v. California, supra, to protect minors from exploitation and abuse in the production of sexual materials.

B. IMPORTANT SPECIAL AREAS OF RESTRAINT OF SEXUAL EXPRESSION

1. Radio and Television

The two media in which the standards laid down in Miller for the suppression of sexual expression need not be applied are radio and television. As to those media the Supreme Court has ruled that violation of a less demanding "indecency" standard is enough to justify both Federal Communications Commission administrative sanctions against and criminal punishment of those who broadcast sexual material or dirty words.

In FCC v. Pacifica Foundation, 438 U.S. 726, 98 S.Ct. 3026, 57 L.Ed.2d 1073 (1978), Pacifica's New York City radio station broadcast in the early afternoon a discussion of the English language which included a recorded satirical monologue by the comedian George Carlin entitled "Filthy Words" which contained a variety of common usages of seven dirty words which Carlin said could not be uttered on the public airwaves—mostly of the four-letter Anglo-Saxon variety. A father and his young son heard this portion of the broadcast and complained to the Federal Communications Commission which, agreeing with the complaint, issued a declaratory order stating that Pacifica had violated Section 1464 of the United States Criminal Code, forbidding the use of "any obscene, indecent, or profane language by means of radio communications." The FCC held the Carlin cut to be "indecent" and subject to sanction. The United States Court of Appeals reversed the Commission's order and that court's judgment was in turn reversed by the Supreme Court.

In upholding the Commission's order, the Court ruled first that the FCC's imposition of administrative sanctions for the broadcasting of indecent material was not itself a violation of Section 326 of the Federal Communications Act of 1934 which prohibits the Commission from censoring radio communications.

The Court then went on to hold that Section 1464 of the United States Criminal Code made the broadcast of indecent material a crime separate from the broadcast of obscene material and that the Pacifica broadcast was indecent, accepting the Commission's definition of indecent as including the exposure of children to language that describes, in patently offensive terms, sexual or excretory activities and organs, at times of the day when there is a reasonable risk that children may be in the audience. Indecency, the Court noted, differs from obscenity mainly in that it does not appeal to prurient interest or sexual longing.

Finally, a majority of the Court held that application of a statutory standard less demanding than the obscenity standard of Miller, i.e., indecency, did not violate the First Amendment rights of broadcasters because their media are (1) unique in their pervasive presence in society and their ability suddenly to confront the audience with material it may not wish to receive and (2) uniquely accessible to children, relying on the rationale presented in Ginsberg v. New York, supra, p. 143. On the constitutional issue, the Court reaffirmed its position suggested earlier in Red Lion Broadcasting Co., Inc. v. FCC, 395 U.S. 367, 89 S.Ct. 1794, 23 L.Ed.2d 371 (1969) that "of all forms of communication, it is broadcasting that has received the most limited First Amendment protection," 438 U.S. at 748, 98 S.Ct. at 3040, 57 L.Ed.2d at 1092.

Despite the above constitutional ruling relying on the nature of the medium involved, the Pacifica decision is relatively narrow in scope because broadcasters may avoid the "indecent" label by broadcasting offensive but not obscene matter at times when children do not constitute a significant portion of the audience. Moreover, the decision is not likely to affect the broadcast of offensive matter through media subject to close control in the home by adults such as subscription television which requires the use of decoder equipment or lock-channel cable television which requires the use of some type of key to open so-called "blue" channels. Finally, it should be noted that the Pacifica decision does not preclude the Commission from using the higher obscenity standard of Miller v. California in imposing administrative sanctions on broadcasters if their programming is obscene. See Illinois Citizens Committee for Broadcasting v. FCC, 515 F.2d 397 (D.C.Cir. 1975).

2. Motion Pictures

A medium of expression which has felt the hand of the censor acutely over the years is the motion picture. Movies have been and are still being censored locally for obscenity prior to exhibition and more often are simply seized in police raids. Some of the leading prior restraint cases have involved motion pictures and a distinct area of obscenity law has been carved out.

a. *Background and Modern Doctrine*

Until 1952 the motion picture was not considered a medium of expression protected by the Constitution and the censors were free to control film exhibition in any way they saw fit. In that year the Supreme Court in Joseph Burstyn, Inc. v. Wilson, 343 U.S. 495, 72 S.Ct. 777, 96 L.Ed. 1098 (1952) rejected earlier doctrine and held that expression by means of motion picture film is protected by the First and Fourteenth Amendments even though it be assumed that motion pictures have a greater impact on the mind than other modes of expression. Thereafter, attempts at censorship for obscenity have generally been measured by prevailing constitutional standards. But since obscenity can be constitutionally suppressed under Roth and Miller, prior licensing and confiscation of films as well as subsequent punishment for their exhibition are permissible under certain circumstances and a general constitutional attack on a local ordinance or state statute requiring submission of motion pictures for prior censorship will fail. See Times Film Corp. v. City of Chicago, 365 U.S. 43, 81 S.Ct. 391, 5 L.Ed.2d 403 (1961).

One indirect approach to controlling "adult" motion pictures and thereby avoiding the constitutional standards of Roth and Miller and necessary procedural safeguards that accompany those

[*147*]

standards is the control of land use in order to concentrate adult movie houses in so-called "combat zones" or, conversely, to prevent concentrations, which have the tendency to destroy commercial and residential neighborhoods. Either way, non-proliferation of such establishments is the goal. This indirect approach was approved by the Supreme Court in Young v. American Mini Theatres, Inc., 427 U.S. 50, 96 S.Ct. 2440, 49 L.Ed.2d 310 (1976) because neither complete suppression of adult movies nor criminal sanctions were involved.

b.   Procedural Safeguards for Film

After the Times Film Corp. case, supra, it was clear that there could be constitutional as well as unconstitutional prior restraint on motion pictures, and the Supreme Court began to evolve the rules under which the censors might operate. Freedman v. Maryland, 380 U.S. 51, 85 S.Ct. 734, 13 L.Ed.2d 649 (1965) involved a challenge by a film exhibitor to a state statute authorizing certain procedures of the now defunct Maryland Board of Censors, including a lengthy appeal process. The Supreme Court struck down the statute as unduly restrictive of protected expression and set out certain procedural safeguards for regulating the censor's business. Prior restraint statutes and ordinances are now required to:

(a) place the burden of proving that the film in question meets constitutional standards for obscenity (i.e., Roth and Miller) on the censor;

(b) provide that the censor will, within a specified very brief period, either issue a license for exhibition or go into court to seek to restrain exhibition and;

(c) assure a prompt final judicial decision in order to minimize the deterrent effect of an interim refusal to license.

In addition, prior restraint legislation whether it involves outright censorship or merely mandatory film classification for the protection of minors, as in Interstate Circuit, Inc. v. City of Dallas, 390 U.S. 676, 88 S.Ct. 1298, 20 L.Ed.2d 225 (1968), must be narrowly drawn, detailed, and precise as to the standards to be employed by the classifier. Anything less will inhibit protected expression and run afoul of the First and Fourteenth Amendments.

Similarly, procedural safeguards have been established for the seizure of films by law enforcement officials. A judicial warrant issued consistent with Fourth and Fourteenth amendment standards must be obtained before any seizure. Failure to obtain such warrant will result in the suppression of the film as evidence of obscenity law violations at subsequent judicial proceedings. Roaden v. Kentucky, 413 U.S. 496, 93 S.Ct. 2796, 37 L.Ed.2d 757 (1973); Lee Art Theatre, Inc. v. Virginia, 392 U.S. 636, 88 S.Ct. 2103, 20 L.Ed.2d 1313 (1968). And it is not sufficient justification for the issuance of the warrant that the prospective seizing officer made conclusory assertions of the film's obscene nature. Rather, the magistrate must concern himself or herself deeply with the question of the film's probable nature before issuing the warrant. Ibid. But an adversary proceeding at this stage is not required. Heller v. New York, 413 U.S. 483, 93 S.Ct. 2789, 37 L.Ed.2d 745 (1973). The seizure of a copy of the film pursuant to a constitutionally valid warrant must be for the limited purpose of preserving it as evidence in a subsequent adversary proceeding and must not prevent continued exhibition of the film until a prompt determination of its nature is made in that proceeding. If there is only one copy at hand, the film seized must be made available to the exhibitor for copying so that he or she may continue its exhibition. Ibid.

These procedural safeguards may not be avoided by legislation providing for indirect prior restraints such as statutes (1) which permit enjoining the operation of adult movie houses as public nuisances because of past exhibition of obscene films; (2) which prohibit the unapproved future exhibition of motion pictures that have not yet been found to be obscene; and (3) which require the judiciary to place its imprimatur on such future exhibitions before the films may be shown to the public without penalty. See Vance v. Universal Amusement Co., 445 U.S. 308, 100 S.Ct. 1156, 63 L.Ed.2d 413 (1980).

While the focus here has been on the constitutional limitations on prior restraint of motion pictures because this is where most of the legal battles have been fought, parallel safeguards have been developed to protect other modes of expression from overzealous censors. See, e.g., Kingsley Books, Inc. v. Brown, 354 U.S. 436, 77 S.Ct. 1325, 1 L.Ed.2d 1469 (1957) (booklets); Marcus v. Search Warrant, 367 U.S. 717, 81 S.Ct. 1708, 6 L.Ed.2d 1127 (1961) (books and magazines).

3. Mail and Customs Censorship

Until fairly recently the United States Post Office Department carried on a largely futile campaign of administrative censorship of the mails in addition to referring certain cases to the Justice Department for criminal prosecution. Unsuccessful administrative devices have included removal of material from the mail, revocation of publishers' second class mailing privilege and refusal to deliver mail to alleged commercial pornographers.

Recently a more indirect approach to the problem of obscenity in the mail has proved both workable and less threatening to first amendment interests. Pursuant to present section 3008 of title 39 of the United States Code, individual addressees who have received "pandering advertisements" which offer for sale matter which the addressee believes to be erotically arousing or sexually provocative may request the Postmaster General to issue an order directing the sender and his or her agents to refrain from further mailings to the named addressee. If after notice and hearing it should be determined by the Postmaster General that the order has been violated, the Postmaster General may request the Attorney General to seek a federal court order directing compliance with the Postmaster's order. Violation of the court order will, of course, subject the sender to sanctions for contempt of court. The constitutionality of this statute was upheld in Rowan v. United States Post Office Department, 397 U.S. 728, 90 S.Ct. 1484, 25 L.Ed.2d 736 (1970).

Customs censorship through seizure and confiscation of incoming materials has had a long history and continues to the present within obscenity standards laid down in Roth and Miller, supra, and pursuant to procedural safeguards required by Freedman v. Maryland, supra.

C. CRIMINAL PROSECUTIONS FOR OBSCENITY

The threat of criminal prosecution can also have a restraining influence on sexual expression. While criminal prosecutions for obscene expression are in general outline much like other criminal prosecutions and the rights accorded defendants are the same, certain special aspects of criminal obscenity proceedings are particularly significant to the eventual outcome.

Before one can be convicted of violating any criminal statute, the statute must give reasonable notice of the conduct that is prohibited. This has presented substantial difficulties for the drafters of criminal obscenity legislation in the past because of the definitional problem; convictions have sometimes been reversed because the statute alleged to have been violated was held "void for vagueness." See, e.g., Winters v. New York, 333 U.S. 507, 68 S.Ct. 665, 92 L.Ed. 840 (1948); cf. Interstate Circuit, Inc. v. City of Dallas, 390 U.S. 676, 88 S.Ct. 1298, 20 L.Ed.2d 225 (1968). This drafting problem may be alleviated by legislatures utilizing the definition of unprotected obscenity set forth in Miller.

As noted earlier in connection with the discussion of the effects of the recent trilogy of obscenity cases, *where* an obscenity prosecution is brought is of the greatest importance because of the Supreme Court's sanctioning of the application of local standards. Because a prosecution for violation of the Comstock Law may be brought in any district from, through or into which the mail in question is carried, federal prosecutors will usually have an advantageous choice as to venue. Reed Enterprises v. Clark, 278 F.Supp. 372 (D.D.C.1967), affirmed 390 U.S. 457, 88 S.Ct. 1196, 20 L.Ed.2d 28 (1968). Similar options as to venue between counties are often available to state prosecutors. And thus a defendant in an obscenity prosecution may be tried far from his or her residence or base of operations.

The burden of proof is always upon the state or federal government and the standard is the

[*153*]

same as in all criminal cases: guilt beyond a reasonable doubt. The burden has been eased somewhat by the Supreme Court's holding in Paris Adult Theatre that the material complained of "speaks for itself" and thus expert testimony as to its obscene nature is no longer required.

An important element of the prosecutor's burden is scienter or guilty knowledge. It may be difficult in certain cases to establish beyond a reasonable doubt that a book seller, magazine dealer or movie exhibitor knew of the obscene nature and contents of the material he or she was purveying. But neither the states nor the federal government may constitutionally eliminate this mental element in their criminal obscenity statutes. Smith v. California, 361 U.S. 147, 80 S.Ct. 215, 4 L.Ed.2d 205 (1959).

The chief defense in most obscenity prosecutions is that the material is protected expression under the prevailing Supreme Court tests. The defense will normally call expert witnesses to testify that the material has serious literary, artistic, political or scientific value and perhaps local psychologists or psychiatrists to testify that the material does not appeal to the prurient interest of the average person in the particular locality. Defense counsel may attempt to establish "tolerant" community standards through expert testimony and the introduction of comparable materials freely available in the local area. This latter defense is meeting with only mixed success before the courts.

D. PRIOR RESTRAINT FOR PURPOSES OF NATIONAL SECURITY

1. The Conflict

Since the founding of the Republic the federal and state governments have laid claim to the right to keep secrets on the ground that disclosures of certain matters would be harmful to the public interest. Obvious examples are troop deployments and diplomatic judgments concerning foreign governments. The working assumption of government officials is that the people would not want to know about sensitive matters if such knowledge would be harmful to their best interest.

While this assumption may have validity, official judgments as to precisely what knowledge would be harmful to the public interest are coming under increasing challenge. The common theme of the advocates of a freer flow of information is "the people's right to know" or "freedom of information."

The conflict has grown sharper with the growth of governmental activity since the New Deal and the increasing distrust of "big government" engendered in part by an unpopular war in Indochina and the Watergate scandal. Representative of the heightened conflict is the willingness of the media, particularly a once deferential press, to publish material which the government wishes to keep secret and a readiness on the part

[*155*]

of governmental officials to retaliate against the media and to seek injunctions against publication of those secrets.

2. Legal Background

There is no question but that the federal government has an inherent right to keep certain matters secret, especially information relating to national security and diplomatic affairs and that it may invoke executive privilege and establish a classification system to prevent disclosure. See United States v. Nixon, 418 U.S. 683, 703–713, 94 S.Ct. 3090, 3105–3110, 41 L.Ed.2d 1039, 1061–1067 (1974) (the Nixon Tapes case); United States v. Reynolds, 345 U.S. 1, 73 S.Ct. 528, 97 L.Ed.2d 727 (1953). Furthermore, there is little doubt that those individuals privy to secret government information or those who come across it accidentally might be enjoined from disclosing what they have learned or, in certain cases, be criminally punished for actually making disclosures to others. And in the process of protecting government secrets the executive's judgment concerning the need for secrecy for the specific material involved will not be reviewed by the judiciary because of the separation of powers doctrine.

The problem becomes considerably more complex, however, when disclosure is made or threatened by the media. In this situation, of course, first amendment considerations first raised in Near v. Minnesota, 283 U.S. 697, 51 S.Ct. 625, 75 L.Ed. 1357 (1931) intervene. While in *Near* prior restraint of the press was generally disapproved as violative of the First and Fourteenth Amendments, the Supreme Court did recognize that such restraint might be permissible in extraordinary situations including the threatened publication of military secrets in time of war. This left the door open for the federal government forty years later to attempt to stop the presses from printing the so called "Pentagon Papers."

3. New York Times Co. v. United States

Disillusioned with the war in Vietnam he had once supported, Daniel Ellsberg, a former Department of Defense official, arranged for the photocopying, without authorization, of a "top secret" multi-volume Department of Defense study of American involvement in the war between 1945 and 1967 entitled "History of U.S. Decision Making Process on Vietnam Policy" and a one volume "Command and Control Study of the Tonkin Gulf Incident" and made them available to selected newspapers throughout the United States. On June 12, 13 and 14, 1971 the New York Times became the first paper to publish summaries and portions of the text of the two studies popularly known as "The Pentagon Papers." The United States Justice Department sought and obtained a temporary restraining order from the United States District Court to prevent the Times from continuing publication of the classified material. This restraining order remained in effect until the

Supreme Court decided the case, thereby preventing further publication of the material for 15 days. At approximately the same time the Washington Post began publishing excerpts from the two studies and the government likewise sought to restrain the Post and for a short time succeeded. But the temporary restraining order binding the Post expired prior to the Supreme Court's resolution of the case and the anomalous situation was then presented of the Post being free to publish while the New York Times was not.

The issue presented to the Supreme Court in the historic case of New York Times Co. v. United States, 403 U.S. 713, 91 S.Ct. 2140, 29 L.Ed.2d 822 (1971) was very simply whether publication by the press of secret matters relating to the history and past conduct of an ongoing war could be enjoined consistent with the First Amendment. The Court by its judgment freed the Times to continue publication along with the Post. But its per curiam opinion is not, as some at first suggested, a ringing endorsement of a free press. The Court stated, " 'Any system of prior restraints of expression comes to this Court bearing a heavy presumption against its constitutional validity.' . . . The Government 'thus carries a heavy burden of showing justification for the imposition of such a restraint.' . . . The District Court for the Southern District of New York in the New York Times case and the District Court for the District of Columbia and the Court of Appeals for the District of Columbia Circuit in the

Washington Post case held that the Government had not met that burden. We agree." 403 U.S. at 714, 91 S.Ct. at 2141, 29 L.Ed.2d at 824–825.

What the Court necessarily implied was that given sufficient proof by the government of some serious effect on the war effort or national security, the media could be enjoined by the government from publishing truthful matters of public interest. What saved the press from being permanently gagged by court order for the first time in our history was the government's inability to prove to the satisfaction of the courts that publication of the papers would clearly result in direct, immediate and irreparable damage to the nation or its people.

The one implication favorable to the media from the per curiam opinion is that publication of government secrets relating to other than military, national security or diplomatic matters is unlikely to be enjoined because the possible consequences to the nation could never be sufficiently weighty to overcome the media's first amendment right to publish. Cf. United States v. Nixon, 418 U.S. 683, 707–713, 94 S.Ct. 3090, 3106–3110, 41 L.Ed.2d 1039, 1063–1067 (1974).

In addition to the per curiam opinion, The Pentagon Papers case is marked by six concurring and three dissenting opinions. An analysis of them must be considered generally discouraging to those favoring a free press.

1. Only three justices, Black, Douglas and Brennan gave strong support for the idea of an unfettered press and even Brennan accepted the constitutionality of prior restraint when publication would "inevitably, directly, and immediately cause the occurrence of an event kindred to imperiling the safety of a [troop] transport already at sea." 403 U.S. at 726–727, 91 S.Ct. at 2148, 29 L.Ed.2d at 831–32.

2. The same three justices were the only ones showing concern that newspapers had been restrained even temporarily from accurately publishing material of public interest, for the first time in the nation's history.

3. At least two of the concurring justices, White and Marshall would apparently have permitted the press to be enjoined permanently if the Congress had legislated to permit injunctions to issue in this type of situation. Their views, taken together with those of the three dissenters, might have formed a majority supporting the issuance of permanent injunctions against the newspapers involved had Congress previously enacted legislation authorizing such injunctions against publication by the press.

4. Six justices expressly agreed that the First Amendment permitted subsequent criminal punishment of individuals and corporations for publication of government secrets, assuming the existence of relevant criminal statutes and regardless of whether prior restraint of the publication would have been constitutionally permissible, thus confirming the Blackstonian dichotomy noted in Near v. Minnesota.

5. The three dissenting justices, Harlan, Burger and Blackmun subscribed to the idea that the First Amendment only commands the judiciary to review the executive's request for an injunction in order to determine whether the subject matter of the threatened publication lies within the boundaries of the President's foreign relations power and whether the determination of irreparable injury from publication was made by the appropriate cabinet officer— here the Secretary of Defense or Secretary of State. Adoption by a majority of the Court of such a restricted judicial review would almost certainly lead to injunctions against the media as a matter of course when sought by the federal government.

Thus, what appeared at first blush to be a great victory for the press is, at best, a pyrrhic one. The Court has given notice that there are limits to the media's right to publish and the people's right to learn government secrets relating

to national security. As a result of this case, the
media may become more wary of publishing classified material obtained without authorization.
At best the Pentagon Papers case encourages
self censorship by the news media and at worst
forms the predicate for successful government
censorship in the future. Indeed, in the three reported cases following the Supreme Court's decision involving censorship on grounds of national
security the government was successful in enjoining disclosure of certain CIA secrets in a book
by a former agency official, (United States v.
Marchetti, 466 F.2d 1309 (4th Cir. 1972), cert. denied 409 U.S. 1063, 93 S.Ct. 553, 34 L.Ed.2d 516;
Alfred A. Knopf, Inc. v. Colby, 509 F.2d 1362 (4th
Cir. 1975)) and information on the workings of
the hydrogen bomb contained in a magazine article (United States v. The Progressive, Inc., 486
F.Supp. 5 (D.Wis.1979)).

4. Other Inhibitions on Publication

Aside from direct injunctive restraints on the
release of national security information attempted in the New York Times Co., Marchetti,
Colby and Progressive cases, the federal government has successfully employed other techniques
to discourage disclosure of sensitive diplomatic,
military and intelligence information.

In Snepp v. United States, 444 U.S. 507, 100
S.Ct. 763, 62 L.Ed.2d 704 (1980) the defendant, a
former CIA agent, published a book ("Decent Interval") about certain CIA activities in South Vi-

etnam without submitting it for prepublication review as expressly required by his employment agreement with the intelligence agency. The Government brought suit to enforce the agreement by, among other things, capturing all profits that Snepp might earn from publishing the book in violation of the agreement. The District Court entered a judgment for the Government, giving it the relief it sought but the United States Court of Appeals refused to approve the turning over of the profits from the book to the Government. The Supreme Court summarily and without benefit of briefs or oral argument on the subject upheld the Government's right to capture all profits from the publication. The financial burden placed upon Snepp to pay off the Government was substantial and should give pause to other government employees considering writing about sensitive official matters.

Perhaps the most chilling aspects of the Marchetti, Colby and Snepp cases is the almost cavaliar subordination of First Amendment interests to "boilerplate" contract clauses in CIA employment agreements. In Snepp, the Supreme Court majority relegated First Amendment considerations to a footnote in rigorously enforcing the CIA employment contract against Snepp.

The denial or revocation of a passport because of expression which the Government perceives as damaging or potentially damaging to national security or foreign policy is yet another of the Government's techniques for inhibiting the release of

[*163*]

undesired information or comment. This technique was approved of by the Supreme Court in Haig v. Agee, 453 U.S. 280, 101 S.Ct. 2766, 69 L.Ed.2d 640 (1981), a case involving an ex-CIA agent's attempt to expose existing CIA agents in foreign countries and have them driven out by anti-CIA groups in those countries.

And finally, the Reagan Administration persuaded a willing Congress in 1982 to make it a federal crime for anyone to publish anything they have reason to know will disclose the identity of United States intelligence agents. See Intelligence Identities Protection Act, P.L. 97–200, 96 Stat. 122, 50 U.S.C.A. §§ 421–426.

CHAPTER V

FREEDOM TO GATHER NEWS AND INFORMATION

A. INTRODUCTION

The freedom of expression guaranteed by the First Amendment would have little meaning if there were nothing to express. The First Amendment assumes that the citizenry will have access to information, particularly concerning their governance, as the grist for meaningful expression in a democratic society. As James Madison wrote, "A popular Government, without popular information, or the means of acquiring it, is but a Prologue to a Farce or a Tragedy; or, perhaps both. Knowledge will forever govern ignorance: And a people who mean to be their own Governors, must arm themselves with the power which knowledge gives." Letter to W. T. Barry, August 4, 1822, quoted in Environmental Protection Agency v. Mink, 410 U.S. 73, 110–111, 93 S.Ct. 827, 847, 35 L.Ed.2d 119, 145 (1973) (dissenting opinion of Douglas, J.).

Nevertheless, since the time of George Washington, the federal and state governments have claimed the right to withhold information about their activities and operations in the "public interest" and to restrict the access of individuals and the media to certain sources of information. But it is clear that not all governmental secrecy and restrictions on the gathering of information are justified. If nothing else the tragedies of Vietnam and Watergate have taught us that much.

A movement to reverse the trend toward secret government, led by the media, began to develop in the 1960s. And by the late 1970s it had resulted in some notable successes in the fight for open government, such as the federal Freedom of Information Act and federal and state open meetings legislation. However, a reaction has set in to the relatively easy access of the press and public to government information. One of the first orders of business of the Reagan Administration was the introduction of a comprehensive package of amendments to FOIA, which could only be described as constricting the flow of information from the government to the press and public.

It is clear, then, that ease of access to government data cannot be taken for granted but depends to a large extent on the good will and grace of the legislative and executive branches of government.

B. THE FEDERAL FREEDOM OF INFORMATION ACT

1. Provisions

A major breakthrough in favor of more open government was the passage by Congress in 1966 of an amendment to the Federal Administrative

Procedure Act. This amendment, Section 552 of Title 5 of the United States Code, popularly known as the Freedom of Information Act (FOIA), requires federal executive agencies and independent regulatory agencies to publish in the Federal Register and make available as a matter of course or upon specific request of any person, information, documents and records concerning agency activities and operations not specifically exempted from disclosure by the Act itself. The language of the Act is affirmative in requiring disclosure; nowhere does the Act require nondisclosure. An agency may, if it chooses, refuse to release information under a claim that the information is covered by one or more of the nine enumerated exemptions, but then it may be required to defend its refusal in federal court where the burden of justification is on the withholding agency and not on the person or organization seeking disclosure. With Congress' bestowal of jurisdiction upon the federal courts to hear complaints of alleged FOIA violations, agency officials are no longer the sole judge of what information should and should not be made available to the public.

The enumerated exemptions from disclosure are found in subsection b of the Act, as amended in 1974, and cover matters that are:

(1) (a) specifically authorized under criteria established by an executive order to be kept secret in the interest of national defense or foreign policy and (b) are in fact

properly classified pursuant to such executive order;

(2) related solely to the internal personnel rules and practices of an agency;

(3) specifically exempted from disclosure by statute;

(4) in the nature of trade secrets and commercial or financial information obtained from a person and privileged or confidential;

(5) in the nature of inter-agency or intra-agency memoranda or letters which would not be available by law to a party other than an agency in litigation with the agency;

(6) in the nature of personnel and medical files and similar files the disclosure of which would constitute a clearly unwarranted invasion of personal privacy;

(7) in the nature of investigatory records compiled for law enforcement purposes, but only to the extent that the production of such records would (a) interfere with enforcement proceedings, (b) deprive a person of a right to a fair trial or an impartial adjudication, (c) constitute an unwarranted invasion of personal privacy, (d) disclose the identity of a confidential source and, in the case of a record compiled by a criminal law enforcement authority in the course of a criminal investigation, or by an agency conducting a lawful national security intelligence investigation, confidential informa-

tion furnished only by the confidential
source, (e) disclose investigative techniques
and procedures, or (f) endanger the life or
physical safety of law enforcement personnel;

(8) contained in or related to examination, operating, or condition reports prepared by,
on behalf of, or for the use of any agency
responsible for the regulation or supervision of financial institutions; or

(9) in the nature of geological and geophysical
information and data, including maps, concerning wells.

Because the purpose of the FOIA is to encourage
agency disclosure the exemptions are supposed to
be construed narrowly by the federal courts but
that has not always been the case, and certain
amendments to the original act considered below
became necessary.

2. Operation of the Original Act

a. In the Courts

Results of litigation under the original act
were mixed. While the courts placed the burden
on the agencies to justify withholding information and exercised the injunctive jurisdiction to
force disclosure when deemed appropriate, they
also construed certain of the exemptions broadly.

In Environmental Protection Agency v. Mink,
410 U.S. 73, 93 S.Ct. 827, 35 L.Ed.2d 119 (1973),

the Supreme Court held in effect that the executive branch had some authority to determine under Executive Order 10501 (setting up the present government classification system) what information was to be kept secret in the interest of national defense or foreign policy. The Court ruled that original exemption (1) did not permit a United States District Court to study in closed chambers classified documents concerning a scheduled underground nuclear test on Amchitka Island in order to isolate non-secret portions and order their release. A classified stamp on a file made everything in that file immune from disclosure.

In FAA Administrator v. Robertson, 422 U.S. 255, 95 S.Ct. 2140, 45 L.Ed.2d 164 (1975), the Court construed exemption (3) as referring to statutes broadly granting discretionary authority to agency officials to withhold unspecified information if in the "public interest" to do so. The Center for the Study of Responsive Law, an organization associated with Ralph Nader, had sought the release of the FAA's Systems Worthiness Analysis Program Reports (SWAP) concerning the operation and maintenance performance of the commercial airlines. The airlines voluntarily provide SWAP information to the FAA, and the industry's trade association, the Air Transport Association, objected to the release of the reports claiming that publication would adversely affect the airlines and make them less cooperative in the future with consequent adverse effect on air safety. The FAA Administrator denied the Center's request under Section 1104 of the Federal Aviation Act of 1958, which provides in relevant part that whenever an objection to release of information such as that of the ATA is made, "the Board or Administrator shall order such information withheld from public disclosure when, in their judgment, a disclosure of such information would adversely affect the interests of such person [objecting] and is not required in the interest of the public."

The Center successfully argued in the district court and the court of appeals that exemption (3) refers only to statutes which specifically designate particular classes of documents which might be withheld by the agencies and the SWAP reports were not so designated in Section 1104. The Supreme Court could find no such narrow limitation to exemption (3) either in its wording or legislative history and held that the FOIA permitted the Administrator to withhold information so long as he or she exercised discretion consistent with the general dictates of Section 1104. The Robertson decision had great potential for limiting the flow of information from the agencies to the public because there are nearly 100 statutes or parts of statutes which restrict public access to the records of executive and independent regulatory agencies in more or less general terms. But the Congress nullified the Supreme Court's construction in the new "Government in the Sunshine Act," P.L. 94–409, 90 Stat. 1241 (1976) and has essentially adopted the Nader group's position. See 5 U.S.C.A. § 552b(c)(3). This aspect of the legislation is discussed in Consumer Product Safety Commission v. GTE Sylvania, Inc., 447 U.S. 102, 121–22, n. 18, 100 S.Ct. 2051, 2063, n. 18, 64 L.Ed.2d 766, 780, n. 18 (1980).

One other exemption had been construed broadly and, as construed, had a substantial impact on the availability of governmental information sought by the media. Exemption (7) as originally enacted permitted the withholding of investigatory files compiled for law enforcement purposes except to the extent they are available by law to parties to subsequent law enforcement proceedings other than the agencies themselves. A number of lower federal courts had construed this exemption as covering files in which no civil or criminal proceeding is ever initiated and files involving matters long since closed. The reasoning behind this broad construction was that the identity of informants and agency investigatory techniques had to be protected. See, e.g., Frankel v. SEC, 460 F.2d 813 (2d Cir. 1972), cert. denied 409 U.S. 889.

In contrast, certain other exemptions have been narrowly circumscribed by the courts, including exemption (4) dealing with trade secrets and commercial or financial information obtained by the government from businesspersons and exemption (5) involving inter-agency or intra-agency memoranda. See, e.g., Soucie v. David, 145 U.S. App.D.C. 144, 448 F.2d 1067 (1971).

b. At the Administrative Level

While litigation or the threat of it is very important to the operation of FOIA, the proof of the legislation is in its day to day administration by the agencies themselves. Litigation is costly and time consuming. Information is needed by the media quickly and at reasonable cost. At the administrative level, too, the results have been mixed. Some agencies such as the Department of Justice (excluding the FBI) and the Department of Defense have promulgated fair and reasonable regulations for the expeditious release of information and are generally following them. Some agencies have not been as conscientious. Charges for searches and copying have too often been exorbitant and extensive delays in releasing information have been frequent. Nevertheless, vast amounts of information have been made routinely available to the public and the media which prior to the Act would have been kept from view.

3. The 1974 Amendments

As a result of experience with the operation of FOIA in court and in the agencies over a period of several years, Congress amended the Act in 1974 in an effort to increase and expedite governmental disclosure. P.L. 93-502, 88 Stat. 1561. The amendments are both substantive and procedural in nature. One substantive amendment enlarges the scope of the Act by defining a federal agency to encompass any executive department; military department; government corporation (such as the Federal Deposit Insurance Corporation); government controlled corporation (such as the Corporation for Public Broadcasting); or other establishment in the executive branch, including the Executive Office of the President itself, and any independent regulatory agency. In the past some administrative units attempted to avoid the strictures of the Act by claiming they were not "agencies." Another amendment requires the agencies to maintain and make available for public inspection and copying current indexes providing identifying information for the public as to any matter issued, adopted or promulgated after July 4, 1967 (the effective date of FOIA) and required by the Act to be made available or published.

Still other substantive amendments override or modify court decisions not consistent with the broad purpose of the Act. Exemption (1) involving national defense and foreign policy matters, has been modified to except from disclosure matters which are "(A) specifically authorized under criteria established by an Executive order to be kept secret in the interest of national defense or foreign policy and (B) are in fact properly classified pursuant to such Executive order." This means that the United States District Courts are directed to go beyond the face of the executive branch's classification of particular records and documents and to determine whether such classification in fact comports with the current executive order on classification. To do this the federal trial courts are also given explicit authority to inspect the material in closed chambers. If portions of the material are not properly classifiable and can be reasonably segregated such portions will be ordered disclosed. This amendment clearly overrides the decision in Environmental Protection Agency v. Mink, supra.

Also overridden are numerous lower federal court decisions construing exemption (7). The exemption, originally devoid of standards for the withholding of investigatory files compiled for law enforcement purposes, now provides six specific alternative bases for such withholding. Following the FOIA's amendment in 1974, these records may now only be withheld if their release would (1) interfere with enforcement proceedings; (2) deprive a person of the right to a fair trial, or impartial adjudication; (3) constitute an unwarranted invasion of personal privacy; (4) disclose the identity of a confidential source and, in certain cases, confidential information furnished by the confidential source; (5) disclose investigative techniques and procedures; or (6) endanger the life or physical safety of law enforcement personnel. As a result of the amendment of exemption (7), it is no longer possible for the courts to permit the agencies to withhold whole files indefinitely simply because some of the materials in them were compiled for law enforcement purposes. To be withheld, records and documents must now meet one or more of the criteria listed by Congress. Whatever in the file does not meet such standards must be released if it is reasonably divisible from the exempted matter.

The procedural amendments may be even more significant because they are designed to speed the release of information and reduce the costs to requesting individuals or organizations. The amendments require the agencies to establish uniform fee schedules, limit fees to reasonable charges for document searches and duplication based upon the agencies' direct costs and require specific time periods for agency determination whether to comply with requests for information (completion and notification within ten days, excluding Saturdays, Sundays and legal holidays) and administrative appeals from refusals to comply (completion and notification within twenty days after receipt of the appeal, excluding the same days as above). Failure of the agency to comply with the time limits or to obtain the short extension permitted by the Act gives the requester immediate access to the appropriate United States District Court. Once it is called into federal court the agency must serve its answer to the requester's complaint within thirty days instead of the sixty days previously allowed, unless the court directs otherwise.

4. New Problems and Assessment of the Act

Despite Congress' efforts in its 1974 amendments to increase the effectiveness of the Freedom of Information Act, problems persist. Perhaps the most significant one involves the statutory requirement that an agency must improperly withhold agency records before the federal courts can order such records to be released to the FOIA requester. In Kissinger v. Reporters Committee for Freedom of the Press, 445 U.S. 136, 100 S.Ct. 960, 63 L.Ed.2d 267 (1980), the Supreme Court ruled that the United States District Court had no jurisdiction to order the Library of Congress to return to the State Department certain telephone records made by Henry Kissinger while Secretary of State and later transferred by him to the Library in apparent violation of the Federal Records Act. Reading the agency "withholding" requirement quite narrowly, the Supreme Court ruled that an agency does not withhold agency records from a requester when it does not physically possess or control them. That being so the refusal of an agency to turn over records no longer in its possession does not violate the FOIA.

This decision creates a rather large loophole in the Act and a potential for agency abuse as Justice Stevens points out in his dissent. "It . . . creates an incentive for outgoing agency officials to remove potentially embarrassing documents from their files in order to frustrate future FOIA requests." 445 U.S. at 161, 100 S.Ct. at 974, 63 L.Ed.2d at 288. Justice Stevens might have added that it also encourages venal federal agency officials to move records out of the agencies that generated them even while they remain in office.

Another problem with the Act came to light in the companion case of Forsham v. Harris, 445 U.S. 169, 100 S.Ct. 978, 63 L.Ed.2d 293 (1980) in which the Court ruled that documents produced by a private medical research group under a federal grant from and with supervision by an agency of the then Department of Health, Education and Welfare but with custody of the documents remaining with the private research group were not "agency records" accessible under FOIA. Thus, it is possible for federal agencies to avoid the reach of the Act by contracting with private organizations for controversial studies and reports so long as physical custody of the documents generated remains with the private contractor.

While the Kissinger and Forsham cases limit the reach of FOIA, Chrysler Corp. v. Brown, 441 U.S. 281, 99 S.Ct. 1705, 60 L.Ed.2d 208 (1979), the so-called "reverse FOIA case" gives an expansive interpretation to the act to permit federal agencies to release, pursuant to FOIA requests, certain classes of information required to be submitted to these agencies by private businesses and organizations, including their trade secrets and confidential statistical data. In so ruling the Court repeated the idea that FOIA is exclusively a disclosure statute and that the exemptions in the act and particularly the one dealing with trade secrets *permit* agencies to withhold records but do not *require* them to do so. This ruling has created problems for the government in collecting privately held confidential business information and has resulted in calls from the business community for amendment of the Act to *require* agencies to withhold certain records. Such amendment would however be inconsistent with the underlying disclosure philosophy of the act.

Finally, criticism of the act exists regarding the uses to which it is put. Claims have been made that the act is under-utilized by journalists, who are more interested in breaking news than painstaking stories about government that can be documented with the aid of FOIA. At the same time, critics of the act assert that it is being abused by private litigants and their lawyers who use it in circumvention of ordinary procedural rules of court governing discovery of information. Journalists and lawyers reject these charges. As one newsperson told a congressional committee, "for every one or two formal requests under the act . . . there are 12 or 14 we didn't have to make. The act is there, and the bureaucrats are aware of it." Nevertheless, the act is under attack, particularly from those who argue that too much information is released under it.

Despite its problems and limitations, FOIA provides the American people and the media which serve them with a significant instrument for holding their government accountable. To date, much information has been released pursuant to its provisions, and it has been estimated that plaintiffs have been successful in 60 to 70 percent of the court cases. The 1974 amendments have improved on this record. Already the new timetables seem to be having the desired effect. From discussions with agency counsel it appears that some of the agencies even defer important projects in order to provide the personnel needed to expedite FOIA requests. And the Act's new limitation on agency charges together with the efforts of private organizations such as the Washington based Freedom of Information Clearinghouse and the Reporters Committee for Freedom of the Press to educate the public and media representatives concerning the Act has encouraged increased utilization. Equally important large amounts of information are obtained by the media without formal request because of the mere existence of the Act. For a more detailed assessment of the original FOIA and the amended version see Clark, "Holding Government Accountable: The Amended Freedom of Information Act," 84 Yale L.J. 741 (1975).

C.   OPEN MEETINGS—OPEN RECORDS LEGISLATION IN THE STATES

Parallel to the Federal Freedom of Information Act are federal and state "govenment in the sunshine" statutes which require federal, state and local governmental units to conduct their business in the open. These statutes, now in force in a large majority of states, vary considerably and journalists and lawyers must acquaint themselves with the provisions in their particular jurisdiction if the legislation is to be effectively utilized. Space limitations do not permit a state by state analysis here but the general outline of the legislation and the basic legal issues may be considered in relation to one state's law.

1. Basic Provisions

One of the more influential "sunshine" statutes is that of Florida. The ten year debate in the Florida legislature prior to its enactment created substantial interest in this type of legislation in a number of other states. In addition, members of the Florida congressional delegation, apparently convinced of the utility and effectiveness of Florida's statute, were instrumental in forcing the Congress to enact federal "sunshine" legislation.

The Florida statute provides:

(1) All meetings of any board or commission of any state agency or authority or of any agency or authority of any county, municipal corporation or any political subdivision, except as otherwise provided in the constitution, at which official acts are to be taken are declared to be public meetings open to the public at all times, and no resolution, rule, regulation or formal action shall be considered binding except as taken or made at such meeting.

(2) The minutes of a meeting of any such board or commission of any such state agency or authority shall be promptly recorded and such records shall be open to public inspection. The circuit courts of this state shall have jurisdiction to issue injunctions to enforce the purposes of this section upon application by any citizens of this state.

(3) Any person who is a member of a board or commission or of any state agency or authority of any county, municipal corporation or any political subdivision who violates the provisions of this section by attending a meeting not held in accordance with the provisions hereof is guilty of a misdemeanor of the second degree, punishable as provided in § 775.082, § 775.083 or § 775.084.

§ 286.011 Fla.Stat.Ann. (1975).

The law was amended in 1978 to allow courts, in certain circumstances, to assess attorneys' fees against public bodies and their individual members found in violation of the act.

Sec. 286.011(4) and (5).

a. Coverage

The Florida statute is one of the most sweeping in terms of coverage. All meetings of nearly all state and local executive and administrative units are required to be open and minutes of those meetings must be taken and made public.

Statutes in other states are not as broad. Some limit coverage jurisdictionally to local units of government while others limit coverage functionally to particular activities of government. Still others limit the reach of the legislation to the culminating stages in the decision-making process such as meetings at which final actions or final votes are taken. The spirit of this latter type of statute may be easily avoided by agencies making the real decisions behind closed doors, then ratifying those decisions in the "sunshine." It seems clear that the broader the coverage the more effective will be the legislation. But sheer breadth without exemptions can cause problems for individuals and the public.

b. *Exemptions*

The Florida statute is not tempered by any clearly defined exemptions as to units of government, their functions or the stages of deliberation. Thus, for instance, internal personnel matters discussed informally by two or more officials of an agency at the water fountain would seem to fall within the mandate of the legislation and could result in delaying or preventing a necessary personnel action. Then, too, charges of misconduct against a state employee would, even at the earliest stage of investigation, have to be aired in public. And material concerning private citizens best left in the file drawers (or even destroyed) might be unnecessarily publicized in the absence of exemption.

The Florida statute seems atypical in failing to delineate any exemptions to its requirements or to provide any procedure for executive sessions. Most state legislation provides specific exemptions from the public meeting requirement or at least contains an "except as otherwise provided" clause which incorporates the authority granted by other statutes to governmental units to conduct certain business in private. The new federal legislation, for instance, contains exemptions parallel to those found in the Freedom of Information Act. P.L. 94–409 § 3(c), 90 Stat. 1241–1242 (1976).

The obvious danger presented by exemption or executive session clauses is that if they are not carefully drafted they can be used to defeat the objectives of the legislation. It is these clauses which will be of most concern to the working journalist and media counsel in their efforts to increase the scope of newsgathering concerning government operations.

c. Public Notice of Meetings

It is axiomatic that unless the public and the media have notice of meeting times and locations, the requirement of open meetings is virtually worthless. Yet Florida and a number of the other "sunshine" states have no provision in their statutes requiring governmental units to set regular times and places for their meetings and to prohibit special or emergency meetings without some advance notice to the public generally or at

least to the local media. Because it is the special
or emergency meeting which often generates
newsworthy actions, the media and the public
need special notice legislation covering at least
the same governmental units as are covered by
the "sunshine" acts themselves. In this connection, California's notice requirement for special
meetings and North Dakota's notice requirements for emergency and special meetings fur-
nish useful models. Section 54956 of the California Government Code requires notice in writing
to local newspapers and radio and television stations of special meetings of covered agencies at
least 24 hours before the time of the meeting as
specified in the notice, provided the media have
previously requested receipt of such notices from
the agencies. The one exception to this notice requirement is in the case of an emergency situation involving matters requiring prompt action by
a legislative body because of the disruption or
threatened disruption of public facilities. Section
54956.5.

North Dakota's open meetings legislation provides that the official calling an emergency or
special meeting of a public body covered by the
act must notify representatives of the news media who have requested to be notified of such
meetings at the same time as the members of the
public body are notified. North Dakota Cent.
Code § 44–04–20 (Cum.Supp.1981).

d. Enforcement and Sanctions

In addition to an adequate notice provision, an open meetings statute must have enforcement provisions and sanctions for violations if it is to be effective. Subsection two of the Florida statute confers jurisdiction on the courts of general jurisdiction of the state to issue injunctions to enforce the act at the behest of any citizen or citizens of the state. There is thus no problem for any Florida citizen to bring suit to enforce the provisions of the Act. Moreover, the same provision eliminates the need for a plaintiff seeking injunctive relief to establish that a violation will cause him or her irreparable injury. If a violation is threatened or is occurring it may be enjoined regardless of the nature of the injury and the normal requirements of equitable jurisdiction.

Subsection three makes willful violation of the statute a misdemeanor punishable by fine, imprisonment or both. In addition, since subsection one states that no resolution, rule, regulation or formal action shall be considered binding except as taken at a meeting conforming to the requirements of the act, such actions would appear to be nullified upon proof that they were taken at meetings not conducted in accordance with the act.

Most of the other states recognize the need for enforcement in their legislation and provide for minor criminal prosecutions or civil actions for injunctive relief or both. A few states provide for the nullification of final actions but most of the states shy away from this extreme enforcement device. Removal of violators from office is another possible sanction and is provided for in a handful of states.

2. Assessment

The "government in the sunshine" statutes are apparently having the desired effect. A survey taken by the Harvard Law Review in the early 1960's indicated that by and large the statutes were making it easier for reporters and other media representatives as well as members of the general public to be admitted to governmental meetings. Reporters and others have forced open what would have been closed meetings by either exhibiting copies of the local act or simply referring to it. When such tactics have failed, the newspapers and other media have often succeeded in opening meetings and records through the use of their editorial power. See Note, "Open Meeting Statutes: The Press Fights for the 'Right to Know'," 75 Harv.L.Rev. 1199, 1216–1217 (1962). If anything, the statutes enacted since the Harvard survey have more teeth in them and should be even more effective in opening state and local government meetings and records. But the cost involved ought not to be ignored in deciding whether to enact new statutes or strengthen old ones. Conducting government business in a fishbowl may interfere with free and frank discussion of the merits of proposed actions at least in the preliminary stages. Government officials, like nearly everyone else, are loathe to go out on limbs in public. There is bound to be some loss of input when nearly every move of the government employee or official is subject to public scrutiny. This loss of input can adversely affect the final product of government. Thus, the public will have to decide whether open government is worth the price.

For a survey of the major legal and political issues involved with the sunshine legislation together with a model statute, see Wickham, "Let the Sun Shine In!," 68 Nw.U.L.Rev. 480 (1973).

D. MEDIA ACCESS TO GOVERNMEN-TALLY RESTRICTED PLACES AND INSTITUTIONS

A field in which the freedom to gather news and information has not expanded in recent years is that of access to governmentally restricted institutions such as military bases and penitentiaries and geographic areas such as unfriendly foreign countries. While the Supreme Court recognized in the abstract in Branzburg v. Hayes, 408 U.S. 665, 681, 92 S.Ct. 2646, 2656, 33 L.Ed.2d 626, 639 (1972), that "without some protection for seeking out the news, freedom of the press could be eviscerated," the Court in that very case appears to have restricted first amendment protection for newsgathering to those areas accessible to the general public.

Such an approach to access assures that the media will not be discriminated against in the gathering of information. But no guarantee is given that public access and, hence, media access to sources of information will not be further curtailed by a security conscious government.

Initially it was thought that because Branzburg involved a claim of indirect restriction on newsgathering (see pp. 224–228 infra for a discussion of the case), the limitation on protection for newsgathering might not be applicable to direct governmental restrictions on media access. This has not proven to be the case. In Pell v. Procunier, 417 U.S. 817, 94 S.Ct. 2800, 41 L.Ed.2d 495 (1974) and Saxbe v. Washington Post Co., 417 U.S. 843, 94 S.Ct. 2811, 41 L.Ed.2d 514 (1974) the California Department of Corrections and the Federal Bureau of Prisons had by regulation barred representatives of the media from interviewing specifically designated penitentiary inmates. The rationale for such restriction is that only a relatively small number of inmates are of interest to the media and those inmates who are conspicuously publicized tend to become the source of substantial disciplinary problems that can affect large portions of the prison population. Certain individual journalists and the Washington Post attacked the state and federal regulations as violative of the First Amendment's protection of newsgathering activities.

In the face of a detailed evidentiary record in the Washington Post case supporting the press' need for interviews with designated prisoners and a powerful dissent by Mr. Justice Powell, the

Court decided by 5–4 votes that both the California and federal regulations totally banning designated interviews were constitutionally valid. Relying on Branzburg the Court held that newspersons have no constitutional right of access to prisons or their inmates beyond that afforded the general public. Since the public is given no general access to the prisons or their inmates the regulations did not abridge the First Amendment. As if to underline the limited constitutional protection afforded the newsgathering function the Court said, "The proposition 'that the Constitution imposes upon government the affirmative duty to make available to journalists sources of information not available to members of the public generally . . . finds no support in the words of the Constitution or in any decision of this Court.' " 417 U.S. at 850, 94 S.Ct. at 2815, 41 L.Ed.2d at 520. This view of the Constitution was reaffirmed by the High Court in Houchins v. KQED, Inc., 438 U.S. 1, 98 S.Ct. 2588, 57 L.Ed.2d 553 (1978).

The principle that journalists are not accorded special access to news sources by the First Amendment is a broad one and would seemingly apply to any situation in which the state or federal government limits public access reasonably and in a nondiscriminatory way. A common situation is the setting up of police lines to seal off a geographic area in the interest of public safety. By definition police lines are designed to keep the public out of even public areas for limited periods

of time and if there exists a reasonable basis for
the lines it would seem to follow that the media
could also be excluded. In practice, accredited
journalists are often permitted by police authorities to cross the lines. If such permission is giv-
en, however, it must be extended on a nondiscriminatory basis to all journalists with proper
credentials and the credentials must be issued in
a fair and nondiscriminatory manner.

An analogous situation was considered by the
Supreme Court in Zemel v. Rusk, 381 U.S. 1, 85
S.Ct. 1271, 14 L.Ed.2d 179 (1965). There, a private citizen contended that he had a First Amendment right to visit the then off-limits nation of
Cuba to inform himself of the conditions on that
island. In rejecting Zemel's contention the Court
upheld Department of State passport regulations
which, in effect, set up exclusionary lines around
an entire country. While media representatives
were not involved in the Zemel case and, in fact
might, by Department of State regulation, be giv-
en special authorization to travel to Cuba and other restricted foreign areas to report the news (see
22 C.F.R. § 51.73(b)(1) (1981)), they could be prohibited from travelling to large areas of the
world pursuant to the rulings in Pell and Washington Post Co. if such prohibition ostensibly
serves some reasonable governmental purpose.

The danger to international newsgathering by
American journalists posed by Zemel is further
emphasized by the recent case of Haig v. Agee,
453 U.S. 280, 101 S.Ct. 2766, 69 L.Ed.2d 640

(1981) in which the Supreme Court upheld the authority of the Secretary of State to revoke passports for conduct and expression which he considers damaging to national security or foreign policy. Presumably this could include newsgathering which the Secretary views as harmful or embarrassing to the country's interests.

Instead of rejecting the special societal interest in the newsgathering function, Justice Powell, in dissent in the Washington Post Co. case, would have recognized it in the context of Pell and Washington Post Co. and would have imposed upon the Government the same heavy burden of justification for denial of access of the press as for prior restraint of publication required in New York Times Co. v. United States, 403 U.S. 713, 91 S.Ct. 2140, 29 L.Ed.2d 822 (1971) (the "Pentagon Papers" case). Of course, the Justice recognized that his approach raises problems avoided by the majority. Prison agencies would have to make individual judgments regarding requests for inmate interviews and would have to define who or what is included in the term "press" for purposes of protecting the societal interest. But these problems, he asserted, are not insuperable.

While the prevailing judicial view refuses to mandate constitutional protection for the media in their newsgathering function beyond that afforded the general public, special consideration may still be accorded the media by legislative or administrative grace. We have already cited the examples of credentialed newspersons being permitted to cross police lines and the Department of State regulation giving professional journalists special authorization for travel to restricted foreign areas if the purpose of the travel is to make information available to the public concerning these areas. Others could be mentioned. But, of course, what is given at the government's discretion may also be withdrawn at its discretion.

E.   MEDIA ACCESS TO COURTS AND GOVERNMENTAL RECORDS

1.   The Impact of Court Decisions

Another major source of concern about media access to governmentally generated information has recently developed, this time in relation to the courthouse. While it had long been our history that the doors of American courtrooms were open to the public and press (see Justice Black's opinion In re Oliver, 333 U.S. 257, 266, 68 S.Ct. 499, 504, 92 L.Ed.2d 682, 690 (1948)), a trend toward closing the courtroom developed in the 1970s as a judicial response to the threat to fair trials allegedly posed by publicity surrounding those trials. By the end of that decade the Reporters Committee for Freedom of Press had documented several dozen cases in which pretrial and trial proceedings across the country had been closed to the public and press by judicial order. This movement to deny access of the media to judicial information and news reached its zenith with the decision in Gannett Co. v. De Pasquale, 443 U.S. 368,

99 S.Ct. 2898, 61 L.Ed.2d 608 (1979). There, the two defendants in a murder case asked the judge to close a pretrial hearing in the case on the ground that the unabated publicity in Gannett's local Rochester, New York newspapers was jeopardizing their ability to receive a fair trial. The prosecuting attorney did not oppose the motion and a Gannett reporter present in the courtroom did not object at the time the closure motion was made and granted. The next day, however, the reporter wrote a letter to the trial judge asserting a "right to cover this hearing." When her request was rejected, Gannett formally moved the court to set aside the closure order. This motion was subsequently denied. On appeal the Appellate Division of the New York Supreme Court vacated the trial court's order but, in turn, the New York Court of Appeals reinstated the closure order.

In affirming the judgment of the New York Court of Appeals upholding the closing of the pretrial hearing, the United States Supreme Court rejected, in a five to four decision, Gannett's contentions that the Sixth and First Amendments, which are applicable to the states through the Fourteenth Amendment, conferred upon the press a right of access to the pretrial proceedings in the case. Regarding the Sixth Amendment claim of access, the majority held that members of the public and press have no enforceable right independent of the parties to the litigation to demand a public trial. Rather, the public trial guarantee of the Sixth Amendment was created for the benefit of the defendant, and he or she may waive that protection.

Alternatively, the majority argued that even assuming that the Sixth Amendment could be understood as embodying the right of the public and press to attend criminal *trials*, it did not apply to *pretrial* proceedings.

Turning to Gannett's First Amendment claim to access, the majority, speaking through Justice Stewart, held that if such a right of access to criminal trials existed, Gannett's assumed right of access was not violated in this case. Justice Stewart asserted that such assumed First Amendment right would not be absolute but would have to be balanced against the defendant's right to a fair trial and that this balancing had been fairly done by the trial judge and he had determined that the balance should be struck in favor of closure of the courtroom in this case.

Moreover, any denial of First Amendment access in the case was temporary, for as soon as the danger of prejudicial publicity had dissipated, a transcript of the suppression hearing was made available to the press and public. Thus, no First Amendment right of Gannett to attend the criminal trial was violated.

Perhaps because of the broad manner in which the majority opinion was written and the seemingly inconsistent concurring opinions by some of the justices who had formed the majority, considerable confusion arose as to whether the decision covered actual trials as well as pretrial proceedings and whether there was or was not a First Amendment right of access.

Fortuitously, a case was already in the judicial system of the State of Virginia which squarely raised these questions and would quickly give the Supreme Court an opportunity to clarify what it had decided in Gannett. In Richmond Newspapers, Inc. v. Virginia, 448 U.S. 555, 100 S.Ct. 2814, 65 L.Ed.2d 973 (1980), a murder trial was closed to the public and the press on the motion of the defendant, who had already gone through three previous mistrials of the same case. The reason given for the motion was that the defense did not want information being shuffled back and forth during recesses as to what particular witnesses had testified to. Neither the prosecutor nor the reporters covering the trial for the Richmond newspapers objected to the closure at the time the trial judge granted the motion. But later that same day, the Richmond Newspapers and their reporters sought a hearing on their motion to vacate the closure order. A hearing was held the next day at which time constitutional objections were raised by Richmond Newspapers and the reporters. The court denied the motion to vacate and ordered the trial to proceed "with the press and public excluded." The media corporation and its employees then appealed to the Virginia Supreme Court which denied the petition for appeal. The United States Supreme Court then granted a petition for certiorari to review the case.

The Court, in reversing the judgment of the Virginia Supreme Court, noted at the outset of its opinion that the Richmond Newspapers case involved exclusion from a trial and not from a pretrial proceeding. The Court then went on to hold that while the Sixth Amendment provided the press with no right of access to trials, the First Amendment, as applied to the states through the Fourteenth Amendment, did. Chief Justice Burger speaking for the Court said, "We hold that the right to attend criminal trials is implicit in the guarantees of the First Amendment; without the freedom to attend such trials, which people have exercised for centuries, important aspects of freedom of speech and 'of the press could be eviscerated.'" 448 U.S. at 580, 100 S.Ct. at 2829, 65 L.Ed.2d at 991–92 (1980).

But Chief Justice Burger made clear that the First Amendment right of access to trials was not absolute. If the trial court could find, as the Virginia trial court did not, that there was a specific overriding interest in closing a trial, then an occasional courtroom closure might pass constitutional muster.

However, he did not state the precise constitutional standards which litigants would have to meet to obtain such closures or whether different standards might be applied to the closing of pretrial proceedings permitted by Gannett. Pretrial proceedings pose greater risks of generating publicity prejudicial to a fair trial because prospective jurors may be influenced by the news stories arising out of such proceedings before they are even chosen and the judicial devices to prevent potential prejudice in such cases are limited. Therefore, the standard for closing a pretrial proceeding might be more relaxed or at least applied in such way as to make it easier for a defendant to meet it.

Precise constitutional standards for the closing of trials and pre-trial proceedings as well as for the calling of in camera (closed) proceedings during trials await further Supreme Court elaborations. But it seems clear at this point from Globe Newspaper Co. v. Superior Court, —— U.S. ——, 102 S.Ct. 2613, 73 L.Ed.2d 248 (1982) that such standards will be difficult for proponents of closed judicial proceedings to meet. In the Globe Newspaper case a rape trial involving minor victims was closed under a Massachusetts statute requiring without exception closure during the victims' testimony.

In striking down the statute as violative of the First Amendment right of access of the press and public to court proceedings, the court said "[T]he circumstances under which the press and public can be barred from criminal trials are limited; the state's justification in denying access must be a weighty one. Where, as in the present case, the State attempts to deny the right of access in order to inhibit the disclosure of sensitive information, it must be shown that the denial is necessitated by a compelling governmental interest, and narrowly tailored to serve that interest." — U.S. at —, 102 S.Ct. at 2620, 73 L.Ed.2d at 257.

Even the compelling interest of the state in that case to protect minor victims of sex crimes from further trauma and embarrassment was held insufficient to justify *indiscriminate* exclusion of the press and public from those portions of criminal trials during which the victims testify.

An attempt to formulate such standards for federal trial courts has been made by the Committee on Rules of Practice and Procedure of the Judicial Conference of the United States in Rule 43.1 of its Preliminary Draft of Proposed Amendments to the Federal Rules of Criminal Procedure. The Committee tentatively proposes to permit a United States District Court to order the exclusion of the public and representatives of the news media if the court finds "that there is a reasonable likelihood that dissemination of information from the proceeding would interfere with the defendant's right to a fair trial by an impartial jury; and that the prejudicial effect of such information on trial fairness cannot be avoided by any reasonable alternative means."

Because the Committee, by its proposal, would establish a substantive First Amendment standard in the guise of procedural rulemaking, it is unlikely that the proposal will ultimately be approved by the Supreme Court as final arbiter of the rules governing lower federal courts. Rather, the Court itself, as in the Globe Newspaper Co. case, will ultimately formulate the substantive standards for court closings of both federal and state courts.

Because the Gannett, Richmond Newspapers and Globe Newspaper cases do permit court closings under the Constitution in at least some cases, whatever the standards may be, state law may be relied upon by newspersons to keep open state pretrial and trial proceedings when that law provides stronger guarantees of public and press access than does the United States Constitution. Thus, in Phoenix Newspapers, Inc. v. Jennings, 107 Ariz. 557, 490 P.2d 563 (1971), the Arizona Supreme Court determined that a provision in the state constitution that "[j]ustice in all cases shall be administered openly" required that preliminary hearings be open to the public except in cases where there is a clear and present threat to the due administration of justice. The court also expressly ruled that the news organization which challenged the order closing the hearing had standing to sue to keep it open.

Just as with state "sunshine laws," supra pp. 180–188, newspersons should be familiar with state constitutional and statutory provisions dealing with open trials and pretrial proceedings and be prepared to invoke them before the trial judge when attempts are made to close such proceedings.

2. Legislation Limiting Access in the Name of Personal Privacy

One other aspect of the growing desire for individual privacy in our society should be mentioned though space does not permit a full exploration. More and more legislation is being placed on the books to shield from public scrutiny information about individuals gathered by government. In 1974, Congress passed the Privacy Act, 5 U.S.C.A. § 552a, to curb abuses by the federal government in its handling of personal information about individual citizens. The idea behind the federal statute has spread to the states and as of 1980 some 16 states had enacted some kind of privacy act. See I Prentice-Hall Government Disclosure Service, p. 30,001 (1980). Seventeen states have legislation providing for expungement of nonconviction arrest records. See Biweekly Comparison of Key Statutes, National Law Journal, February 11, 1980, pp. 12–14. Instances of lessened press access to governmental records because of privacy claims abound, particularly with regard to arrest records.

Though the intent of these statutes to protect citizens from abusive treatment by federal, state and local government is laudatory, journalists must recognize that the more restrictive the treatment of government-collected information the less access the press will have to it. This will undoubtedly affect the press' historic function of overseeing government operations on behalf of society as a whole.

One specific example of this growing threat to newsgathering will suffice. Under the federal FOIA, all government documents and records must be disclosed upon request unless the agency involved chooses to invoke an exemption (of which there are nine). Before the passage of the Privacy Act an agency could, in its discretion, waive applicable exemptions and release the information anyway. The Privacy Act requires the Federal Government to keep from disclosure certain information in its possession about individual citizens unless there is an exemption permitting its release. 5 U.S.C.A. § 552a(b). One of these exemptions permits the release of such information when it is *required* to be disclosed under FOIA. The apparent implication here of the Privacy Act as it intersects the FOIA is that a government agency may no longer release personal information about individuals to others if such information is subject to one or more of the nine FOIA exemptions, as, for instance, the personnel and medical files exemption (5 U.S.C.A. § 552(b) (6).

More generally, federal and state privacy statutes impose penalties on government agencies which improperly release information but do not penalize the agencies or their employees when information which should be disseminated is not released. It is likely then, that government personnel responsible for release of information will err in favor of nonrelease when there is any question as to the propriety of such release. For a thorough discussion of the relation of the Federal Privacy Act to the Freedom of Information Act and the problems created by that relation see 2 J. O'Reilly, Federal Information Disclosure § 20.13 (Sheppard's 1977).

F.   MEDIA ACCESS TO COPYRIGHTED MATERIAL

1.   Legal Protection for Intellectual Property as a Limitation on Access to Information

a.   Introduction

The legal concepts of American copyright law and the provisions of the new copyright statute, 17 U.S.C.A. § 101 et seq., 90 Stat. 2541 (1976) are to be summarized in another volume of the "Nutshell" series and will not be generally repeated here.

It is enough to say that the Congress, pursuant to constitutional authority can and does protect the owners of intellectual property in fixed form such as writings, photographs, and sight and sound recordings from having their creations copied and appropriated by others. Such copying and appropriation of copyrighted works constitutes infringement for which the copyright holder may seek civil remedies and the federal government may in certain cases seek criminal sanctions.

While the aim of copyright law to encourage the production of intellectual property is laudable, it does have the effect of limiting access to copyrighted material produced by others even in the face of First Amendment claims to use of the material by the newsmedia.

Thus in Roy Export Co. v. Columbia Broadcasting System, Inc., 672 F.2d 1095 (2d Cir. 1982), CBS's claim of First Amendment protection in the use, on the occasion of Charlie Chaplin's death, of a special compilation of excerpts from Chaplin's motion pictures in which Roy Export Co. held the copyright was rejected by the United States Court of Appeals. In affirming that CBS had been guilty of copyright infringement in using "the compilation" originally prepared for the 1972 Academy Award Presentations during which Chaplin received a special "Oscar," the Second Circuit made clear that it would be a very rare case in which copyrighted material was so imbued with news value as to subordinate the copyright holder's protection to First Amendment claims. An example of this, according to the court, might be the Zapruder home movie of the assassination of President Kennedy. But normally, the news media would have to rely on the nonconstitutional "fair use" defense to copyright infringement to gain access to copyrighted material. See discussion of "fair use" infra, pp. 208–212.

However, it must be noted that raw news and information are not subject to copyright and are in the public domain for anyone to disseminate. See International News Service v. Associated Press, 248 U.S. 215, 39 S.Ct. 68, 63 L.Ed.2d 211

(1918) in which the Supreme Court recognized that the substance of the news of the day was not copyrightable because of the obvious public policy that such history should be made freely available to all. But the *way* news or information is organized, including the words used and the manner chosen by the reporter or publisher to express the news or information gathered, is copyrightable. For instance, the news that the University of Southern California has beaten another football opponent by a certain score is not copyrightable but the words of a Los Angeles Times sportswriter describing Southern Cal's victory would be.

b. Copyright Infringement

Actions for infringement of statutory copyright are brought in the federal courts since under Title 28 of the United States Code Section 1338(a), the United States District Courts have jurisdiction "over any civil action arising under any Act of Congress relating to patents, copyrights and trademarks."

In order to prevail in an infringement action, the plaintiff must prove that he or she is the owner of the copyright and that the rights granted to him or her by the copyright statute have been violated. Ordinarily, the plaintiff will not be able to proffer direct eyewitness testimony of copying; all he or she can offer is proof that the alleged infringing work is substantially similar and that the defendant had the opportunity to copy the plaintiff's creation.

The element of "substantial similarity" clearly excludes from consideration as infringement trivial or slight similarities between the defendant's work and the plaintiff copyright holder's work. But what is actually included in this element is not always clear. Analytically, there are four types of similarity which may be found to be substantial:

(1) comprehensive literal similarity, wherein the defendant's work is an almost verbatim replication of the plaintiff's work. This is the most obvious case and infringement may even be established in the absence of direct proof of access to the plaintiff's work;

(2) comprehensive paraphrase. It must be emphasized that paraphrasing another's work will not protect the defendant against liability for copyright infringement. While the appropriation of a theme or basic idea of another's creation such as the idea of ungrateful children in Shakespeare's "King Lear" is not actionable, the copying of the sequence of events, the pattern of the work and the characterizations may be. See, e.g., Nichols v. Universal Pictures Co., 45 F.2d 119, 121 (2d Cir. 1930), wherein the author of the stage play "Abie's Irish Rose," about a Jewish boy who marries an Irish girl over the objection of both fami-

[*206*]

lies, was unsuccessful in an infringement action against a motion picture company which had used a similar theme but different events and characters in a movie entitled "The Cohens and the Kellys;"

(3) noncomprehensive literal similarity, wherein the defendant has copied only a portion of the copyright holder's work, as for instance one scene in a play or eight bars of a musical composition. Plaintiff may recover for the appropriation of his or her work if the portion taken is important to the totality of the plaintiff's work, regardless of its quantity. Thus, theoretically the taking of the central four note theme from Beethoven's Fifth Symphony might be considered an infringement were it not in the public domain;

(4) noncomprehensive paraphrase. The same standard as for noncomprehensive literal similarity applies where the similarity involves a paraphrase of a portion of the copyright holder's work, i.e., whether the portion taken is of importance to the plaintiff's work taken as a whole. See, e.g., Universal Pictures Co. v. Harold Lloyd Corp., 162 F.2d 354, 360–61 (9th Cir. 1947) (infringement found where defendant paraphrased 20 percent of plaintiff's work).

Once substantial similarity and access are proven, the defendant must either shoulder the heavy burden of proving that the work was not copied or must establish one or more affirmative defenses which bar liability for the defendant's copying. These defenses include the statute of limitations, abandonment of the copyright, estoppel and "fair use."

2. The "Fair Use" Defense as an Access Tool

It should be clear that copyright protection provides a serious limitation on use of existing material by the news media. But some access of journalists to copyrighted material for purposes of republication is afforded by the "fair use" defense to copyright infringement suits.

This defense is not statutory in origin but was created by the courts apparently in the belief that public policy requires persons other than the copyright owner to be able to use the owner's work under strictly limited conditions in certain contexts in which it will be of value to the public. This defense has often been misunderstood by the courts and has not been defined with any great precision. Nevertheless, certain features of the defense can be discerned. One may be protected in copying another's copyrighted work where the copying is not likely to hurt the present and potential markets for the copyrighted work and where the copying is likely to be of substantial benefit to the public. In determining whether the use of another's creation is a "fair use," the purpose of the defendant's work, the amount of copying involved, the public interest in the copyrighted material, the nature of the media involved and the effect of the copying on the market value of the plaintiff's work are all factors to be considered. An example of the balancing of these factors is Time, Inc. v. Bernard Geis Associates, 293 F.Supp. 130, 144–146 (S.D.N.Y.1968), in which a book publisher reproduced several frames of the Zapruder home movie of the Kennedy assassination in a book about the assassination. In holding the reproduction of the frames a fair use the court balanced the great public interest in information concerning the assassination against the doubtful effect of the reproduction on the market value of Time, Inc.'s copyright in the entire film.

At bottom what is evolving from the judiciary's recognition of these factors is a market value test of whether the defendant copier's use of the plaintiff copyright holder's material tends to reduce the plaintiff's potential profit from his or her literary property in present and potential markets. Professor Nimmer in his leading work on copyright law calls the effect of copying on market value the "central question." 3 Nimmer on Copyright Sec. 13.05[A][4] (1981). Thus, it would seem that where the defendant's work is or would be in substantial competition with the plaintiff's work the copying would normally not be a fair use.

These principles have now been given explicit statutory recognition in Section 107 of the 1976 Copyright Act which states that in determining whether the use made of a work in any particular case is a fair use, the following factors shall be considered:

"1. the purpose and character of the use, including whether such use is of a commercial nature or is for nonprofit educational purposes;

2. the nature of the copyrighted work;

3. the amount and substantiality of the portion used in relation to the copyrighted work as a whole; and

4. the effect of the use upon the potential market for or value of the copyrighted work."

These common law factors were discussed soon after their incorporation in the 1976 act in the case of Quinto v. Legal Times of Washington, Inc., 506 F.Supp. 554 (D.D.C.1981). There, a Harvard law student had written an article describing the summer employment experiences of Harvard law students. The article was published in and copyrighted by the Harvard Law Record, a student newspaper at Harvard Law School. The defendant Legal Times, the publisher of a commercial newspaper aimed at the legal profession, republished verbatim 92 percent of the article in its pages. In rejecting the defendant's claim that the republication constituted a fair use the court concentrated on the extent of the copying but also noted that republication was for commercial rather than educational purposes and that the reprinting eliminated the possibility that the writer could sell his article to legal newspapers such as the Legal Times, and those newspapers represented the entire market for his work.

Here, the limited public interest in knowing about the experiences of Harvard law students in summer jobs with law firms was far outweighed by the amount of the copying, the commercial purpose involved in the copying and the damage done to the writer's property interest.

The public interest concept is central to a successful invocation of the fair use defense. Statutory protection of expression encourages authors and artists to continue to produce original works; continued production and dissemination of these works aids the flow of ideas throughout society. But statutory protection can also retard the flow of ideas, offering a work so much protection that the ideas contained therein are no longer free to enter the marketplace. The fair use defense moderates this overprotection, thus stimulating the circulation in society of the ideas and information that the copyrighted work contains. This rationale for the defense explains some of the more common examples of fair use, such as the quotation or paraphrase of passages from books in book reviews and the limited quotation of copyrighted materials in news stories.

At bottom, then, two elements predominate in determining the availability of the fair use defense: (1) the intensity of the public interest in the free dissemination of portions of particular copyrighted works (e.g., the desire of the public for as much opinion and information about the Kennedy assassination as possible); and (2) the effect such free dissemination will have on the property value of or income from the particular copyrighted work (e.g., parody of a literary work or motion picture in such detail that an audience exposed to the parody will have little desire to pay for the privilege of reading or viewing the original).

G. THE EFFECT ON NEWSGATHERING OF SEARCHES AND SEIZURES IN THE NEWSROOM

1. Zurcher v. Stanford Daily

Searches and seizures in the newsrooms of the nation by law enforcement officers pursuant to properly issued search warrants have been rare in American history. Normally, prosecutors seeking evidence of crimes which they believe can be found in the desks or files of a newsroom have simply subpoenaed someone associated with the news operation to bring the evidence, if any, to court. This procedure avoids the disruption of a search of the newsroom, avoids the chilling effect on the gathering of sensitive news and information and gives the subpoenaed party an opportunity to move to quash the subpoena.

But in Zurcher v. Stanford Daily, 436 U.S. 547, 98 S.Ct. 1970, 56 L.Ed.2d 525 (1978), a local district attorney obtained a search warrant issued on a judge's finding of probable cause to believe that the Stanford Daily, a student newspaper, possessed photographs and negatives revealing the identity of demonstrators who assaulted and injured police officers who were attempting to quell a riot at the Stanford University Hospital. A search of the paper's newsroom was undertaken pursuant to the warrant but no incriminating evidence was found. Thereafter, the paper and certain staff members sought a judicial declaration that the search had deprived them of their constitutional rights and an injunction against further searches. The United States District Court denied the injunction but granted the declaratory relief sought. The United States Court of Appeals affirmed the judgment of the District Court.

In the Supreme Court, the Stanford Daily argued that such searches of newspaper offices for evidence of crimes committed by others seriously threatened the ability of the press to gather, analyze and disseminate news, thereby violating the First Amendment. More specifically the newspaper argued that (1) searches are physically disruptive to orderly publication; (2) confidential sources of information will dry up and access to various news events will be denied because of fear that press files will be readily available to law enforcement authorities; (3) reporters will be dissuaded from recording and preserving their recollections for verification and future use; (4)

the processing of news and its dissemination will be chilled by the prospect that searches will disclose internal editorial deliberations; and (5) the press will resort to self-censorship to conceal its possession of information of potential interest to the police.

While Justice Stewart in dissent generally agreed with the newspaper's contentions, a majority of the Court led by Justice White held that searches and seizures in newsrooms pursuant to warrant did not violate First Amendment guarantees because the drafters of the Constitution had not, under the Fourth Amendment, forbidden search warrants directed to the press, did not require special showings that subpoenas would be impractical before warrants could be issued to search the premises of the press and did not insist that if a press organization was named in a search warrant, the police would first have to show the organization's complicity in the alleged offense being investigated.

Justice White argued in support of his conclusion that if law enforcement officers and the courts properly administer search warrants, the preconditions for their issuance—probable cause, specificity with respect to the place to be searched and the things to be seized, and overall reasonableness in searches and seizures—should afford sufficient protection against infringement of First Amendment interests. Further, Justice White doubted, in the face of numerous press organization affidavits to the contrary, that confidential sources would dry up or that the press would suppress news because of fears of warranted searches.

2. Federal Legislation in the Wake of Zurcher

Less than three years after the decision in Zurcher, a Congress less sanguine about the dangers posed by searches and seizures in newsrooms enacted P.L. 96–449, the Privacy Protection Act of 1980, 42 U.S.C.A. 2000aa–1 et seq. This act substantially restricts the situations in which a newsroom search and seizure may legally occur. Title I of the statute divides evidence subject to possible seizure into two categories (1) work product materials possessed by newspaper persons, authors or broadcasters and (2) all other documentary materials possessed by these same classes of persons. The Privacy Protection Act makes it unlawful for federal and state government officers or employees to search for or seize materials in the first category except in two cases: (1) where there is probable cause to believe that the person possessing such materials has committed or is committing the criminal offense to which the materials relate unless the criminal activity involved is simply the reception, possession, communication or withholding of the work product material itself or the information contained therein; and (2) where there is reason to believe that the immediate seizure of such materials is necessary to prevent the death of, or serious bodily injury to, a human being.

The act also makes it unlawful for federal and state government officers or employees to search for or seize materials in the second category with four exceptions. The first two exceptions are exactly the same as the exceptions for the first category of material. The two additional exceptions permitting lawful searches and seizures of second category material are first that there is reason to believe that the giving of notice pursuant to a subpoena of the material would result in its destruction, alteration or concealment; and second that such materials have not been produced in response to court order and all appellate court remedies have been exhausted or that "there is reason to believe that the delay . . . occasioned by further proceedings relating to the subpoena would threaten the interests of justice." As to the quoted portion of the last exception, the person possessing the sought after material is afforded an opportunity under the act to oppose the issuance of the search warrant.

The act further provides for certain civil remedies against the federal and state governments or, where states have not waived their governmental immunity, against state employees, for violating its provisions. Finally, Title II of the act directs the United States Attorney General to issue guidelines for the procedures to be followed by federal officers and employees in obtaining documentary evidence of crimes in the private possession of all persons not just newspersons, authors or broadcasters when such persons are not believed to be suspects themselves or related by blood or marriage to those suspected of the criminal activity being investigated. Congress' reason for mandating these guidelines was to protect the personal privacy of all persons residing in the United States by restricting the use by federal law enforcement officers of search warrants when less intrusive means such as subpoenas, summons or informal requests for documentary material would likely be effective. The Attorney General issued his guidelines on April 17, 1981. 46 Fed.Reg. 22362. They can be found in 28 Code of Federal Regulations §§ 59.1–59.5.

CHAPTER VI

NEWSPERSONS' PRIVILEGE, SUBPOENAS AND CONTEMPT CITATIONS

A. SUBPOENAS V. CLAIMS OF PRIVILEGE

1. The Contemporary Problem

Until relatively recently the subpoenaing of newspersons by various branches and agencies of federal, state and local governments to testify as to their sources and other information did not pose much of a problem for the media. Until the 1950's, there were only a handful of cases involving attempts by government to force disclosure from unwilling members of the press. And as late as the advent of the Nixon Administration the problem was not one of major concern.

But then a number of social and political forces combined to embolden prosecutors, judges, legislators and other government officials to seek unpublished information of interest to them in the hands and heads of newspersons. Mutual distrust and even enmity between public officials and reporters began to grow, particularly in the large urban areas, fueled at least in part by the Vietnam war, a troubled economy, widespread graft and corruption at all levels of government, leaks of secret government information, doubtful media coverage of government and its personnel and what some might characterize as anti-establishmentarianism by some elements of the media. Then, too, stories about the drug and sex subcultures and violence prone anti-government organizations became of greater interest to the press. As a result, reporters became privy to information concerning law violations that prosecutors wanted and could not obtain through traditional means. In addition, "law and order" concerns began to grip the land in the wake of an ever increasing crime rate and public posturing by former President Nixon and other members of his administration. The widespread attitude of government officials now appears to be that if reporters have unpublished information concerning crimes and anti-establishment conduct, they have the same legal duty as anyone else to disclose it.

This attitude poses special problems for newspersons. First, the ethics of their profession require that they not divulge information obtained in confidence. Second, any disclosure or appearance of disclosure of sources or other information obtained in confidence will mark the reporter as "unreliable" in the view of those from whom he is obtaining information and will have an inhibiting effect on his or her ability to gather and disseminate news. Third, like lawyers, the professional status of newspersons gives them a basis for claiming protection from disclosure of their nonpublished work product, and they wish to protect that status.   Therefore, news media personnel insist that the law must accord them a privilege not to testify or produce materials under compulsion of subpoena when their testimony would run counter to their ethical obligations or professional status or have an adverse effect on their ability to gather the news.   In many cases today, newspersons are refusing to obey subpoenas and choosing to face jail for contempt when the claimed privilege is denied.

There is now a serious and growing confrontation between those who would gather the news and those who would use these newsgatherers to provide information for governmental purposes. What makes the problem especially difficult is that both sides to the dispute may say, with some justification, that by their actions they are serving the public interest.

2. Legal Background

a.   Common Law Privilege

The common law, while recognizing testimonial privileges for the attorney-client, doctor-patient and marital relationships, has never accorded a like privilege to the newsperson-news source relationship or any other aspect of the newsgathering process.   A strong policy argument can be made that a newsperson's privilege is at least as necessary to the public welfare as the recognized privileges are because of its societal benefit in encouraging a freer flow of news and information to the public. But the law has accepted the strong opposing policy that the public, in the words of the master of the law of evidence, Dean Wigmore, "has a right to every man's evidence." The more testimonial privileges that are recognized, the less evidence will be available to those who must attempt to reconstruct the truth in a judicial proceeding or establish public policy in the halls of a legislature or in an executive office. Not surprisingly, then, the common law courts have consistently refused to expand the number of recognized privileges in order to cover newspersons.

b. *Newspersons' Shield Statutes*

An alternative to persuading the courts to fashion a newsperson's privilege is to convince legislatures to enact statutes embodying such privilege. The first so-called newspersons' shield law was enacted in Maryland in 1898 to protect the confidentiality of news sources. It remained unique for more than three decades before New Jersey adopted a similar statute. Thereafter, lobbying campaigns by the newspaper industry have resulted in the enactment of shield statutes of one type or another in approximately one half the states. These acts are analyzed below at pp. 186–191.

Though such legislation is now widespread, the statutes at best provide uncertain protection for the newsperson because they are subject to interpretation and application by the state courts which have generally been hostile to their aim.

They are, with few exceptions, narrowly construed and sharply limited as to the protection they afford.

The first federal shield statute was proposed in 1929 but though bills have been introduced in Congress with increasing frequency since then, no federal statute extending a testimonial privilege to newspersons has been enacted. Perhaps this is because no consensus has ever developed within the media as to either the necessity for such legislation or its proper scope.

c. *Claims of Privilege Under the First Amendment*

A comparatively recent claim of newspersons to immunity from testimonial compulsion is based on the Constitution. The argument is that compelling reporters to testify in judicial and other proceedings will have a detrimental effect on their access to sensitive and confidential news sources and consequently restrict the flow of news to the public in violation of the First Amendment.

The argument was first made in Garland v. Torre, 259 F.2d 545 (2nd Cir. 1958), cert. denied 358 U.S. 910, 79 S.Ct. 237, 3 L.Ed.2d 231. Judy Garland had brought an action against the Columbia Broadcasting System alleging, inter alia, that the network had authorized and induced the publication of false and defamatory statements about her. Some of the allegedly defamatory statements appeared in a radio-TV column in the New York Herald Tribune written by Marie Torre and were attributed by her to an unnamed CBS executive. When Garland's attorney deposed Torre she refused to disclose the name of the executive, asserting that to do so would violate a journalistic confidence. Court proceedings were initiated to compel her to disclose the name. Again Torre refused to make disclosure. She was held in criminal contempt and sentenced to ten days imprisonment. On appeal she raised the constitutional issue. In affirming her conviction Judge (later Mr. Justice) Stewart, while recognizing that compulsory disclosure of a journalist's confidential sources might entail an abridgment of press freedom, held that such abridgment had to be balanced against the obvious need in the judicial process for testimonial compulsion. And where, as here, the need for the testimony sought went to the heart of the plaintiff's claim, the Constitution conferred no right on Torre to refuse to answer.

In his opinion for the Second Circuit Justice Stewart pointed out that the judicial process was not being used to force wholesale disclosure of a news source or to discover the identity of a source of doubtful relevance or materiality. He thereby implied that there might be situations in which the First Amendment would provide the newsperson with a qualified privilege not to testify under compulsion of legal process.

On the other hand some state court decisions after Garland and prior to 1972 held that the First Amendment provided no testimonial privilege of any kind. See In re Taylor, 412 Pa. 32, 193 A.2d 181 (1963); State v. Buchanan, 250 Or. 244, 436 P.2d 729 (1968), cert. denied 392 U.S. 905, 88 S.Ct. 2055, 20 L.Ed.2d 1363. Thus, the existence of even a limited first amendment testimonial privilege for the newsgatherer was in doubt and the issue could only be decided by the Supreme Court.

3. The Branzburg-Pappas-Caldwell Trilogy

The issue was finally presented to the Supreme Court in three different contexts in Branzburg v. Hayes, In re Pappas and United States v. Caldwell and eventually decided in one consolidated opinion at 408 U.S. 665, 92 S.Ct. 2646, 33 L.Ed.2d 626 (1972). In addition to the impact on newsgathering from its dictum that "the First Amendment does not guarantee the press a constitutional right of special access to information not available to the public generally," 408 U.S. at 684, 92 S.Ct. at 2658, 33 L.Ed.2d at 641 discussed at pp. 188–193, supra, the majority opinion in this trilogy of cases denied to newsgatherers a testimonial privilege to refuse to appear before grand juries and testify as to possible criminal activities they may have witnessed in the course of their professional responsibilities and the identity of those who engaged in such activities.

a. What the Supreme Court Decided

What the Court decided in the trilogy of newsperson privilege cases is not entirely clear because of the failure of Justice White, the author of the majority opinion, to relate his lengthy reasoning to the three cases at hand and to make distinctions between them and because of the presence of what appears to be a conflicting concurring opinion of Justice Powell, a member of the five person majority.

It is clear that the majority recognized no basis for a newsperson to refuse to appear and answer *some* questions when summoned by a grand jury. And it is also clear that the majority held that members of the news media may be compelled to provide information concerning their witnessing of criminal activity. It also seems to follow from these holdings that the appearance and testimony of newspersons would be compelled in criminal and civil trials. If immunity against compelled testimony is denied in a closed and freewheeling grand jury proceeding, it would be difficult to justify its extension to open public trials controlled by strict evidentiary rules. The Court thus rejected the idea that the First Amendment confers an absolute privilege upon newspersons not to appear and testify in judicial proceedings.

Less clear is whether the majority ruled that not even a qualified privilege may be claimed by the newsperson. Justice White's opinion rejected the idea of the existence of such a privilege and

[*225*]

gave two reasons: first, the lack of efficacy of a qualified privilege in protecting news sources because of the uncertainty prior to court test of the availability of the privilege in specific cases and, second, the difficulties presented for judicial administration by the privilege, including the delineation of the newsgatherers to be covered and the necessity of applying in each case a multiplicity of tests and value judgments to determine the availability of the privilege.

To become binding authority the rejection of the qualified constitutional privilege must be adhered to by at least five justices. It is here that Justice Powell's concurrence takes on particular significance. Justice Powell's short opinion stated that the Court did not hold that newspersons before grand juries are without first amendment rights with respect to the gathering of news or the safeguarding of sources. Becoming more specific, Justice Powell observed:

> Indeed, if the newsman is called upon to give information bearing only a remote and tenuous relationship to the subject of the investigation, or if he has some other reason to believe that his testimony implicates confidential source relationships without a legitimate need of law enforcement, he will have access to the court on a motion to quash and an appropriate protective order may be entered.

The Justice then concluded:

> The asserted claim to privilege should be judged on its facts by the striking of a proper balance between freedom of the press and the obligation of all citizens to give relevant testimony with respect to criminal conduct. The balance of these vital constitutional and societal interests on a case-by-case basis accords with the tried and traditional way of adjudicating such questions.

408 U.S. at 710, 92 S.Ct. at 2671, 33 L.Ed.2d at 656.

Thus, Justice Powell would recognize protection for the newsperson from testimonial compulsion before grand juries in certain situations. But in a footnote Justice Powell made clear that for him the balancing process begins only after the newsperson appears and refuses to answer specific questions on first amendment grounds. He dissociated himself from the approach of dissenters Stewart, Brennan and Marshall which requires a balancing before a reporter is required to appear. Under their approach the government, in a proceeding to quash the subpoena, would have to: (1) show that there is probable cause to believe that the newsperson has information that is clearly relevant to a specific probable violation of law; (2) demonstrate that the information sought cannot be obtained by alternative means less destructive of first amendment rights; and (3) demonstrate a compelling and overriding interest in the information. 408 U.S. at 743, 92

S.Ct. at 2681, 33 L.Ed.2d at 676. But though they differ as to the extent of the qualified privilege and the point at which it may be invoked, Justice Powell and the other three justices accept the idea that the First Amendment confers some protection from testimonial compulsion upon the press. And when Justice Douglas' view is added, there seems to have existed at the time Branzburg was decided a majority of the court favoring recognition of at least a qualified constitutional privilege. In any event, Justice White's rejection of the qualified privilege does not have the force it appears to have. This may explain the continued interest of lower federal and state court judges after Branzburg in determining the scope of a qualified constitutional privilege for newspersons.

b.   *The Legal Situation After Branzburg*

(1) In Detail

Most lower federal and state courts are limiting the application of Branzburg in civil cases and in certain aspects of criminal proceedings. In the leading civil case of Baker v. F & F Investment, 470 F.2d 778 (2d Cir. 1972), cert. denied 411 U.S. 966, 93 S.Ct. 2147, 36 L.Ed.2d 686 (1973), plaintiffs, alleging racial discrimination in the sale of houses to blacks in Chicago, sued certain local real estate organizations and sought prior to trial to depose Alfred Balk, a writer and editor, as to the true identity of the ficticiously named "Norris

Vitchek," a real estate agent and the main source
for Balk's article published in the Saturday Evening Post on "blockbusting" in Chicago. Balk
and his publisher had previously promised Vitchek that they would not reveal his true identity.
Consequently Balk, while highly sympathetic to
the plaintiffs' cause, refused to provide Vitchek's
true identity, claiming first amendment protection. The plaintiffs sought an order from the
United States District Court directing Balk to
provide the information. The order was denied
and the Second Circuit handed down a decision after Branzburg affirming that denial. Recognizing that the compelling of disclosure of newspersons' confidential sources has a "chilling effect"
on the flow of news to the public, the court of
appeals balanced the competing interests along
the lines suggested by Justice Stewart in his dissent in Branzburg, thereby recognizing the existence of a qualified constitutional privilege in civil
cases. Accord: Silkwood v. Kerr-McGee Corp.,
563 F.2d 433 (10th Cir. 1977) (documentary film-
maker treated as a reporter); Loadholtz v. Fields,
389 F.Supp. 1299 (M.D.Fla.1975) (disclosure of unpublished background background materials
sought and refused); Democratic National Committee v. McCord, 356 F.Supp. 1394 (D.D.C.1973)
(disclosure of unpublished background materials
sought and refused); Apicella v. McNeil Labora-
tories, Inc., 66 F.R.D. 78 (E.D.N.Y.1975) (disclosure of identity of anonymous author sought and
refused). Los Angeles Memorial Coliseum v. Na-

tional Football League, 89 F.R.D. 489 (C.D.Cal. 1981). Contra: Dow Jones and Co. v. Superior Court, 364 Mass. 317, 303 N.E.2d 847 (1973); Caldero v. Tribune Publishing Co., 98 Idaho 288, 562 P.2d 791 (1977); Matter of Farber, 78 N.J. 259, 394 A.2d 330 (1978), cert. denied 439 U.S. 997, 99 S.Ct. 598, 58 L.Ed.2d 670 (1979).

Of course, the balance may, on occasion, be struck in favor of compelling the newsperson to reveal confidential sources and to provide unpublished background materials and work product. See, e.g., Wingard v. Oxberger, 258 N.W.2d 847 (Iowa 1977), cert. denied 436 U.S. 905, 98 S.Ct. 2234, 56 L.Ed.2d 402 (1978). The above cited cases involved only the claim of reportorial privilege at the pretrial discovery or motion stage in civil proceedings. At that stage the relevance and materiality of the journalist's information may not be as clear and the possibility of the existence of alternative sources for the same information will likely not have been thoroughly explored.

It is not yet clear whether the newsperson will be protected as regularly and to the same degree at the *trial* of a civil case when a litigant seeks confidential information from a journalist which will likely make or break his or her case. In such situation the interests of the individual litigant and the public in fair and peaceable settlement of private disputes comes into direct confrontation with the first amendment interest of the public in the free flow of news.

In addition, the cited cases did not involve journalists as party defendants. Availability of the qualified privilege can be affected by this factor. The courts are not likely to be very sympathetic to a reporter defendant sued for libel or invasion of privacy who asserts the qualified privilege to prevent an allegedly wronged plaintiff from proving his or her case. In this context Garland v. Torre, 259 F.2d 545 (2d Cir. 1958), cert. denied 358 U.S. 910, 79 S.Ct. 237, 3 L.Ed.2d 231 discussed earlier, states the applicable principle: the balance is to be struck in favor of disclosure if the information sought goes to "the heart of the plaintiff's claim."

This principle has taken on increased importance with the advent of the New York Times v. Sullivan line of defamation cases requiring the plaintiff, if a public official or public figure, to establish knowing falsity or reckless disregard for the truth on the part of the defendant. Proof of this may be made impossible if the plaintiff cannot gain access to the defendant's background materials and work product and examine his or her sources for the defamatory communication. This was the concern of the Court of Appeals in Carey v. Hume, 160 U.S.App.D.C. 365, 492 F.2d 631 (1974) in which the increased burden for a plaintiff in a defamation action was recognized and the defendant-reporter's claim of privilege to protect news sources made during the pretrial discovery proceedings was disallowed. A similar concern was expressed by the United States Su-

preme Court in Herbert v. Lando, 441 U.S. 153,
99 S.Ct. 1635, 60 L.Ed.2d 115 (1979), discussed in
detail in Chapter II, supra. There, an editor-pro-
ducer of CBS' "Sixty Minutes" television program who was being sued by an admitted public
figure claimed a privilege under the First Amendment at the time he was deposed not to divulge
his thought processes or state of mind involved in
the editing and producing of the program segment complained of. Though the claim of privilege was somewhat different than the one made
in Carey, the Supreme Court rejected it for the
same reason expressed in Carey: that acceptance
of the privilege would substantially enhance the
plaintiff's burden of establishing actual malice as
required by New York Times Co. v. Sullivan. It
would appear then that whatever evidence a
newsperson possesses relevant to the actual malice issue in a defamation action brought by a public figure and which evidence cannot be otherwise
obtained goes to the "heart of the case" and is
simply not protected by a qualified privilege.

The one caveat to the Garland principle is that
if it is clear to the trial judge at the preliminary
stage in the proceedings that the plaintiff has little hope of success even with the testimony of the
defendant journalist such testimony need not be
compelled. Cervantes v. Time, Inc., 464 F.2d 986
(8th Cir. 1972), cert. denied 409 U.S. 1125, 93 S.Ct.
939, 35 L.Ed.2d 257 (1973).

The lower federal and state courts are generally following the narrow holding of Branzburg

in criminal proceedings and are denying the privilege when newspersons assert it before grand juries to protect (1) the identity of sources who may have engaged in criminal activity and (2) their unpublished background materials, information, and work product which might lead to the discovery of those engaged in such activity. See, e.g., In re Lewis, 501 F.2d 418 (9th Cir. 1974), cert. denied 420 U.S. 913, 95 S.Ct. 1106, 43 L.Ed.2d 386 (1975) (claim of privilege by radio station manager to withhold original document of Weather Underground and tape recording of Symbionese Liberation Army from federal grand jury rejected); In re Bridge, 120 N.J.Super. 460, 295 A.2d 3 (1972), cert. denied 410 U.S. 991, 93 S.Ct. 1500, 36 L.Ed. 2d 189 (1973) (claim of privilege by reporter to refuse to answer five specific questions propounded by a local grand jury concerning an alleged offer of a bribe to a public official rejected). Because the grand jury has evolved by and large into a prosecutorial device, prosecutors have been quite successful both before and after Branzburg in having claims of constitutional privilege rejected during the preliminary stages of criminal investigations.

On the other hand, the cases since Branzburg indicate that such reportorial claims may meet with a greater degree of success when it is the defendant in a criminal prosecution who is seeking disclosure of a reporter's sources, unpublished information and material or work product. See, e.g., People v. Marahan, 81 Misc.2d 637, 368

N.Y.S.2d 685 (1975) (claim of privilege by reporter at hearing to suppress evidence not to present background information and notes and memos relative to his story concerning a police raid uncovering illegal weapons upheld); State v. St. Peter, 132 Vt. 266, 315 A.2d 254 (1974) (claim of privilege by television news reporter at a pretrial deposition not to reveal the source of his prior knowledge of a drug raid upheld); Brown v. Commonwealth, 214 Va. 755, 204 S.E.2d 429 (1974), cert. denied 419 U.S. 966, 95 S.Ct. 229, 42 L.Ed.2d 182 (claim of privilege by a reporter at a criminal trial for murder not to disclose her confidential source upheld because such information was not material to the accused's defense); Zelenka v. State, 83 Wis.2d 601, 266 N.W.2d 279 (1978) (claim of privilege by a reporter in a first degree murder case not to disclose source of story about the murder upheld despite defendant's claim that knowledge of the source might help him establish entrapment defense). But compare Matter of Farber, 78 N.J. 259, 394 A.2d 330 (1978) (claim of privilege by reporter not to disclose sources and confidential documents and materials underlying newspaper stories leading to murder prosecution rejected). One close observer of the entire privilege problem has suggested that this peculiar pattern of acceptance or nonacceptance of the qualified privilege by the courts in criminal proceedings stems not from deficient protection of the interests of criminal defendants but from an overgenerous grant of discretion to prosecutors in determining when compelled disclosure of press confidence is required. Murasky, "The Journalist's Privilege: *Branzburg* and Its Aftermath," 52 Tex.L.Rev. 829, 898 (1974).

(2) In Summary

While generalization in the field of reportorial privilege is risky, the following principles and rules are suggested in summary:

(1) There is no absolute first amendment newspersons' privilege.

(2) The recognition by the courts of a qualified newspersons' privilege depends to a great extent on the legal context in which the claim of privilege is made.

(3) The courts will not honor the claim of privilege made before grand juries and trial courts when it would protect sources and others who have been seen by the reporter engaging in the suspected criminal activity under investigation.

(4) The courts will not honor such claim made before grand juries when the reporter is asked to produce physical evidence in his or her possession of suspected criminal activity under investigation such as tape recordings and documents.

(5) The courts will not honor such claim at a criminal trial or collateral hearing when the information or evidence is sought by

the prosecutor and it is relevant and material to his or her case.

(6) The courts will honor such claim at a criminal trial or collateral hearing when the confidential information or evidence is sought by the accused and it is not clearly critical to his or her defense.

(7) The courts will generally honor such claim in civil pretrial proceedings and trials unless the information or evidence sought by the litigant goes to the heart of his or her case and there is no alternative source for that information.

(8) When the newsperson is a party defendant in civil litigation (usually defamation or invasion of privacy actions), the courts are more likely to find that the information or material sought to be protected under the privilege goes to the heart of the plaintiff's case and cannot be obtained from alternative sources.

(9) When the newsperson is a party plaintiff in civil litigation and claims the qualified privilege to prevent the defendant from obtaining information relevant to his or her defense, the claim of privilege will be denied. See Anderson v. Nixon, 444 F.Supp. 1195 (D.D.C.1978).

(10) If the newsperson's claim to a qualified privilege in the particular context is not accepted, he or she will have to choose be-

tween revealing confidential information or material and accepting the consequences of disobedience of a lawful court order.

c. *The Practical Effect of Branzburg on Newsgatherers*

Despite the limitation placed on the scope of Branzburg by Justice Powell's concurring opinion and the well meaning efforts of lower federal and state courts to carve out a qualified privilege particularly in civil cases, the holding in Branzburg has had a serious effect on newsgatherers. The majority's rejection of an absolute privilege has left the newsperson to guess whether and to what extent the courts will protect confidences subsequent to their creation. At the time assurances of secrecy are given to sources a reporter will often be unable to determine in what legal context he or she will be asked to breach such confidences. Thus, even assuming the rules of the game to be clearly established after Branzburg, the reporter cannot always be sure which rule or rules will be applicable when his or her testimony is sought to be compelled.

This uncertainty must necessarily lead to greater caution on the part of the newsperson in making commitments to protect sources in return for information of interest to the public. Where such commitments are made they are leading to increased confrontation between the press and the judiciary. Hardly an issue of The News Media and the Law published by the Reporters Committee for Freedom of the Press goes by without the detailing of numerous cases involving contempt citations against reporters who have refused to testify pursuant to subpoena. This abrasive confrontation between two of the most important institutions in our free society has prompted renewed interest in legislative approaches to the problem of the newspersons' privilege.

B. NEWSPERSONS' SHIELD LAWS

In Branzburg Justice White indicated in dictum that Congress and the state legislatures were free to extend a privilege against testimonial compulsion to newspersons by statute so long as such "shield" legislation did not run afoul of the First Amendment. Since the Branzburg decision there has been renewed interest in legislative action, with a number of states joining the ranks of those with shield statutes and with numerous bills being introduced in Congress to provide some kind of protection for newsgatherers.

1. State Shield Laws

a. Statutory Analysis

At the time this is written 25 states have enacted some form of shield legislation, and one state—California—has adopted a constitutional provision protecting newspersons. Although they vary somewhat in their language and provisions, these statutes usually address the follow-

[*238*]

ing essential issues: (1) who should be protected
against testimonial compulsion (reporters only or
others communicating to the public and those aid-
ing and abetting in such communication)?; (2)
which kinds of media should be covered (newspapers only or radio, television, motion pictures)?;
(3) what information should be protected (the
identity of confidential sources or other unpublished matter as well)?; (4) at what types of government proceedings and at what stages in these
proceedings is the privilege against testimonial
compulsion available (judicial proceedings alone
or legislative, executive and administrative proceedings)?; (5) whether there are any exceptions
or conditions to the availability of the privilege
(e.g., the need for regular publication and general
circulation, thereby excepting many nonestablish-
ment publications)?; and (6) whether the privilege
may be waived by the protected individual (e.g.,
by disclosing the identity of a source to third persons)? In analyzing one's local shield legislation,
these are the issues that determine the availability and scope of the privilege afforded.

State shield statutes are divided into three
main groups, according to a study of the Freedom of Information Center of the University of
Missouri School of Journalism. The first group
of statutes provides for the unqualified protection
of reporters against having to divulge the source
of information obtained in the course of employment. An example of a statute in this group is
that of Pennsylvania. The Pennsylvania statute

provides that "no person, engaged on, connected
with, or employed by any newspaper of general
circulation . . . or any press association or
any radio or television station, or any magazine
of general circulation for the purpose of gathering, procuring, compiling, editing or publishing
news, shall be required to disclose the source of
any information procured or obtained by such
person, in any legal proceeding, trial or investigation" before any governmental unit. Pa.Stats.
Ann., title 42, section 5942(a) (Cum.Supp.1981).
Within this first group there is a subgrouping of
statutes which limit the unqualified or absolute
protection of sources to those newsgatherers connected with newspapers and press associations.
An example of this subgroup is found in title 27
section 2739.12 of the Ohio Revised Code Anno-
tated, 1953 edition. It should be noted that most
statutes in the first group refer only to sources
and do not expressly cover the reporter's work
product or unpublished information and materials. Given the propensity of the courts to construe shield statutes narrowly, it is not safe for
the reporter to assume that these matters are also protected by such statutes.

The second group of shield laws provides a
privilege against disclosure of the source of information actually published or broadcast. An example is the Maryland statute. It provides that
"A person engaged in, connected with or employed on a newspaper or journal or for any radio
or television station may not be compelled to dis-

close in any legal proceeding or trial or before any committee of the legislature or elsewhere, the source of any news or information procured or obtained by him for and published in the newspaper or disseminated by the radio or television station . . ." Md.Cts. and Jud.Pro.Code Ann. § 9–112 (1974). While absolute in their terms, statutes in this group are very weak in protecting sources and facilitating the flow of news since rarely will the source or, for that matter, the reporter be certain at the time the information is to be passed that it will be actually published or broadcast. Moreover, like the statutes in the first group, these statutes do not protect the information itself. See, e.g., Lightman v. State, 15 Md.App. 713, 294 A.2d 149 (1972), affirmed 266 Md. 550, 295 A.2d 212, cert. denied 411 U.S. 951, 93 S.Ct. 1922, 36 L.Ed.2d 414 (1973).

The third group includes statutes which are conditional in their grant of privilege to newspersons or which provide a basis for the waiver of the privilege. An example of a conditional statute is that of Illinois which makes the grant of privilege to protect a source dependent on "the nature of the proceedings, the merits of the claim or defense, the adequacy of the remedy otherwise available, if any, the relevancy of the source, the possibility of establishing by other means that which it is alleged the source requested will tend to prove." Ill.Rev.Stat.1971 ch. 51, § 116. New Jersey is a state which permits the waiver in certain situations of an absolute privilege protecting a newspaper reporter's sources. See N.J.Stat. Ann. §§ 2A:84A–21 and 2A:84A–29 (1976). The statutes in this final category are also generally narrow in scope, protecting only sources and often only sources connected with the print media. More important, even when a privilege in this category appears to cover a particular reporter's situation there is no certainty that it will be held by the courts to be available when the reporter actually invokes it.

In short, by their express terms most state shield laws, however categorized, provide only limited protection for the newsperson against testimonial compulsion. And the availability of this limited protection may be uncertain. Still worse from the reporter's point of view is the attitude of the courts toward these statutes.

b. *Judicial Treatment*

The common law tradition of hostility toward the creation of testimonial privileges, whose effect is to deny the judicial, legislative and administrative processes desired information, has been carried over by the state courts to the interpretation and construction of newsperson shield statutes. The courts, for the most part, construe these statutes very narrowly and refuse to extend their protection beyond the literal words of the acts. Thus, where the Maryland statute speaks in terms of protecting a newsperson against being compelled to disclose "the source of any news or information procured or obtained by

him," the information itself is not protected by
the privilege. See Lightman v. State, 15 Md.App.
713, 294 A.2d 149 (1972), affirmed 266 Md. 550,
295 A.2d 212, cert. denied 411 U.S. 951, 93 S.Ct.
1922, 36 L.Ed.2d 414 (1973). Even where the literal wording of a statute would seemingly provide protection for the newsperson, courts have
been known to construe it otherwise. Thus,
while the Kentucky statute also speaks in terms
of protecting a newsperson against being compelled to disclose "the source of any information
procured or obtained by him," the Kentucky Supreme Court has construed the word "source" to
exclude those who permit the newsperson to ob-
serve their criminal activities. Branzburg v.
Pound, 461 S.W.2d 345 (Ky.1971) affirmed sub
nom. Branzburg v. Hayes, 408 U.S. 665, 92 S.Ct.
2646, 33 L.Ed.2d 626 (1972).

The classic illustration of limitation of a newsperson's shield statute by judicial construction is
provided by New York. In its express terms the
New York shield statute (N.Y.Civ.Rights Law §
79–h(b) (Cum.Supp.1975)) is one of the broadest in
coverage and most absolute in protection of any
in the nation. Nevertheless, in a quick succes-
sion of cases following the statute's enactment,
the New York courts ruled that the privilege
could only be claimed when (1) the information or
material sought by the government is received by
the newsperson under a pledge of confidentiality
(though the requirement of confidentiality is not
mentioned in the statute); (2) the information or

material has not been previously published (though the statute contains no waiver provision); (3) the newsperson has not personally observed the criminal activities, including the persons involved, about which the government is making inquiry (though the statute expressly makes privileged "any news or the source of any such news" coming into the newsperson's possession); and (4) the information or material to be protected has been affirmatively sought out by the newsperson and not dropped in his or her lap (though, again, the statute makes no such requirement). People v. Wolf, 39 A.D.2d 864, 333 N.Y.S.2d 299 (1st Dept. 1972); People by Fisher v. Dan, 41 A.D.2d 687, 342 N.Y.S.2d 731 (4th Dept. 1973); In re WBAI–FM, 68 Misc.2d 355, 326 N.Y.S.2d 434 (Albany County Ct.1971), affirmed sub nom. WBAI–FM v. Proskin, 42 A.D.2d 5, 344 N.Y.S.2d 393 (3d Dept. 1973).

Apart from limiting the scope and efficacy of shield statutes through narrow and distorted construction of their meaning, a generally hostile judiciary has also begun to question the very constitutionality of such legislation. In Ammerman v. Hubbard Broadcasting, Inc., 89 N.M. 307, 551 P.2d 1354 (1976), the New Mexico Supreme Court ruled that the state's shield law created a rule of evidence in judicial proceedings and as such was violative of the New Mexico constitution which reposed the exclusive power to create and administer rules of evidence in the judicial branch of the state government. Thus in New Mexico, at

[244]

least, it is constitutionally impossible for the legislature to create a statutory privilege protecting newspersons or anyone else. Other states have similar "separation of powers" clauses in their constitutions and it would not be too difficult for this constitutional interpretation to spread beyond the boundaries of New Mexico.

But the most damaging constitutional ruling so far has come from the New Jersey Supreme Court. In the highly publicized shield law-privilege-contempt case of New York Times reporter Myron Farber, the New Jersey court ruled that the state's shield legislation violated the state constitutional provision that in all criminal prosecutions the accused shall have the right "to have compulsory process for obtaining witnesses in his favor." The court interpreted this provision as affording defendants in criminal prosecutions the right to compel the attendance of witnesses, including newspersons, at trial and to compel the production of documents and other material for which the defendant has, or believes he has, a legitimate need in preparing a defense. Testimonial privileges found in modern shield legislation were thus held by the court to violate the state's constitution when they are invoked by newspersons to prevent criminal defendants from obtaining testimony, documents and other material relevant to their defense. Matter of Farber, 78 N.J. 259, 394 A.2d 330, cert. denied sub nom. New York Times Co. v. New Jersey, 439 U.S. 997, 99 S.Ct. 598, 58 L.Ed.2d 670 (1978).

The Farber decision is potentially very harmful to legislative attempts to protect newspersons' sources and confidential information and materials because the New Jersey compulsory process clause is identical to that found in the Sixth Amendment to the United States Constitution. Should the Supreme Court ever interpret the Sixth Amendment in the same way the New Jersey Supreme Court interpreted the state's constitutional provision, statutory shield privileges would be rendered ineffective everywhere when invoked to prevent criminal defendants from obtaining testimony or other evidence. This is so because the Supreme Court has previously ruled that the compulsory process clause of the Sixth Amendment is applicable to the states through the Fourteenth Amendment. Of course, the statutory newspersons privilege would still be available in civil matters, non-trial proceedings and even in criminal trials when the demand for evidence does not come from the defendant. In fairness it should be noted that where Sixth Amendment compulsory process is not implicated, the New Jersey Supreme Court is one of the few courts to read the protections to newspersons afforded by a state shield law very broadly. See Maressa v. New Jersey Monthly, 89 N.J. 176, 445 A.2d 376 (1982).

The moral of all this is that a legitimate newsgatherer cannot rely with confidence even upon the plain language of his or her jurisdiction's shield law but must also be aware of the case law construing such statute. Even then the newsperson should assume, particularly in a sensitive case, that the courts will not uphold his or her claim to the statutory privilege and therefore should act as cautiously as possible consistent with "getting the story."

2. Administrative Protection for the Newsperson: The Department of Justice Guidelines

Though no federal shield legislation has ever been enacted, the United States Department of Justice, by administrative regulation, has voluntarily set restrictions on its prosecutors when they deal with news media personnel. The Department of Justice guidelines as presently stated in Section 50.10 of Title 28 of the Code of Federal Regulations require that before a federal prosecutor requests authorization from the Attorney General to obtain a subpoena directed toward a member of the media, he or she must consider the competing interests of the public in the free dissemination of information and in effective law enforcement and fair administration of justice. In striking the balance the following matters must be considered by Department of Justice personnel: (1) there should be reasonable belief based on non-media information that a crime has occurred; (2) there should be reasonable ground to believe that the information sought is essential to a successful investigation—particularly with reference to directly establishing guilt or innocence;

[247]

(3) the government should have unsuccessfully attempted to obtain the information from alternative non-media sources; (4) except under exigent circumstances subpoenas should be limited to verification of published information; (5) even the appearance of harassment of media personnel should be avoided if at all possible; (6) subpoenas should, wherever possible, be directed at material information regarding a limited subject matter, should cover a reasonably limited period of time, and should avoid requiring production of a large volume of the newsperson's unpublished material.

The Department of Justice guidelines also emphasize that negotiations with newspersons for the obtaining of desired information or material should be pursued before subpoena authorization is sought; that only the attorney general may authorize subpoenas aimed at media personnel, unless the newsgatherer in negotiations promised to supply materials already published; and that only the attorney general may authorize the questioning, arrest or indictment of members of the news media in connection with criminal conduct allegedly engaged in by them within the scope of or arising out of their newsgathering activities.

In 1980 the guidelines were extended to afford similar protection in civil actions and to telephone toll records of journalists.

While the guidelines reflect the Department's sensitivity to the problem of compelling testimony from newspersons, they provide only minimal and uncertain protection because they are limited in scope to federal criminal prosecutions and are construed by government officials whose main concern must, of necessity, be for effective law enforcement.   Moreover, the protection afforded is by administrative grace and that protection can be modified or withdrawn by the Department of Justice almost at will.

C.   CONTEMPT FOR UNPRIVILEGED REFUSAL TO TESTIFY

1.   The Real Importance of the Privilege

The existence of a privilege in a particular case of a refusal to testify or produce material is important in shielding a newsperson from the sanctions associated with the contempt power of courts and legislatures.   Without a privilege to refuse to comply with a judicial or legislative subpoena, the newsperson will almost surely be held in contempt if the information sought is deemed relevant and material to the work of the governmental unit seeking the information.   Depending on the type of contempt involved, the sanctions may include determinate and indeterminate jail sentences, criminal fines and civil payments to parties injured by the contemptuous conduct.

2.   Types of Contempt

Traditionally, contemptuous conduct is categorized in two ways.   First, there is the distinction drawn between direct and indirect contempt.

[*249*]

This distinction is based primarily on whether the disapproved conduct occurred within the presence of the court or legislature or outside such presence. It is essentially a question of location and the significance of the place of the contempt lies in the procedural disposition. If, for instance, a reporter at a trial were to refuse without privilege to testify, this refusal would constitute contempt in the presence of the court and could be dealt with by the court summarily. The reporter could be held in contempt immediately and punishment within constitutional limits could be imposed without further proceeding.

If, on the other hand, the refusal to testify occurred in a grand jury proceeding, this would ordinarily be taken to be a contempt outside the presence of the involved court, and, before a sanction could be imposed by the court, the reporter would be entitled to some notice as to what is complained of together with a hearing on the matter before the appropriate judge.

The other major distinction is between civil and criminal contempt. This dichotomy is based on the purpose for which the sanction is imposed. If the sanction is designed, for example, to force the contemnor to testify, the sanction is viewed as coercive and nonpunitive and hence civil in nature. If the sanction is imposed to uphold the dignity and authority of the court and its orders without concern for coercion, it is deemed punitive in nature and thus the contempt is considered criminal.

The significance of the dichotomy is two-fold. First, in a civil contempt the period of incarceration must, of necessity, be indeterminate. Since the sanction is coercive the contemnor may purge himself or herself of contempt at any time by agreeing to comply with the court's order, thereby effecting his or her release from custody. If the civil contemnor does not choose to purge himself or herself, release from custody theoretically comes only when the information sought is no longer of value as when a grand jury term or trial proceeding has actually ended or the information is obtained from an alternative source. In contrast, a sentence of imprisonment for criminal contempt is of determinate duration and though the contemnor may have a change of heart and wish to obey the court's order once the jailhouse doors close, he or she will have to serve the sentence imposed. Such was the case of Marie Torre who refused to divulge the identity of the CBS executive who had allegedly libeled Judy Garland. The trial judge could have treated the refusal as a civil contempt and ordered her to jail until she talked. Instead he ordered Torre imprisoned for a definite period to protect the authority of his orders. See Garland v. Torre, 259 F.2d 545 (2d Cir. 1958), cert. denied 358 U.S. 910, 79 S.Ct. 237, 3 L.Ed.2d 231.

Second, if the contempt is treated as criminal and does not occur in the presence of the court, procedural safeguards peculiarly associated with a criminal prosecution such as proof beyond reasonable doubt are applicable to the contempt proceeding. Within the criminal contempt category a further dichotomy exists between serious and petty contempts. If the contempt is serious, as defined by the length of the prison sentence which might be or actually is imposed, the alleged contemnor is entitled to a jury trial under the United States Constitution. See Bloom v. Illinois, 391 U.S. 194, 88 S.Ct. 1477, 20 L.Ed.2d 522 (1968); Muniz v. Hoffman, 422 U.S. 454, 475, 95 S.Ct. 2178, 2190, 45 L.Ed.2d 319, 334 (1975). The point of division between the serious contempt proceeding which requires a jury trial and the petty contempt proceeding which does not is a prison sentence in excess of six months. See Cheff v. Schnackenberg, 384 U.S. 373, 86 S.Ct. 1523, 16 L.Ed.2d 629 (1966); Muniz v. Hoffman, supra. Whether the imposition of a fine only against news organizations and personnel as punishment for criminal contempt would be considered serious and entitle them to jury trial is an open question. See Muniz v. Hoffman, supra.

3. The Impact of Contempt on Newspersons

The number of contempt citations issued against newspersons for refusal to testify before or otherwise cooperate with government units has increased dramatically in the last decade. But while the number of newspersons actually languishing in jails around the country is not yet great, the potential for such a situation is. The courts know that the imposition of fines or civil payments is not likely to intimidate or chasten the reporter who, for principle, refuses to cooperate in a grand jury or judicial proceeding.

Only imprisonment is at all likely to have the desired effect. And thus the newsperson who digs in his or her heels must be ready to accept incarceration of either determinate or indeterminate duration. About the only comforting note from the newsperson's perspective is that if the contempt is treated as criminal the likelihood of a sentence in excess of six months is remote because of the burden on the judicial system of granting the newsperson a jury trial.

4. Alternatives to Contempt Citations and the Jailing of Newspersons

Courts are learning that imprisonment for contempt is rarely effective in achieving the goal of disclosure by newspersons of confidential information. The courts are slowly changing tactics and choosing alternatives to contempt in an effort to enforce their disclosure orders. One new tactic utilized in libel actions against newspapers and their reporters when the reporters refuse to divulge the identity of sources for their stories is for the courts to presume that such sources do not in fact exist. Such presumption aids the public figure plaintiff in establishing actual malice as required by New York Times Co. v. Sullivan and aids the private figure plaintiff in making the showing of negligence on the part of the defendant as required by most jurisdictions following Gertz v. Robert Welch, Inc. See Downing v. Monitor Publishing Co., 120 N.H. 383, 415 A.2d 683 (1980); De Roburt v. Gannett Co., 507 F.Supp. 880 (D.Haw.1981).

Another device to force compliance by reporters with judicial disclosure orders employed by at least one state trial court is to strike the newspaper defendant's pleadings and to enter a default judgment for the plaintiff in its libel action. Because this device raises a serious question as to the deprivation of due process, courts must be very careful to employ it only when the information sought is absolutely essential to the plaintiff's case and cannot be obtained by less drastic means. See Sierra Life Insurance Co. v. Magic Valley Newspapers, Inc., 101 Idaho 795, 623 P.2d 103 (1980).

CHAPTER VII

THE FREE PRESS—FAIR TRIAL CONFLICT

A. THE PROBLEM

1. Introduction

The Sixth Amendment guarantees that in criminal prosecutions the accused shall be entitled to a speedy and public trial "by an impartial jury." A necessary implication of this constitutional mandate is that jurors must not be influenced in their determination of the guilt or innocence of the accused by forces outside the courtroom or by information or material not admitted into evidence at the trial.

But news stories concerning a criminal case published before or during trial, particularly those containing information adverse to the accused not presented to the jury at trial such as a past criminal record or some incriminating statement or confession may influence individual jurors and destroy their impartiality. Because accused persons are entitled only to "impartial" juries and not favorably biased ones, the constitutional requirement binding on the states through the Fourteenth Amendment may also be violated by publicity adverse to the prosecution.

In addition, the Fifth Amendment guarantees to every person, including criminal accused, that they will not be deprived of life, liberty or property without due process of law. Due process may be affected by the media and their representatives by both the generation of pressures on the trial judge through editorial content and by disruption of the repose of the courtroom, making fair procedure and calm deliberation difficult if not impossible.

The problem for the courts in attempting to safeguard an accused's fifth and sixth amendment rights arises out of the potentially conflicting guaranty of the First Amendment that the Congress shall make no law abridging freedom of the press. This guaranty is interpreted to include court orders. Therefore, orders designed to assure fair and impartial trials and which directly or indirectly restrict the newsgathering and news disseminating functions of the press may run afoul of the First Amendment. Some restrictive orders, particularly those that bar newspersons from the courtroom, may also violate the "public trial" requirement of the Sixth Amendment itself.

While most of the potential conflicts between fair trial and free press might be avoided by the exercise of restraint and common sense by the media, judiciary, trial participants and law enforcement officials, these qualities are sometimes in short supply in relation to criminal cases of great public interest. Then the conflict becomes real and troublesome. One example will suffice to illustrate the extreme bounds of the problem.

2. A Case Study: Sheppard v. Maxwell

The classic case of excessive and abusive pre-trial and trial publicity and improper courtroom behavior by the media is Sheppard v. Maxwell, 384 U.S. 333, 86 S.Ct. 1507, 16 L.Ed.2d 600 (1966). Correlatively, it is a classic case of abdication of responsibility by a member of the judiciary to safeguard the rights of an accused.

Dr. Samuel Sheppard's pregnant wife, Marilyn, was brutally bludgeoned to death in an upstairs bedroom of her home in a suburb of Cleveland. Dr. Sheppard's story was to the effect that at the time of the murder he was asleep on a couch in the living room. He heard his wife cry out and he rushed upstairs where, in the dim light from the hall, he saw a "form" standing near his wife's bed. As he struggled with the "form" he was struck on the back of the neck and fell to the floor unconscious. When he regained consciousness he found his wife dead.

From the beginning the coroner and the police believed Sheppard guilty of murder and interrogated him at great length and without benefit of counsel. He was also pressed by the police to take an "infallible" lie detector test or an injection of "truth serum" or to confess. Sheppard resisted. The local newspapers, which took great interest in the case, played up Sheppard's refusal to subject himself to a lie detector test and the injections, as well as a so-called "protective ring" thrown up around him by his family.

Thereafter, an editorial writer opened fire with a front page charge that somebody was "getting away with murder." The editorial attributed the ineptness of the investigation to "friendship, relationships, hired lawyers, a husband who ought to have been subjected instantly to the same third-degree to which any other person under similar circumstances is subjected." The following day another front page editorial was headed: "Why No Inquest? Do It Now, Dr. Gerber." The coroner called the inquest the same day. It was staged in a school gymnasium, televised live to the people of the Cleveland area, covered by a swarm of reporters and photographers and ended after three days in a public brawl.

Throughout the period prior to Sheppard's arrest the newspapers emphasized facts that tended to incriminate Sheppard and highlighted discrepancies in his statements. Much of this "evidence" was never introduced at trial and the editorials became more insistent as to Sheppard's guilt. An editorial entitled "Why Don't Police Quiz Top Suspect" demanded that Sheppard be taken to police headquarters and another asked: "Why Isn't Sam Sheppard in Jail?" Immediately thereafter Sheppard was arrested and charged with murder. Then the publicity intensified. Cartoons, editorials, news stories and features, most unfavorable to Sheppard, poured forth from the local presses and radio and television stations. Headlines announced, among other things, "Sheppard 'Gay Set' Is revealed by Houk [Sheppard's neighbor and mayor of the town in which the murder took place]," "Blood Is Found In Garage," "New Murder Evidence Is Found, Police Claim," "Dr. Sam Faces Quiz At Jail On Marilyn's Fear Of Him." The publicity continued unabated until Sheppard's conviction in December 1954 and the press clippings alone from the three Cleveland newspapers filled five volumes of the record.

The conduct of the trial was equally depressing. Before the case was set the names of the prospective jurors were published along with their addresses. Consequently, anonymous letters and telephone calls concerning the prosecution were received by all of the prospective jurors. Most of the space in the small courtroom was set aside for the use of the media, including a large area inside the bar where traditionally only those directly involved in the conduct of trials are permitted. Representatives of the news media used all the rooms on the courtroom floor, and private telephone lines and telegraphic equipment were installed in these rooms for their convenience. Live newscasts were made from a temporary broadcasting facility set up on another floor of the courthouse. Everywhere around the courthouse and nearly everywhere within, there were newsreel and still photographers with all of their paraphernalia, intent on capturing all the participants on film as often as possible.

All of these arrangements with the representatives of the media were permitted to continue throughout the nine weeks of trial and the courtroom remained crowded to capacity with news personnel. The confusion caused by their movement in and out of the courtroom made it difficult for witnesses and counsel to be heard. Because of the close quarters and crowding it was almost impossible for Sheppard and his counsel to hold confidential discussions in the courtroom. Participants in the trial had to run a human gauntlet of media representatives just to get into and out of the courtroom. It was all reminiscent of the circus atmosphere that pervaded the Bruno Hauptmann trial for kidnapping and murder of the Lindbergh child some thirty years earlier. The trial judge, who was running for reelection, did nothing to stop it. He failed to sequester the jury during the presentation of evidence. Consequently, the jurors were exposed to the publicity generated during the trial. The Supreme Court in its opinion in the Sheppard case listed several instances of highly prejudicial publicity during that period. Repetition of only a few of them will suffice to suggest the environment in which the jurors decided Sheppard's fate.

On the second day of voir dire examination of the prospective jurors a debate was presented over WHK radio. The participants, newspaper reporters, accused Sheppard's counsel of throwing roadblocks in the way of the prosecution and claimed that Sheppard had admitted his guilt by hiring a prominent criminal lawyer to defend him. When defense counsel complained about the broadcast to the judge, he refused to take any protective action. During the trial, a Cleveland police officer gave testimony that tended to contradict portions of Sheppard's written statement made to the police. Two days later, in a broadcast again over WHK, Robert Considine, Hearst feature writer and radio personality, likened Sheppard to a perjurer and compared the episode to Alger Hiss' confrontation with Whittaker Chambers. Defense counsel asked the judge to question the jury to determine how many had heard the broadcast and, again, the judge refused and overruled a motion for a continuance based on the same incident. Later, a story dealing with the defendant's temper appeared under an eight column headline reading "Sam Called A 'Jekyll-Hyde' By Marilyn, Cousin To Testify." No such testimony was ever produced at trial. Similarly, two weeks later a police captain not at the trial and never called as a witness denied certain trial testimony given by Sheppard under the headline " 'Bare-Faced Liar', Kerr says of Sam."

Only after the case was submitted to the jurors were they sequestered. However, after the guilty verdict was returned, defense counsel discovered that jurors had been allowed to make telephone calls every day and no record was kept of the calls. The trial judge had failed to instruct the bailiffs to prevent such calls. Defense counsel moved for a new trial. The motion was overruled. Sheppard's initial state appeals were unsuccessful and review by the United States Supreme Court was denied. He served ten years in the Ohio penitentiary before obtaining a review of his conviction in the federal courts under a habeas corpus application. In those ten years the Supreme Court's attitude toward trial and pretrial publicity had been changing. In 1959 in Marshall v. United States, 360 U.S. 310, 79 S.Ct. 1171, 3 L.Ed.2d 1250, the Supreme Court, exercising its supervisory authority over the lower federal courts, reversed a conviction for unlawfully dispensing drugs because jurors had seen newspaper stories indicating that the defendant had two prior convictions, one of which was for practicing medicine without a license. The Court ordered a new trial despite assurances from the jurors that they would not be influenced by these stories. Then in Irvin v. Dowd, 366 U.S. 717, 81 S.Ct. 1639, 6 L.Ed.2d 751 (1961), the Supreme Court held for the first time that the exposure of jurors to massive and highly inflammatory pretrial publicity (including news stories that the accused had confessed to six murders) violated the accused's right to a fair trial guaranteed by the due process clause of the Fourteenth Amendment. Again, in Rideau v. Louisiana, 373 U.S. 723, 83 S.Ct. 1417, 10 L.Ed.2d 663 (1963), a conviction was reversed because of pretrial publicity undermining a fair trial, this time in the form of a televised "interview" of the accused by the local sheriff during which the accused admitted to bank robbery, kidnapping and murder. Finally, in Estes v. Texas, 381 U.S. 532, 85 S.Ct. 1628, 14 L.Ed.2d 543 (1965), a conviction for large scale fraud was reversed because pretrial and trial proceedings were televised and filmed. The Court held that such coverage denied to the accused a fair trial because of the psychological impact on and the distraction of the jurors, judge, witnesses and the accused himself.

In requiring a new trial in Sheppard's case, the Supreme Court signalled its determination to end free-wheeling media coverage of important criminal cases. Its decision intensified the conflict between the judiciary and the media. While noting that a responsible press is regarded as an indispensible handmaiden of fair and effective judicial administration, the Court in Sheppard recognized that in cases involving probable jury exposure to massive publicity relating to information not introduced in evidence at trial, jurors might be improperly influenced in their deliberations and decisions. The Court then ruled, relying on almost a decade of precedent, that in cases involving a high probability of prejudice to one or the other of the parties stemming from pretrial and trial publicity, such prejudice could be presumed to exist and actual evidence of the exposure to and the effect on individual jurors of such publicity need not be presented. Sheppard's case was held to be one of those in which the presumption would apply.

The Court further stated that the trial judge compounded the problem of undue publicity in the case by acting pursuant to the erroneous belief that he lacked power to control it in any way. The Supreme Court catalogued a number of approaches and tactics that the judge might have utilized to guarantee Sheppard a fair trial without imposing restrictions or sanctions *directly* against the press. These will be discussed shortly.

The idea that massive trial and pretrial publicity automatically results in the denial of a fair trial to one or the other of the parties is not unqualified. Otherwise the more notorious the crime the less the likelihood of obtaining a valid conviction in this age of mass communications. It has often been suggested that had Lee Harvey Oswald lived he could not have been convicted for the assassination of President Kennedy because a fair trial would have been impossible anywhere. But the judicial system will not allow itself to be paralyzed. If the presumed prejudice is clearly rebutted on voir dire examination of the prospective jurors and the atmosphere in the local community and the circumstances surrounding the trial do not betray inflamed community sentiment, there is no denial of a fair trial merely because of the publicity. This is made clear in Murphy v. Florida, 421 U.S. 794, 95 S.Ct. 2031, 44 L.Ed.2d 589 (1975). Because of the notoriety of the defendant, his case was heavily covered by the local and national media and his prior felony convictions were widely reported. But the jurors chosen were emphatic that they would not be influenced by the publicity and only 20 of the 78 potential jurors questioned were excused as indicating an opinion as to the defendant's guilt. In contrast, in Irvin v. Dowd 268 of the 430 veniremen were excused. In addition, unlike the Sheppard, Rideau and Estes cases, the conduct of the trial and atmosphere in and around the courthouse was proper. In such circumstances, the Supreme Court held that the defendant had not been deprived of his constitutional rights to a fair trial. The importance of the Murphy case lies in its necessary implication that claims of prejudicial publicity will be considered on a case by case basis, with careful scrutiny by the courts of the circumstances surrounding the trials. Convictions will not be reversed automatically because of the presence of substantial publicity.

Even so there is still a serious free press-fair trial problem created by media coverage of criminal and other proceedings. The blame for the existence of the problem can be widely apportioned among prosecutors and defense counsel who violate their code of professional responsibility by trying their cases in the news media, law enforcement officals seeking glory for their agencies, judges who cannot resist the limelight, prominent uninvolved parties such as Presidents of the United States who pass judgment on accused in advance of trial and, of course, media representatives who aid, abet and encourage these sources.

B. APPROACHES TO THE PROBLEM

1. Voluntary Cooperation Between Bench, Bar and Media

a. *Press Councils*

One non-legal mechanism designed to eliminate unfairness and impropriety in reporting generally is the press council. Its functions include hearing grievances brought by members of the public, including lawyer groups, concerning the media, passing judgment on those grievances and, in the process, laying down guidelines for fair reporting and proper behavior in the future. There are two such councils in the United States, the National and Minnesota Press Councils. Each is a private organization headed by a distinguished jurist with membership divided between journalists and lay persons. Having no power to sanction the media or its representatives for unfairness in the coverage of criminal cases and other matters, the councils must rely on friendly persuasion and the leverage inherent in publicizing their opinions.

b. *Voluntary Guidelines for Criminal Trial Coverage*

A more widely accepted non-legal approach is voluntary adherence to general guidelines and policies for covering criminal proceedings drafted jointly by bench, bar and media representatives. Voluntary guidelines are in effect in more than half of the states and are strongly backed by organizations such at the American Bar Association, the American Society of Newspaper Editors and the American Newspaper Publishers Association.

An example of these guidelines is the California Joint Declaration of Principles and Policy, which begins with a declaration supporting both first amendment principles and fair criminal proceeding. Concrete policies for news coverage then follow, including restraint by the media in characterizing slayings as "murders" until a formal charge is made and characterizing those brought in for questioning as "suspects." Restraint is also urged in reporting confessions. If confessions are reported they are to be called "statements" thus leaving to the jury the decision whether the accused really confessed. Generally, under the California guidelines prior criminal records should not be reported. Recognizing a major source of prejudicial publicity, the guidelines caution reporters not to let prosecutors, police or defense attorneys use the media as "a sounding board for public opinion or personal publicity."

Being voluntary and non-binding, the guidelines provide no sanctions for violation beyond adverse publicity and peer disapproval for the offending subscriber. Moreover, assuming good faith adherence to the enunciated principles and policies by the bar and media, an irreducible number of problems will still arise, and the danger exists that some judges may choose to treat the guidelines as mandatory upon the press and condition access to their courtrooms upon adherence to the guidelines. See, e.g., Federated Publications v. Swedberg, 96 Wash.2d 13, 633 P.2d 74 (1981), cert. denied, ___ U.S. ___, 102 S.Ct. 2257, 72 L.Ed.2d 862 (1982).

2. Resort to Judicial Procedural Devices

In his opinion for the Court in Sheppard, Mr. Justice Clark listed certain procedural devices available to judges to neutralize the possible prejudicial effect of publicity and behavior of media representatives without *direct* limitation on them. These include postponing the case until the danger of prejudice abates, transferring it to another county if the publicity has not saturated the entire state, sealing off or sequestering the jury as soon as it is empaneled to shield the jurors from trial publicity, sequestering the witnesses or at least admonishing them not to follow the proceedings in the media until they have testified, strictly controlling the courtroom and courthouse environment and, if all else fails, ordering a new trial. The last device is an extreme one not to the judiciary's liking. But the others may not, in given circumstances, be fully effective in insuring a fair trial. For instance, postponements and venue changes will have little effect if the publicity is dramatic and pervasive and sequestration does not shield the jurors from prejudicial publicity before they are selected.

3. Limiting Access of the Media to Information About Pending Legal Matters

a. The Suggestions in Sheppard

Justice Clark seemed to recognize the shortcomings of these devices for he also recognized the constitutionality of action to eliminate the need for new trials by restricting the sources of much potentially prejudicial publicity. Speaking for a majority of the Court, he would permit trial judges to issue restrictive orders prohibiting the prosecuting and defense attorneys, parties, witnesses and court and law enforcement officials from divulging prejudicial matters to the media such as statements made by the accused, the identity and probable testimony of witnesses and comments concerning the merits of the case. In addition, trial judges were encouraged to admonish reporters who wrote or broadcast prejudicial stories of the impropriety and danger of publishing matters not introduced at trial. But it is important to note that Justice Clark did not authorize direct restrictions on and sanctions against the media. He left that issue open for later consideration by the Court.

b. *The American Bar Association's Reardon Report*

The Court's endorsement of restrictive orders to reach the sources of much prejudicial publicity was quickly seconded by the American Bar Association with its adoption of the so-called "Reardon Report." The report, based on a study made by the ABA Advisory Committee on Fair Trial and Free Press, which was created in response to suggestions by the Warren Commission, recommended that the courts adopt strict standing rules for all cases to regulate the conduct of counsel, parties, witnesses, court personnel and law enforcement officers in releasing information to the press. Enforcement of such standing orders against members of the bar would be effectuated by invoking the legal profession's canons of ethics (now code of professional responsibility) enacted as law in most states. Law enforcement officers could be regulated and sanctioned by their respective agencies, which should be encouraged to adopt regulations on the release of information concerning court cases or potential court cases. Court personnel could be controlled by rules of court. And those less amenable to control by the court and other governmental agencies such as witnesses and members of the news media might be sanctioned directly through the exercise of the courts' criminal contempt power to punish the release and publication of information willfully designed to influence the outcome of criminal prosecutions. This last suggestion to breathe life into the dormant contempt power as a means of controlling what the media publishes went beyond Sheppard and made the report controversial and subject to vigorous attack by the press and even segments of the bar and bench.

c.   Other Institutional Reactions Favoring Restrictions on News Flow to the Media

The Judicial Conference of the United States, the agency responsible for formulating policy for the federal courts made a report to the Chief Justice of the United States also in the late 1960's recommending that the United States District Courts firmly regulate both the physical courtroom environs and the release of information by members of their bars and by federal court personnel. The Judicial Conference also rejected the use of the contempt power to prevent unwanted publicity. The recommendations of the Judicial Conference have generally been adopted by the federal trial courts in the form of local rules governing the behavior of counsel and court personnel.

In 1965, the United States Department of Justice promulgated a Statement of Policy Concerning the Release of Information by Personnel of the Department of Justice Relating to Criminal Proceedings. The statement, more commonly known as the Katzenbach Rules, for the Attorney General who approved it, applied to the release of

[271]

information from the time a person is arrested or charged with a crime until the proceeding terminated by trial or otherwise and condemned all release of information designed to influence the outcome of a defendant's trial. Authorized personnel were generally permitted to release only uncontrovertible factual information concerning a defendant's identity and age, residence and other basic background information, the criminal charge, the identity of the investigating and arresting agencies, the length of the investigation and the circumstances immediately surrounding the arrest.

The same personnel were urged to refrain from making available to the media observations about a defendant's character, statements, admissions, confessions or alibis, references to investigative procedures such as laboratory tests, statements about the identity, credibility or testimony of prospective witnesses, statements concerning evidence or legal argument in the case and photographs of the defendant unless a law enforcement function would be served thereby. Nor were members of the Justice Department to volunteer information about a defendant's prior criminal record or to encourage or assist the news media in photographing or televising a defendant in federal custody.

Certain strengthening amendments to the rules have been subsequently approved, including ones to control the release of information in civil and criminal cases in which the United States is a party. See 28 C.F.R. § 50.2 (1980).

While the Katzenbach Rules apply only to the Department of Justice, the ABA's Code of Professional Responsibility establishes standards for all attorneys. Consistent with the Reardon Report, new Code disciplinary rule DR 7–107 provides guidelines for prosecutors and defense counsel alike regarding the release of information concerning pending criminal cases roughly parallel to the Katzenbach Rules. Guidelines are also provided for professional disciplinary proceedings, juvenile justice proceedings, civil cases and administrative proceedings. In those states that have adopted DR 7–107 by statute or court rule attorneys may be disciplined for violating its precepts. While the ultimate sanction of disbarment has yet to be invoked for violation of DR 7–107, harsher disciplinary penalties can be expected in the future.

d. *Exclusion of Camera Operator and Equipment from the Courtroom and Environs*

For 45 years the American Bar Association had vigorously opposed cameras in the courtroom and for much of that time the ABA's position was followed by the nation's judges. ABA Canon of Judicial Conduct No. 3A(7) stated that a judge should prohibit the broadcasting, recording or photographing of proceedings in the courtroom. The only exceptions recognized were ceremonial proceedings or those recorded for educational purposes. Canon 3(7) was preceded by ABA Canon of Judicial Ethics No. 35 adopted in 1937. Canon 35 stated that broadcasting, televising or recording of active court proceedings detracted from the essential dignity of the proceedings, distracted the witnesses and attorneys, and created misconceptions in the public's mind. But though the thrust of old Canon 35 was endorsed by a plurality of the United States Supreme Court in Estes v. Texas, 381 U.S. 532, 85 S.Ct. 1628, 14 L.Ed. 2d 543 (1965), the Court subsequently held in Chandler v. Florida, 449 U.S. 560, 101 S.Ct. 802, 66 L.Ed.2d 740 (1981) that the United States Constitution did not prohibit a state from authorizing the use of cameras in the courtroom even in criminal cases in which the defendants object to the presence of electronic and still photographic equipment to record such trials. The Court said that an absolute constitutional ban on broadcast and still photographic coverage of trials could not be justified simply because there is a danger that, in some cases, the ability of jurors to decide the issue of guilt or innocence on an impartial basis may be impaired. Rather, the appropriate safeguard against such prejudice is the defendant's right to demonstrate that media coverage compromised the ability of the jury in his or her case to adjudicate fairly.

The Chandler opinion was written by Chief Justice Burger, perhaps the leading judicial authority opposing cameras in courtrooms, particularly his own. It is not surprising then that the opinion is very narrow, saying no more than that the due process clause of the Fourteenth Amendment does not per se prohibit photographic coverage of judicial proceedings. Certainly the opinion does not endorse the idea that cameras should be permitted in courtrooms.

Despite ABA Judicial Canon 3A(7) and the opinions of a plurality of justices in the Estes case, a survey taken shortly after Chandler indicated that 31 states had begun to permit cameras in some or all of their courts on a permanent or experimental basis and another five were thinking about it. This turnabout is quite extraordinary, since as late as 1976 only three states were permitting camera access. See News Media and the Law, p. 64 (Oct.–Nov. 1981).

As a result of this change of judicial attitude toward the use of cameras in the courtroom, the American Bar Association, bowing to the inevitable, revoked Canon 3A(7) in 1982 and in its place adopted a guideline stating that judges should be able to authorize unobtrusive camera use under carefully devised local court rules.

e. Sealing Arrest and Other Public Records

Another increasingly popular tactic of the judiciary in restricting access of the news media to information potentially affecting criminal prosecutions is the sealing of arrest and other public records. The premier example of this approach is the trial of the Watergate defendants in which Judge Sirica sealed many of the documents and tapes in the case from public view. When officials of the Reporters Committee for Freedom of the Press wrote the Judge a letter requesting that the material be unsealed and made available for inspection by the news media as representatives of the public the letter itself was ordered sealed.

But while secrecy in judicial proceedings is increasing, the press is beginning to attack the practice of sealing public records and removing them from public inspection. In Miami Herald Publishing Co. v. Collazo, 329 So.2d 333 (Fla.App. 1976), the Miami Herald successfully challenged a trial court order entered at the request of all parties to a negligence action sealing the settlement agreement between the parties to prevent the press and public from learning its terms. In reversing the order the Florida Court of Appeals said, "An informed public depends on accurate and effective reporting by the news media. . . . [T]he 'open court' concept is an indispensable part of our system of government and our way of life." 329 So.2d at 337. And in an unreported case involving the federal prosecution of the Governor of Maryland and certain associates for political corruption, a trial court order sealing pretrial papers and proceedings was modified on appeal within four days of the Washington Post's initial legal challenge so as to open all previously and subsequently filed pretrial papers to public scrutiny. See Wash. Post, June 30, 1976, p. A34, col. 1; ibid. July 3, 1976, p. A1, col. 7. It is clear from these and other recent cases that affected representatives of the media are now recognized as possessing legal standing to assert the public's right to be informed about judicial proceedings when individual judges choose to conceal those proceedings.

f. Closing the Courtroom

Parallel to the sealing of public records is the exclusion of the public and the news media from the courtroom during trial and pretrial proceedings, usually in sensational criminal cases. This device, though once rarely if ever resorted to by American courts (see In re Oliver, 333 U.S. 257, 266, 68 S.Ct. 499, 504, 92 L.Ed. 682, 690 (1948)), became increasingly popular following the Supreme Court's imposition of strict limits on trial court's power to issue injunctive orders preventing publication of news concerning pending criminal trials in Nebraska Press Association v. Stuart, 427 U.S. 539, 96 S.Ct. 2791, 49 L.Ed.2d 683 (1976), discussed infra, pp. 280–283. The problems engendered by judicial resort to the court-closing device are considered in detail in Chapter V at pp. 193–200, supra.

4. **Prior Restraint of the News Media**

The devices previously discussed are employed to prevent the news media from obtaining information about judicial proceedings which the judiciary believes would prejudice such proceedings. An even more difficult legal question than restricting access to news is posed by the judiciary restraining the media from publishing news that they have already obtained. The media's pejorative term for such judicial conduct is "gag order" and, indeed, the effect of judicial restrictive orders is prior restraint of the press.

a. *Problems Engendered*

Once the news media obtain information about pending judicial proceedings which, if published, might seriously affect their conduct and outcome, the courts must choose between previously discussed procedural devices designed to minimize or eliminate the impact of publication and the issuance of restrictive or "gag" orders directly against the news media. Increasingly during the late 1960's and the 1970's the trial courts chose to restrict publication. While all restrictive orders which were challenged on appeal were ultimately reversed, they created serious problems for the media and news personnel. Not the least of these problems arose when news personnel refused to obey even constitutionally invalid orders enjoining publication of the news. In United States v. Dickinson, 465 F.2d 496 (5th Cir. 1972), cert. denied 414 U.S. 979, 94 S.Ct. 270, 38 L.Ed.2d 223 (1973), two reporters assigned by their news service to cover a federal hearing challenging the legality of an allegedly baseless Louisiana murder conspiracy prosecution against a black civil rights worker were orally ordered by the presiding judge not to report the details of the evidence given in open court in the case. Notwithstanding the order, the two reporters wrote articles summarizing the testimony in detail. They were subsequently found guilty of criminal contempt and each was fined $300. On appeal of the contempt convictions the restrictive order was held to violate the First Amendment but the United States Court of Appeals further held that even constitutionally invalid injunctive orders must be obeyed until they are successfully challenged on appeal. This means that reporters, editors and publishers may properly be prosecuted for knowingly ignoring restrictive orders obviously violative of the First Amendment while such orders are ostensibly in effect. The principle enunciated in the Dickinson case that one must, under threat of criminal penalties, obey unconstitutional judicial orders until they are dissolved has generally been recognized in the state courts as well. See Annot., 12 A.L.R.2d 1059, 1107–16 (1950). But see State ex rel. Superior Court of Snohomish County v. Sperry, 79 Wash.2d 69, 483 P.2d 608 (1971) (criminal contempt convictions of two reporters for violation of patently unconstitutional restrictive order vacated on appeal). See also Note, "Defiance of Unlawful Authority," 83 Harv.L. Rev. 626, 633–638 (1970). The only legally safe recourse open to affected news media personnel when they are bound by judicial restrictive orders is to appeal the issuance of such orders directly. As a practical matter, however, few appeals can be expedited sufficiently to strike down the orders while the information suppressed remains newsworthy. Thus, the choice normally confronting media personnel will be to publish what they have and risk imprisonment and fines or not to publish and likely lose the story.

b. *Nebraska Press Association v. Stuart*

Fortunately for the news media the indiscriminate issuance of restrictive orders directly binding their representatives was finally halted by the United States Supreme Court in Nebraska Press Association v. Stuart, 427 U.S. 539, 96 S.Ct. 2791, 49 L.Ed.2d 683 (1976). There the Court unanimously reversed restrictive orders of Nebraska courts barring newspersons from (1) reporting testimony and evidence presented in an open preliminary hearing concerning a ghastly multiple murder; (2) reporting the existence and nature of any confessions or admissions made by the accused to law enforcement officers or others; and (3) reporting any other facts "strongly implicative" of the accused. This was the first time the Court had considered the question of judicial restrictive orders aimed directly at the press. It took the opportunity to make clear that its distaste for prior restraints on the press first expressed in Near v. Minnesota, 283 U.S. 697, 51 S.Ct. 625, 75 L.Ed. 1357 (1931) had not abated.

Terming prior restraints on expression "the most serious and the least tolerable infringement on First Amendment rights" (427 U.S. at 559, 96 S.Ct. at 2802, 49 L.Ed.2d at 697), the Court reaffirmed the idea expressed in the "Pentagon Papers" case (pp. 157–162, supra) that every form of prior restraint comes to the Court with a strong presumption of its unconstitutionality. But a majority of the justices explicitly rejected the idea that the First Amendment (at least at this time) absolutely bars all prior restraints of the press when first and sixth amendment interests are in competition. Instead the majority set out certain considerations to aid trial courts in determining whether in a given and obviously rare case the proponents of a judicial restrictive order might meet their heavy burden of justifying prior restraint of the media on sixth amendment grounds.

First, the courts must seriously examine the alternatives to prior restraint of publication which may be available to them such as change of venue and postponement of the trial and make findings supported by probative evidence that alternatives short of prior restraint orders will not be effective.

Second, even where the courts believe that they can establish the ineffectiveness of less drastic alternatives, they must also assess the probable effectiveness of prior restraint on publication as a method of safeguarding the accused's right to a fair trial. If, as a practical matter, a prior restraint order will not safeguard the accused's rights it should not be entered. In the Nebraska Press Association case the facts militated against entry of such orders. Among other things, the issuing courts could not obtain jurisdiction over all news media organizations and persons reporting on the murder case and thus might not be able to enforce their orders uniformly and effectively and, because the murders took place in a small community of 850 persons, mouth to mouth rumors would saturate the community anyway and might be more prejudicial to a fair trial than reasonably accurate news accounts.

Third, trial courts must consider whether proposed restrictive orders would prevent the reporting of events transpiring in open court. To the extent they have this effect, such orders are constitutionally invalid.

Finally, the courts must consider carefully the terms of such orders. The prohibitions on the media must be precise and not overbroad. In the Nebraska Press Association case one restriction on the news media was that they not disseminate information "strongly implicative of the accused as the perpetrator of the slayings." This language was held too vague and too broad to avoid abridgment of the First Amendment.

Regarding this last consideration, a restrictive order to be valid must be appropriately narrow and precise and yet must also be effective in safeguarding the accused's sixth amendment rights. Walking this constitutional tightrope will not be easy. It is safe to say that the matters which must be considered before a prior restraint order may be entered will severely curtail resort to such orders in the future. For this reason and because of the Supreme Court's unanimous reaffirmation of its attitude of hostility toward prior restraints, Nebraska Press Association v. Stuart must be termed an important victory for the press.

5. Subsequent Criminal Punishment of the News Media

Subsequent criminal punishment of the news media may be just as dangerous to the media's ability to inform the public about judicial matters as prior restraints such as "gag orders." In Landmark Communications, Inc. v. Virginia, 435 U.S. 829, 98 S.Ct. 1535, 56 L.Ed.2d 1 (1978) the Supreme Court struck down as unduly restrictive of press freedom a Virginia statute making it a crime to divulge information regarding proceedings before a state judicial review commission hearing complaints alleging the disability or misconduct of sitting judges. In this case a newspaper corporation was convicted of violating the statute by accurately reporting on a pending commission inquiry and identifying the judge involved. The corporation was fined $500 plus costs.

In reversing the conviction the Court made it clear that subsequent punishment of the press for the publication of accurate information of interest to the public can be just as dangerous a violation of the First and Fourteenth Amendments as judicial and legislative attempts to prevent publication in the first instance. Compare the media contempt cases of Bridges v. California, 314 U.S. 252, 62 S.Ct. 190, 86 L.Ed. 192 (1941); Pennekamp v. Florida, 328 U.S. 331, 66 S.Ct. 1029, 90 L.Ed. 1295 (1946); Craig v. Harney, 331 U.S. 367, 67 S.Ct. 1249, 91 L.Ed. 1546 (1947); Wood v. Georgia, 370 U.S. 375, 82 S.Ct. 1364, 8 L.Ed.2d 569 (1962).

A case similar in effect to the Landmark decision is Smith v. Daily Mail Publishing Co., 443 U.S. 97, 99 S.Ct. 2667, 61 L.Ed.2d 399 (1979) in which a newspaper publishing corporation was indicted for violating a West Virginia statute which makes it a crime for a *newspaper* to publish, without the written approval of the juvenile court, the name of any youth charged as a juvenile offender. The corporation then sought and received from the West Virginia Supreme Court of Appeals an order prohibiting prosecution under the indictment. The state high court's ruling that the statute on which the indictment was based violated the First and Fourteenth Amendments was upheld by the United States Supreme Court.

Both Landmark and Smith require a balancing of the media's interests in free dissemination of information against the state's interests in confidential judicial proceedings. In Landmark, the Supreme Court held that the state's interests in

[*284*]

confidentiality of investigations of members of the judiciary simply did not outweigh First Amendment interests while in Smith the Court held that the state's interests were not weighty enough and further that whatever the weight of the state's interest in confidentiality of juvenile proceedings, it would not be furthered by a criminal statute which permitted media other than newspapers to disclose the names of alleged juvenile offenders.

C. THE FREE PRESS—FAIR TRIAL ISSUE TODAY: A SUMMARY

We now summarize what we believe to be the major aspects of the legal situation following Nebraska Press Association v. Stuart, supra:

1. Except in the most extreme cases, judicial orders directly restraining the dissemination of news by the media concerning judicial proceedings will be held invalid.

2. However, presumptively invalid prior restraint orders must be obeyed by media personnel under penalty of criminal contempt until they are judicially dissolved. Thus, the possibility still exists that some judges may continue to issue unconstitutional restrictive orders against the media for the temporary advantage such action may gain.

3. News media personnel may not be excluded from open judicial proceedings and may

[285]

not be restricted in the reporting of what transpires in open court.

4. Affected news media personnel and organizations have legal standing to challenge the closing of a criminal trial even when the accused chooses to waive his or her constitutional right to an open and public trial, and only in certain very narrow circumstances may the trial judge be allowed to exclude the public and the media. See Richmond Newspapers, Inc. v. Virginia, 448 U.S. 555, 100 S.Ct. 2814, 65 L.Ed.2d 973 (1980).

5. Where statutes and state constitutional provisions permit, the courts may, consistent with the First, Sixth and Fourteenth Amendments of the United States Constitution, close pretrial proceedings to the public and the press. See Gannett Co., Inc. v. De Pasguale, 443 U.S. 368, 99 S.Ct. 2898, 61 L.Ed.2d 608 (1979).

6. An increasing practice of the courts in criminal cases is to seal pretrial and trial papers and transcripts and physical evidence such as the Nixon tapes. While affected members of the news media have legal standing to question individual "sealing" orders, in appropriate and narrowly circumscribed situations, such orders will be upheld.

7. Restraining orders restricting those involved in criminal prosecutions such as witnesses and lawyers from extrajudicially communicating certain matters to the news media are constitutionally valid if the exigencies of a fair trial demand their entry (Sheppard v. Maxwell, 384 U.S. 333, 361–62, 86 S.Ct. 1507, 1521–22, 16 L.Ed.2d 600, 619–20 (1966)) and the orders meet appropriate constitutional standards of precision and narrowness. See Chicago Council of Lawyers v. Bauer, 522 F.2d 242 (7th Cir. 1975), cert. denied, sub nom. Cunningham v. Chicago Council of Lawyers, 427 U.S. 912, 96 S.Ct. 3201, 49 L.Ed.2d 1204 (1976).

8. A newsperson who receives information proscribed by this type of restrictive order may be subpoenaed and compelled to disclose the source of such information under penalty of criminal contempt if he or she is not protected by a newspersons' shield statute. Such subpoena will be enforced in order to allow the issuing court to determine whether anyone bound by the order had violated it. See Farr v. Pitchess, 522 F.2d 464 (9th Cir. 1975), cert. denied 427 U.S. 912, 96 S.Ct. 3200, 49 L.Ed.2d 1203 (1976); Rosato v. Superior Court, 51 Cal. App.3d 190, 124 Cal.Rptr. 427 (Dist.Ct.App. 1975), cert. denied 427 U.S. 912, 96 S.Ct. 3200, 49 L.Ed.2d 1204 (1976).

9. State and federal statutes and court rules and state constitutional provisions which prevent resort to changes of venue, postponement of trial and other devices designed to avoid undue publicity and to insure fair trial may be held unconstitutional in specific applications.

10. Extensive publicity surrounding a criminal case without more does not result in a denial of a fair trial to the accused.

11. But news media misconduct in and around the courtroom and television and film coverage of pretrial and trial proceedings together with other extensive publicity may result in mistrial or reversal of convictions. Such misconduct is censurable and newspersons may be found guilty of criminal contempt for violation of reasonable regulations governing the physical conditions under which criminal trials are to proceed.

12. The broader power of the courts to hold members of the news media in criminal contempt for disseminating information outside the courtroom and its environs in the absence of the violation of any prior existing order restraining publication is in serious doubt since Bridges v. California, 314 U.S. 252, 62 S.Ct. 190, 86 L.Ed. 192 (1941) and its use seems unlikely to be revived, the ABA's Reardon Report to the contrary notwithstanding.

Two philosophical strands of thought can be discerned as underlying many of the above principles and rules. The first is the Blackstonian distinction between prior restraint of the press and subsequent press responsibility for what is published. The second is the Supreme Court's largely unarticulated belief that the First Amendment is more concerned with free dissemination of information than it is with assuring access to the information in the first place. However, the Court's reliance on the First Amendment in Richmond Newspapers to support access of the public and press to criminal trials suggests the possibility that the Court's orientation might ultimately change. But unless and until these two major philosophical approaches to the First Amendment do change, the outlines of the free press-fair trial issue will remain much as they are now.

*

PART TWO

REGULATION OF THE MEDIA

CHAPTER VIII

THE REGULATION OF COMMERCIAL SPEECH

A. CONSTITUTIONAL HISTORY

First Amendment protection for commercial speech—particularly commercial advertising—has had a checkered history in the Supreme Court. First the Court refused to recognize any such protection. Then, after recognizing some protection utilizing the language of ad hoc balancing, the Court appeared to move toward absolutist protection of such speech qualified only by time, place and manner considerations. Now the Court, for the present at least, has settled upon a well defined balancing approach, though the special problems of advertising by professionals may cause some deviations from this approach.

The chronology begins with Valentine v. Chrestensen, 316 U.S. 52, 62 S.Ct. 920, 86 L.Ed. 1262 (1942), in which the Court unanimously sustained an ordinance which banned the distribution of commercial handbill advertising. After being prohibited by local authorities from distributing a handbill announcing the exhibition of a submarine, the promoter had printed on the reverse side of the handbill a protest against an official refusal to allow him to use city wharfage facilities for such exhibition. The court found this supposed political protest to be a mere subterfuge to evade the ordinance and suggested that "purely commercial advertising" was not protected by the First Amendment. In short, the government could constitutionally regulate product or service advertising without abridging the First Amendment.

This distinction between types of expression has been a controversial one. In Cammarano v. United States, 358 U.S. 498, 514, 79 S.Ct. 524, 534, 3 L.Ed.2d 462, 472 (1959), Justice Douglas said that the Chrestensen opinion was "casual, almost offhand" and "has not survived reflection." But thereafter the Court reiterated the distinction between purely commercial advertising and all other expression in New York Times v. Sullivan, 376 U.S. 254, 84 S.Ct. 710, 11 L.Ed.2d 686 (1964).

This was the state of commercial speech until Bigelow v. Virginia, 421 U.S. 809, 95 S.Ct. 2222, 44 L.Ed.2d 600 (1975). Jeffrey C. Bigelow was the managing editor of the Virginia Weekly, a newspaper published in Charlottesville, Virginia. The Weekly ran a referral service for an abortion clinic in New York City. Bigelow was convicted for violating a Virginia statute which made it a misdemeanor for any person by advertisement to encourage or promote the procuring of abortions. His conviction was reversed by the Supreme Court which held that merely because an advertisement is labeled commercial speech does not mean that it is stripped of all first amendment safeguards, as had been implied in Valentine v. Chrestensen. Such speech retains some degree of constitutional protection which must be weighed against the state's interest in regulating the particular advertisement. Justice Blackmun, writing for the Court, then found some value in the abortion referral ad as a vehicle for conveying information of potential interest to Virginia Weekly readers. According to Justice Blackmun, the ad did more than fulfill Bigelow's profit motive. His interest coincided with the constitutional interests of certain of his audience who might need the service offered, or who were concerned about New York's laws or who were seeking abortion law reform in Virginia. Justice Blackmun noted that the availability of legal abortion in New York was information of value to the public and that, as previously decided, the right to early term abortion itself involved a woman's constitutional right to privacy. See Roe v. Wade, 410 U.S. 113, 93 S.Ct. 705, 35 L.Ed.2d 147 (1973) and Doe v. Bolton, 410 U.S. 179, 93 S.Ct. 739, 35 L.Ed.2d 201 (1973).

On the other side of the balance, Virginia contended that abortion referral agencies breed practices such as fee splitting that tend to decrease the quality of medical care and that advertising these agencies will encourage women to seek abortions from those interested only in financial gain and not in providing professional medical service. Virginia, however, made no claim that this advertisement would in any way affect the quality of medical care within its own boundaries, and the Court reasoned that the state was actually asserting an interest in regulating what Virginians hear or read about another state's services. This interest, in the Court's view, was entitled to little, if any, weight. Consequently, the state's interest was not sufficient to permit it to punish Bigelow for running the ad and his conviction was reversed.

Bigelow seemed to say that if First Amendment protection was to be accorded to commercial speech, it would be on an ad hoc balancing basis. But in Virginia State Board of Pharmacy v. Virginia Citizens Consumer Council, Inc., 425 U.S. 748, 96 S.Ct. 1817, 48 L.Ed.2d 346 (1976), the Court appeared to adopt an absolutist approach to the protection of commercial speech in a case where the state statutorily prohibited pharmacists from advertising the prices of prescription drugs which they offered for sale—advertising which, unlike that in Bigelow is *purely* commercial in nature.

In striking down the Virginia statute, Justice Blackmun, speaking for the Court, appeared to reject the balancing process when he said, "There is no claim .   .   . that the prohibition on prescription drug price advertising is a mere time, place, and manner restriction. We have often approved restrictions of that kind provided that they are justified without reference to the content of the regulated speech, that they serve a significant governmental interest, and that in so doing they leave open ample alternative channels for communication of the information . . . . Whatever may be the proper bounds of time, place, and manner restrictions on commercial speech, they are plainly exceeded by this Virginia statute, which singles out speech of a particular content and seeks to prevent its dissemination completely." 425 U.S. at 771, 96 S.Ct. at 1830, 48 L.Ed.2d at 363–64. To similar effect are Linmark Associates, Inc. v. Township of Willingboro, 431 U.S. 85, 97 S.Ct. 1614, 52 L.Ed.2d 155 (1977) (local ordinance forbidding display of "for sale" signs in front of houses struck down); Carey v. Population Services International, 431 U.S. 678, 700–702, 97 S.Ct. 2010, 2024, 52 L.Ed.2d 675, 694–95 (1977) (statute prohibiting advertisement of contraceptives struck down).

B. THE FOUR–PART COMMERCIAL SPEECH ANALYSIS OF CENTRAL HUDSON

Following Bigelow, Virginia Pharmacy Board, Linmark and Carey, the issue is no longer whether purely commercial speech is protected expression but rather what First Amendment philosophy and analysis would govern the extension of

[*295*]

such protection. That question was answered in Central Hudson Gas and Electric Corp. v. Public Service Commission, 447 U.S. 557, 100 S.Ct. 2343, 65 L.Ed.2d 341 (1980).

There, a regulation promulgated by the New York Public Service Commission banned electric utilities in the state from engaging in advertising which promoted the increased use of electricity. In striking down the regulation as violative of the First and Fourteenth Amendments, a bare majority of the Court enunciated a four part test for determining the availability of constitutional protection for commercial speech. The test emphasizes the balancing of state interests in the regulation of commercial speech against individual free speech interests.

In short, the four-part test includes first a determination whether the expression is at all protected by the First Amendment. Commercial speech which involves or advertises unlawful activity or is false or misleading is *not* protected. For examples of this idea see Pittsburgh Press Co. v. Pittsburgh Commission on Human Relations, 413 U.S. 376, 93 S.Ct. 2553, 37 L.Ed.2d 669 (1973) (ordinance prohibiting newspapers from carrying help wanted ads categorized by gender upheld); Princess Sea Industries, Inc. v. Nevada, 635 P.2d 281 (Nev.1981), cert. denied ___ U.S. ___, 102 S.Ct. 1972, 72 L.Ed.2d 441 (1982) (statute prohibiting advertising of prostitution service in Nevada counties in which such service is illegal upheld); Friedman v. Rogers, 440 U.S. 1, 99 S.Ct.

887, 59 L.Ed.2d 100 (1979) (statute prohibiting practice of optometry under a trade name upheld because ill-defined association of trade name with price and quality could be manipulated by user of trade name to mislead the public).

If the commercial speech does not involve illegality and is neither false or misleading, then the second part of the analysis comes into play. The test here is whether the asserted governmental interest in regulation or prohibition of certain commercial speech is substantial. If the state's interest is substantial, then regulation or complete prohibition of the particular commercial expression may be permitted, depending on the results of the third and fourth parts of the test.

The third part asks whether the state's regulation directly advances the governmental interest involved. Such regulation will not be upheld unless it is actually effective in advancing the state's interest directly. Indirect or speculative advancement of the state's interest will not suffice.

The final part of the test and the one the New York Public Service Commission failed in the Central Hudson case is whether the state's regulation is only as broad as is necessary to serve the state's substantial governmental interest. In Central Hudson, the Court's five-member majority was not persuaded that the Commission's complete suppression of promotional advertising by New York electric utilities was necessary to further the State's interest in energy conservation.

The majority pointed out that the Commission had made no showing that a more limited restriction on the content of promotional advertising would have been inadequate to serve the state's interests.

The second and third parts of the Court's four-part test clearly call into play the ad hoc balancing of First Amendment interests against conflicting legitimate state interests while the fourth part attempts to limit the degree of conflict and the extent of intrusion into the First Amendment area posed by the second and third parts.

In his concurring opinion Justice Blackmun pointed out the contradictions of the four-part balancing test with the more absolutist approach taken earlier in Virginia Pharmacy, Linmark and Carey. He noted that such test would permit a complete ban on utilities advertising, for instance, the advantages of air conditioning, assuming that a more limited restriction on such advertising would not effectively deter members of the public from cooling their homes.

The four-part test of the Central Hudson case is not quite as mechanical as it may seem because a number of the present Supreme Court Justices also consider the *kind* of commercial speech involved and the *medium* of expression utilized. The belief is expressed by some of the Court's present members that there exists a hierarchy of expression, meaning that some speech is more important than other speech, and, hence, entitled to more First Amendment Protection. "We have

not discarded the 'common sense' distinction between speech proposing a commercial transaction
. . . and other varieties of speech." Ohralik
v. Ohio State Bar Association, 436 U.S. 447,
455–456, 98 S.Ct. 1912, 1918, 56 L.Ed.2d 444, 453
(1978). See also FCC v. Pacifica Foundation, 438
U.S. 726, 745, 98 S.Ct. 3026, 3038, 57 L.Ed.2d
1073, 1090 (1978) (opinion of Justice Stevens).

As to the means of expression, members of
the Court have long suggested that while every
medium was entitled to First Amendment protection, the nature of the medium could be considered in determining the *scope* of that protection.
See Metromedia, Inc. v. City of San Diego, 453
U.S. 490 n.8, 101 S.Ct. 2882, 2889 n.8, 69 L.Ed.2d
800, 811 n.8 (1981) (opinion of Justice White); Joseph Burstyn, Inc. v. Wilson, 343 U.S. 495,
502–503, 72 S.Ct. 777, 781, 96 L.Ed. 1098, 1106
(1952) (the motion picture medium); Kovacs v.
Cooper, 336 U.S. 77, 97, 69 S.Ct. 448, 458, 93
L.Ed. 513, 528 (1949) (sound trucks) (concurring
opinion of Justice Jackson).

Thus, the Court, or at least some justices, will
be inclined to treat a purely commercial message
on a matchbook or a billboard with less deference
than, say, a ,paid political compaign announcement made over the radio. Compare, e.g., Metromedia, Inc. v. City of San Diego, supra, in
which a plurality of the Court believed that a city
ordinance banning nearly all off-site billboards
met the four-part Central Hudson test for regulating commercial speech but was otherwise too

intrusive of First Amendment interests to stand, with First National Bank of Boston v. Bellotti, 435 U.S. 765, 98 S.Ct. 1407, 55 L.Ed.2d 707 (1978) in which a Court majority readily struck down a state statute forbidding banking and business corporations from spending money, inter alia, for advertising in any medium in order to influence the vote on referendum proposals.

C. THE SPECIAL PROBLEM OF PROFESSIONAL ADVERTISING

Advertising by professionals had been generally frowned upon in the twentieth century and individual members of a number of the learned professions such as law and medicine were prohibited by the states at the behest of professional organizations such as the ABA and the AMA from advertising their services, ostensibly because such advertising was unseemly and unprofessional but more realistically because such bans reduced economic competition within the professions.

1. Advertising by Lawyers: A Case Study

After the Supreme Court's decisions in Bigelow and Virginia Pharmacy Board according First Amendment protection to commercial speech, it was inevitable that bans on professional advertising would come under attack. As might be expected the first legal challenges came from members of the legal profession.

As the legal profession began to change and develop new forms of delivery systems for legal services such as legal clinics for the less affluent in society, advertising became an important tool in achieving volume business to sustain lower fee schedules. But use of such tool was in direct conflict with established law.

In Bates v. State Bar of Arizona, 433 U.S. 350, 97 S.Ct. 2691, 53 L.Ed.2d 810 (1977), two Phoenix legal clinic attorneys, in seeking business from persons of modest income in need of legal services, placed an ad in the Arizona Republic, a daily general circulation newspaper saying "Do You Need a Lawyer? Legal Services at Very Reasonable Fees" and listing the services available, the charges for such services and the name of the clinic, the address and the telephone number. The ad clearly violated the American Bar Association Disciplinary Rule 2–101(B), embodied in Rule 29(a) of the rules of Arizona Supreme Court. The president of the state bar immediately filed a complaint with the Arizona Supreme Court and ultimately that court censured the two attorneys.

By a narrow 5–4 vote, the United States Supreme Court reversed that portion of the state court order which had upheld the total ban on advertising. In so ruling the majority emphasized the consuming public's First Amendment interest in receiving truthful information about available services and products. Justice Blackmun, writing for the majority, noted that the ABA itself had reported that the middle 70 percent of the population on the economic scale was not being reached or adequately served by the legal profession. According to Justice Blackmun, advertising could help solve that problem.

But in holding that lawyer advertising could not under the First Amendment be subjected to blanket suppression, Justice Blackmun made clear that such advertising was too risk-filled not to be regulated. Regulation would be permitted to insure truthful advertising by lawyers for the protection of the public. Reasonable restrictions on the time, place and manner of advertising would be permitted, as would the suppression of false and misleading information and even accurate advertising concerning illegal transactions. In addition, advertising via electronic broadcast media might warrant special consideration and control. Justice Blackmun expected that the organized bar would have "a special role to play in assuring that advertising by attorneys flows both freely and cleanly." 433 U.S. at 384, 97 S.Ct. at 2709, 53 L.Ed.2d at 836.

Emphasizing cleanliness over freedom, the American Bar Association responded to the Bates decision by promulgating two alternative substitutes for the now dead letter DR 2–101(B). "Plan A"—the preferred alternative—listed 25 categories of information that a lawyer could include in his or her advertising. Nothing more could be included. The less restrictive "Plan B" simply permitted advertising that did not run afoul of a small number of general guidelines designed to

prevent fraud, deception or the misleading of the
public.

Despite warnings from legal scholars that
"Plan A" was too restrictive to pass constitutional muster, a majority of the states that considered the ABA's alternative proposals adopted
"Plan A" or some variation of it.

Missouri was one of them. The Missouri Supreme Court's Rule 4 listed only ten categories of
information that could be included in newspaper,
periodical and telephone directory ads. When attorney R_____ M. J_____ placed ads in local
newspapers and the St. Louis telephone directory
containing material not included in Rule 4 such as
the fact that he was licensed in Illinois and had
been admitted to practice before the United
States Supreme Court, the Advisory Committee
of the Missouri Bar filed a complaint in the Missouri Supreme Court seeking the imposition of
sanctions. Following a hearing the attorney was
officially reprimanded by the Missouri Supreme
Court and required to pay the costs of the action
despite his contention that his advertising was
protected speech.

On appeal the United States Supreme Court,
reflecting the principles laid down in Central
Hudson and Bates, voted unanimously to reverse
the judgment of the Missouri court. First
Amendment protection was accorded the lawyer's
advertising because none of the information contained therein was shown to be misleading nor
did the Missouri Supreme Court identify any sub-

stantial state interest in so sharply limiting lawyer advertising that would outweigh the lawyer's or the public's interest in such advertising. In the Matter of R_____ M. J_____, 455 U.S. 191, 102 S.Ct. 929, 71 L.Ed.2d 64 (1982). As a result of this decision the constitutionality of state bar advertising rules based upon restrictive "Proposal A" of the American Bar Association is now in doubt.

One of the special problems of professional advertising is that at some point it shades off into personal solicitation of business. The prohibition of these personal attempts by professionals to generate business has been upheld by the Supreme Court in the face of First Amendment claims because of the inherent dangers of fraud, undue influence, intimidation, overreaching and vexacious conduct. See Ohralik v. Ohio State Bar Association, 436 U.S. 447, 98 S.Ct. 1912, 56 L.Ed. 2d 444 (1978). However, the mailing by a lawyer of truthful professional brochure announcements, letters and information to a targeted group of persons who the lawyer believes may have need for his or her services is likened to general advertising and protected to the same extent. See Kentucky Bar Association v. Stuart, 568 S.W.2d 933 (Ky.1978); Koffler v. Joint Bar Association, 51 N.Y.2d 140, 412 N.E.2d 927, 432 N.Y.S.2d 872 (1981), cert. denied 450 U.S. 1026, 101 S.Ct. 1733, 68 L.Ed.2d 221 (letters to real estate owners and agencies from real estate attorneys); In re Appert, 315 N.W.2d 204 (Minn.1981) (brochures and letters to possible Dalkon Shield users from attorneys representing other such users suing the manufacturer because of uterine injuries).

The separation between protected commercial speech and prohibited solicitation appears to be at the point where the expression is so immediate and personal that danger exists that the potential client's privacy may be invaded or the potential client may not be able to exercise his or her free will in deciding whether to accept a particular professional's services.

2. The Effect of the Lawyer Advertising Cases on the Other Professions

The principles espoused in the lawyer advertising cases seem generally applicable to restraints on advertising imposed on the other professions. Responding to these cases, the American Dental Association, for instance, has entered into a consent decree with the Federal Trade Commission agreeing not to engage in unfair competition by unduly restricting the advertising of its members. This agreement was contingent upon the success of the FTC's litigation with the American Medical Association to eliminate the AMA's restrictions on price advertising and advertising of the availability of individual and alternative medical services. The FTC prevailed in American Medical Association v. FTC, 638 F.2d 443 (2d Cir. 1980), affirmed per curiam by an equally divided Supreme Court, ____ U.S. ____, 102 S.Ct. 1744, 71 L.Ed.2d 546 (1982).

Overall, there has been a decided loosening of strictures on professionals advertising their services. This trend should be given fresh impetus by the Supreme Court's affirmance of the FTC's victory over the AMA in the Second Circuit unless the Congress decides to exempt professional associations from regulation by the Commission as these associations have been advocating.

D. ACCESS OF THE PUBLIC TO THE PRIVATE ADVERTISING MEDIA

Thus far in this chapter the thrust of discussion has been the constitutional protection afforded to individual and corporate commercial speech. But it is important to remember that the First and Fourteenth Amendments are directed only to governmental action and do not compel private media interests to communicate commercial expression. Indeed, the Supreme Court has held that those Amendments do not require newspapers and broadcasters to accept paid editorial messages let alone purely commercial advertising. See CBS Inc. v. Democratic National Committee, 412 U.S. 94, 93 S.Ct. 2080, 36 L.Ed.2d 772 (1973); Miami Herald Publishing Co. v. Tornillo, 418 U.S. 241, 94 S.Ct. 2831, 41 L.Ed.2d 730 (1974).

Thus, while the Constitution limits governmental regulation of commercial speech, there is no guarantee that it will be heard if the speaker is dependent on private means of communications controlled by others.

[*306*]

The fact that until very recently commercial speech generally was not accorded First Amendment protection and false and misleading speech specifically has never been constitutionally protected accounts, at least in part, for the rise of statutory and administrative controls on advertising at both the state and federal levels designed to protect the public from commercial loss. In the remaining sections of this chapter we consider the agencies that exercise these controls, the nature of the controls, available sanctions against commercial wrongdoers and limitations on the imposition of these sanctions.

E. STATE STATUTORY REGULATION

As manufacturing began to dominate the early American agrarian economy and the frontier pushed westward, the distances between the manufacturers and their markets constantly expanded, making regional and national advertising increasingly necessary. Gradually the use of brand names, trademarks, magazine advertising and even advertising agencies grew to fulfill this need. Along with this dramatic growth of advertising use came flagrant advertising abuses. The patent medicines were the epitome of this advertising era, with elixirs such as Dr. J. W. Poland's White Pine Compound, claiming to cure "sore throat, colds, coughs, diphtheria, bronchitis, spitting of blood, and pulmonary afflictions generally." Flamboyant misleading copy writing, false testimonials, slogans, jingles and trade characters quickly became the rule in local and national advertising. Advertisers could, and did, promise anything and everything.

Common law and early state statutory remedies proved inadequate to curb advertising abuses. See E. Kintner, A Primer on the Law of Deceptive Practices: A Guide for The Businessman 7–8, 405–407. Today a majority of the states have added legislation similar to the Federal Trade Commission Act, discussed below, to encourage criminal prosecutions and to provide civil remedies for aggrieved consumers.

F.   FEDERAL STATUTORY AND ADMINISTRATIVE REGULATION

1.   The Federal Trade Commission

a.   *Nature and Jurisdiction*

The original Federal Trade Commission Act was not directed toward false advertising but rather toward the prevention of monopolistic and unfair methods of competition in interstate commerce. Despite the absence of a clear congressional mandate in the advertising area, the early commissioners regulated deceptive ads by labeling them "unfair methods of competition." They took the position that exaggerated or misleading claims for an advertiser's product gave him or her an inequitable competitive advantage over those sellers who told the truth. This position was affirmed by the Supreme Court in Federal

Trade Commission v. Winsted Hosiery Co., 258 U.S. 483, 42 S.Ct. 384, 66 L.Ed. 729 (1922). Justice Brandeis, speaking for the Supreme Court, upheld an FTC determination that when a manufacturer labels its underwear "Natural Wool" and "Natural Worsted" the product must be all wool, not merely 10 percent wool. The Court agreed that when misleading ads are marketed in competition with truthful ads, potential customers are unfairly diverted from the honest advertiser's products. By 1925 three quarters of the Federal Trade Commission's orders concerned false and misleading advertising.

All of the Federal Trade Commission's orders of this period were tied to the concept of unfair competition. The question remained whether the Commission could protect the public from false advertising directly, without having to demonstrate economic injury to a business competitor. Finally, in Federal Trade Commission v. Raladam Co., 283 U.S. 643, 51 S.Ct. 587, 75 L.Ed. 1324 (1931), the Supreme Court answered that question in the negative. In a unanimous decision the Court held that the Commission had no authority to ban purely false advertising, unless it could be shown to be an unfair method of competition. The Raladam decision prompted Congress in 1938 by the Wheeler-Lea Act to amend the Commission's enabling act to permit regulation of "unfair or deceptive acts or practices in commerce" that injure the consumer. Congress also provided for substantial civil fines for violations of Commission orders to "cease and desist" from proscribed advertising practices and for criminal penalties for and injunctions against the dissemination of false advertising pertaining to cosmetics, therapeutic devices and drugs.

b.　Organization and Enforcement

The Federal Trade Commission is an independent regulatory agency with five commissioners appointed by the President for renewable seven-year terms. No more than three members can belong to the same political party. It has more than 1500 employees divided primarily among three bureaus. The one most concerned with advertising is the Bureau of Consumer Protection. Through this bureau the Commission may institute an investigation upon the receipt of even a single letter of complaint from a member of the public. Unfortunately, because of its large workload and reduced budget, investigations often take a considerable length of time to commence and complete, if commenced at all.

If, as a result of the investigation, the Commission feels a formal hearing is necessary to determine the issues, it will draft a detailed complaint specifying the alleged false or deceptive practices and will hold a hearing. At the hearing an administrative law judge will make an initial decision after both sides present their respective positions. The judge's decision is final unless it is reviewed by the Commissioners. If the decision is unfavorable to the advertiser the Commission may issue a cease and desist order which, if violated, will subject the advertiser to an action in a federal district court for civil fine. The advertiser may seek review of the cease and desist order in the United States Court of Appeals.

Because of the delays inherent in such formal proceedings, the Commission has developed faster, less expensive methods of halting or preventing deceptive advertising. Indeed, the general policy has been to avoid litigation if possible by offering some form of settlement to offenders. This settlement can be effected through an "assurance of voluntary compliance" wherein the advertiser merely signs an affidavit that it will discontinue the practices involved. A second and more common approach is the use of the consent decree. Under this procedure the Commission drafts a proposed complaint together with a cease and desist order and attaches them to a notice of intent to commence formal proceedings. This package is sent to the alleged offender who must advise the Commission within 10 days if it is willing to forego a formal hearing and have the issues resolved by consent decree. Once a settlement is negotiated and accepted by the parties, it has the same effect as an order issued after a formal proceeding.

These settlement methods are made palatable to the businesses involved because they do not have to admit any violations of law. As an indication of their popularity, between 150 and 200 decrees have been issued every year since 1961.

Another individualized approach, involving antici-
patory regulation, is the advisory opinion. This is
simply an informal nonbinding statement of advice from a responsible member of the Commission staff to assist the businessperson in determining in advance the legality of proposed
conduct such as a future advertising campaign.
The request must anticipate the act; the Commission will not give advice concerning current business practices.

The Commission also employs certain indus-
try-wide approaches to illegal advertising and
other business practices. One generalized
method the Commission utilizes to promulgate its
views on advertising is the publication of practical manuals or "Guides." The Guides, in pam-
phlet form, are disseminated to both industry and
public to inform them of the Commission's position on certain business practices such as bait and
switch advertising, testimonial advertising and
deceptive pricing. These Guides reflect the view
of the Commission as to what might be considered illegal practices. Violation of a guideline is
not itself a violation of law. Rather, where a
guideline has not been followed, the Commission
must plead and prove that the accused business
violated a provision of the Federal Trade Commission Act itself. For litigation purposes, it is as if
the Guide did not exist.

This is in marked contrast to cases involving
violations of Commission Trade Regulation Rules
which state the types of conduct that will be

deemed unfair or deceptive by the Commission under the Federal Trade Commission Act. In these cases the Commission need only show that its Trade Regulation Rules have been violated. Thus, these Rules are treated as having the force of law and their violation may result in civil penalties of up to $10,000 for each offense.

c. The Federal Trade Commission Improvement Act of 1974

Another major grant of power to the Commission was effected by the Magnuson-Moss Act, 15 U.S.C.A. § 2301 (1975). The 1938 amendments to the Federal Trade Commission Act had placed deceptive advertising squarely within the Commission's jurisdiction, but the advertising was required to be "in commerce." In most other areas of federal regulation the quoted phrase, drawn from the Constitution, has been expanded by court decision to allow federal regulation of matters which merely "affected" interstate commerce. This liberal interpretation was denied to the Commission in Federal Trade Commission v. Bunte Brothers, 312 U.S. 349, 61 S.Ct. 580, 85 L.Ed. 881 (1941). The Bunte Brothers decision declared that only a congressional amendment could expand the scope of the Commission's powers to permit regulation of local business activity "affecting" interstate commerce. Thirty-three years later that amendment was made in the Magnuson-Moss Act. Accordingly, the Commission now has clear regulatory power over advertising reaching down to the local level and may, of course, control local advertising by Trade Regulation Rule, if necessary. In addition, as a result of a "rider" attached to the Trans-Alaskan Pipeline Act of 1973, violations of Commission rules outlawing certain trade practices can now be enjoined. See 15 U.S.C.A. § 53 (Cum.Supp. 1976).

d.   Constitutional Limitations on the Federal Trade Commission's Power to Impose Sanctions

Even before the Central Hudson case supra, it was accepted constitutional doctrine that no protection was afforded false or deceptive advertising. Nevertheless, several United States Courts of Appeal have held that the First Amendment limits the *remedies* the Federal Trade Commission can fashion to protect the public against the risks created by such advertising. And thus it is not correct to assume that the FTC (and state agencies as well) are free to wield unlimited power against fraudulent or misleading advertising. These courts, while mindful that the First Amendment does not shield false or deceptive commercial speech from governmental control, insist that the Commission's exercise of that control be no greater than necessary to protect the public.

For example, in Beneficial Corp. v. FTC, 542 F.2d 611 (3d Cir. 1976), cert. denied, 430 U.S. 983, 97 S.Ct. 1679, 52 L.Ed.2d 377 (1977), the Commission ordered a combined loan and income tax preparation company to stop using the words "Instant Tax Refund Plan" or "Instant Tax Refund Loan" in its advertising because such terms mislead the public as to the nature of the transaction by which consumers received amounts of money from the company equivalent to their prospective tax refunds (actually loan transactions with a substantial interest charge). While not questioning the correctness of the Commission's findings that Beneficial's ads were misleading, the Court refused to approve the Commission's complete ban on the use of the delineated phrases. Rather, the court permitted advertising with the inclusion of those phrases provided they were sufficiently qualified so as not to mislead the audience. The Court said, "The Commission, like any governmental agency, must start from the premise that any prior restraint is suspect, and that a remedy, even for deceptive advertising, can go no further than is necessary for the elimination of the deception." 542 F.2d at 620.

Similar rulings modifying FTC remedial orders were made in National Commission on Egg Nutrition v. FTC, 570 F.2d 157 (7th Cir. 1977), cert. denied 439 U.S. 821, 99 S.Ct. 86, 58 L.Ed.2d 113 (1978) (FTC order requiring a trade association whose advertising on the risks of egg consumption was misleading to present arguments in its future advertising in opposition to its own position disapproved); Warner–Lambert Co. v. FTC, 562 F.2d 749 (D.C.Cir. 1977), cert. denied 435 U.S.

950, 98 S.Ct. 1575, 55 L.Ed.2d 800 (1978) (FTC order requiring corrective advertising to counteract previous false claims that a mouthwash prevented or moderated the common cold modified so as to delete the prefatory phrase "Contrary to prior advertising").

2. The Federal Communications Commission

The Federal Communications Commission licenses radio and television broadcasters to operate in the "public interest, convenience and necessity." This includes broadcast advertising, but historically the FCC has relied on self-regulation by the broadcasters to avoid the specter of government censorship forbidden by Section 326 of the Federal Communications Act of 1934. Until recently there was an absence of any clear boundary between the FCC's authority over advertising through commercial broadcasting facilities and the FTC's general authority over advertising. This issue has now been resolved by agreement between the two agencies. The FCC has responsibility for assuring that commercials are neither objectionably loud nor excessive in number and that a separation is maintained between advertising and programming, especially during children's programs. Misleading or deceptive advertising on radio or television is to be controlled by the FTC.

CHAPTER IX

THE FEDERAL COMMUNICATIONS COMMISSION—WHAT IT DOES AND DOES NOT DO

One of the most important government agencies which affects the communication of information, and which has played an increasingly important role in shaping what we see and hear is the Federal Communications Commission. However, because its activities are often so technical, and because much of its work is phrased in language not susceptible to easy comprehension, there is much confusion in the public mind as to the precise role which the Commission plays in communications regulation. We will see that the Commission is more limited in its impact in certain areas, and more expansive in other areas than is generally believed by the public.

A. HISTORY OF THE FEDERAL COMMUNICATIONS COMMISSION

The existence of the Commission is, in effect, a typical American reaction to a practical and scientific problem. Government regulation of radio began in 1910 at a time when radio was perceived primarily as a safety device in maritime operations and as a potential advance in military technology. The government's primary concern was to assure itself of efficient use of this safety and defense technology, and its role was roughly analogous to that played by the police in registering automobiles. Persons desiring to use radio frequencies would register with the Department of Commerce and frequencies would be assigned to them. Pervasive regulation of the type we have come to accept as routine did not exist because there was no need.

Radio technology made quantum leaps during World War I and the commercial possibilities of radio began to be recognized by entrepreneurs. By the mid 1920's there were hundreds of radio stations operating for commercial use and frequencies were set aside by the Secretary of Commerce for commercial application. However, the powers of the Secretary to regulate such broadcasting were questionable, particularly the Secretary's power to require a radio applicant to broadcast on a particular frequency at a particular power. Two opinions, one by the courts (United States v. Zenith Radio Corp., 12 F.2d 614 (1926)) and one by the Attorney General, (35 Ops.Atty. Gen. 126 (1926)), concluded that the legislation then in force did not permit the Secretary to limit applicants in the use of power and frequencies. The Secretary could only record the applications and grant frequencies, but he did not possess the expansive powers required to regularize radio operations.

These decisions threatened to throw the emerging radio industry into chaos and led to repeated requests by the industry itself for a government agency with greater power than had been possessed by the Secretary of Commerce— an agency which could assign applicants to specific frequencies, under specific engineering rules and with the power to enforce these rules through its licensing function. These efforts culminated in the Radio Act of 1927, which established the Federal Radio Commission and which transformed licensing from a ministerial act to a judgmental one, empowering the Commission to create and enforce standards for the broadcasters' privilege of using the public's airwaves.

The Federal Radio Commission created by the Radio Act of 1927 to supervise broadcasting was, pursuant to the Communications Act of 1934, merged into what is today the Federal Communications Commission. The 1934 Act, modeled largely after the Interstate Commerce Commission Act, and embodying much of the law that had already been made by the 1927 Radio Act, remains the organic legislation which controls American commercial and educational broadcasting. The Communications Act prescribes the basic task of the Federal Communications Commission to be that of "regulating interstate and foreign commerce in communication by wire and radio so as to make available, so far as possible, to all the people of the United States a rapid, efficient, Nationwide and world-wide wire and radio communication service with adequate facilities at reasonable charges for the purpose of the national defense, for the purpose of promoting safety

[*319*]

of life and property through the use of wire and radio communication . . . " 47 U.S.C.A. § 151. The standard to which the Commission must conform in carrying out this responsibility is that of action "consistent with the public interest, convenience [and] necessity." 47 U.S.C.A. § 307. The courts have repeatedly emphasized that the standard is sufficiently broad to allow the Commission to act dynamically in areas of changing or emerging technology while, at the same time, sufficiently precise to prevent the Commission from acting in a wholly arbitrary, unreasonable or capricious manner.

B. SCOPE OF THE COMMISSION'S POWER

It is important, at the outset, to recognize that the Commission's jurisdiction and power are strictly limited in scope to that which is granted by its enabling legislation, the Communications Act of 1934. It can only act in those areas in which it is specifically empowered to act.

This limitation has numerous practical implications. There are many areas which might be considered part of the "communications realm," but with which the Commission does not treat on a primary basis. Perhaps most important, and least known, is the fact that the Commission does *not* have jurisdiction and power over the entire radio spectrum space available to the United States under international treaty. In fact, the Commission has jurisdiction of only approximately one-half of this available radio space. Section 305 of the Communications Act exempts from the Commission's power or jurisdiction all "radio stations belonging to and operated by the United States." The United States government, through its various agencies, offices and departments (military and civilian), operates a host of radio services occupying approximately one-half of the total available frequency space. This allocation of spectrum space among the various governmental branches is made through a governmental coordinating group which is now housed in the National Telecommunications and Information Administration (NTIA), a division of the Department of Commerce. The Commission coordinates with this group but exercises no jurisdiction over the government's stations. It is only that part of the spectrum allocated to non-federal government use over which the FCC exercises jurisdiction. It is instructive to recall this fact when the concept of a "scarcity" of frequency space is discussed. At least in part, the scarcity of frequency space for commercial broadcasting is man-made and its dimensions are initially defined by the Executive Office of the White House. For a fuller discussion of the problem of radio frequency allocation between governmental and non-governmental uses, see Metzger and Burrus, "Radio Frequency Allocation in the Public Interest: Federal Government and Civilian Use," 4 Duquesne L.Rev. 1 (1966).

But even when dealing with those frequencies over which the FCC clearly possesses jurisdiction, there are large areas in which it is forbidden to or has chosen, as a matter of policy, not to exercise power. Thus, for example, the Commission is not empowered by the Act to enforce or decide antitrust issues as embodied in the Clayton and Sherman Antitrust Acts; it has been explicitly forbidden to do so by the courts. United States v. Radio Corp. of America, 358 U.S. 334, 79 S.Ct. 457, 3 L.Ed.2d 354 (1959). Although the Commission may, and sometimes must take into consideration, as part of its public interest standard, economic considerations involving such matters as competition, merger, market share, and the like, it is nevertheless free to ignore the policies favoring competition underlying the Sherman and Clayton Acts if to do so would be in the public interest, convenience and necessity. Federal Communications Commission v. RCA Communications, Inc., 346 U.S. 86, 73 S.Ct. 998, 97 L.Ed. 1470 (1953).

Similarly, the Commission does not determine whether a particular advertising message is "false and misleading." That question has been delegated by law to the Federal Trade Commission. Of course, the FCC would act where a licensee continues to broadcast an advertisement which has been finally adjudicated by the FTC to be false and misleading. But the Commission regularly refuses to make the initial determination as to the nature of the advertising. See

FTC–FCC Liaison Agreement, Current Service, Pike and Fisher Radio Reg., p. 11:212 (hereafter cited as Pike and Fisher R.R.).

In addition, the FCC does not ordinarily become involved in civil or contractual litigation between broadcasters. It does not set advertising rates or oversee ordinary and usual business practices such as production charges, commission arrangements, and salaries of artists. It does not regulate rates which may be charged the public by pay television or cablevision system owners. It does not regulate closed circuit television or radio. It does not license networks. There are many other areas which might appear to fall within its power but which do not.

The reason is at once simple and complex. The American system of broadcasting is an attempt to introduce state regulation of the radio spectrum while, at the same time, allowing as much free market play as possible. The Commission sets the ground rules by which stations can be licensed. It will choose between applicants for conflicting licenses, set up a framework which attempts to insure some competition, and then allow the free market to determine, as well as possible, such matters as advertising costs, expenses, cost of equipment and, perhaps most important, choice of programming by broadcasters. The simplicity of the system breaks down at those points where free market considerations simply do not work well. A free marketplace does not automatically serve up programming for

[*323*]

minority, ethnic or cultural groups. At a number of points (many of which are discussed later), the government has chosen to intervene; more recently (as the number of media types and outlets have grown) the government has "deregulated" some areas. Much of communications law cannot be understood unless it is recognized that the basic bias of our communications system is toward allowing, where possible, the free market to determine matters. See Report and Order, Deregulation of Radio, 46 Fed.Reg. 13888 (1981).

C. STRUCTURAL ORGANIZATION OF THE FEDERAL COMMUNICATIONS COMMISSION

Having been delegated broad powers to make rules and regulations as may be necessary to carry out the provisions of its enabling legislation, the Commission faces the task first of attempting to satisfy the differing demands for communications in a modern industrial economy. Although most familiar to the public in the role of a regulator of commercial and educational broadcasting, the Commission has the equally demanding responsibility of regulating non-broadcast use of communications facilities such as interstate common carrier systems, radio systems for industrial use such as truck to truck communications, taxi cab networks, communications between central plant and repairmen or servicemen, communications between hospital and doctor, marine and ship radio, aviation frequencies, citizen band radio, international "ham" communications, police and fire communications networks, computer to computer communications, and emerging new technologies such as cable television, pay television and satellite communications. In the case of common carriers, the FCC acts as a rate making agency for interstate common carriage in a manner similar to state public utilities commissions.

The Commission itself is composed of five commissioners, appointed by the President with the advice and consent of the Senate. The President designates the chairman. Not more than three members of the Commission can be members of the same political party. Commissioners are appointed for a term of seven years on a staggered basis. See 47 U.S.C.A. § 154(a).

To meet its responsibilities, the Commission has established a number of bureaus to carry out its functions. The most important of these bureaus and a descriptions of the matters with which they deal are as follows:

1. Mass Media. This bureau handles all matters which we normally associate with commercial broadcasting, i.e., initial licensing of applicants, processing of applications for periodic renewal of licenses, inspection and supervision of stations to determine their compliance with technical and operational rules and regulations, and development of rules covering broadcasting. It also handles cable television matters and items associated with emerging television

delivery technologies. We will emphasize the work of this bureau and its review by the courts in the pages that follow.

2. Common Carrier Bureau. This bureau regulates the interstate and foreign common carrier wire and radio system (telephone, telegraph, facsimile, telephoto and satellites), and acts not only as a licensing and regulatory agency, but also as a rate making agency for interstate and foreign services. It also acts, in some respects, as a coordinating body for the various state public utilities commissions which regulate intrastate common carrier services.

3. Private Radio Bureau. This is the bureau which handles other types of radio uses not regulated by the other three. This bureau regulates such matters as industrial use, police and fire use, aviation and marine use, and citizens band radio.

D. ALLOCATION OF FREQUENCIES

The Commission handles the problem of allocation of frequencies between uses in a rather straightforward manner. Certain frequencies are specifically allocated to commercial "broadcasting uses"; other frequencies are specifically allocated to common carrier uses (i.e., telephone, telegraph and other communications services for hire); other frequencies are dedicated to uses such as industrial communication, marine and ship radio, aviation and medical services. These initial allocations are quite important, for they establish the relative "scarcity" of frequencies which, as we will see, is the basic justification for governmental action in the broadcasting realm.

E. JURIDICAL BASIS FOR COMMISSION REGULATION OF BROADCASTING

Government regulation of broadcasting is anomalous. We accept a depth and type of regulation over broadcast facilities which we do not, as a Constitutional matter, tolerate with respect to print media. The most obvious example is governmental licensing of broadcast stations. The First Amendment flatly forbids any such licensing requirement for newspapers, books or magazines. See Near v. Minnesota, 283 U.S. 697, 51 S.Ct. 625, 75 L.Ed. 1357 (1931); New York Times Co. v. United States, 403 U.S. 713, 91 S.Ct. 2140, 29 L.Ed.2d 822 (1971). Yet the licensing of radio stations has long been upheld. Federal Radio Commission v. Nelson Brothers Bond and Mortgage Co., 289 U.S. 266, 53 S.Ct. 627, 77 L.Ed. 1166 (1933). Broadcasters operate under the constraints of the Fairness Doctrine, requiring them not only to air controversial issues of public importance, but to do so in a manner allowing presentation of contrasting views. See Red Lion Broadcasting Co. v. Federal Communications Commission, 395 U.S. 367, 89 S.Ct. 1794, 23 L.Ed. 2d 371 (1969). No such requirement could constitutionally be enforced against the print media.

Moreover, "indecent" (though not obscene) material, which would be protected under the First Amendment if seen in a movie or magazine, may nevertheless be prohibited from broadcast over the air. The Supreme Court has noted that " . . . of all forms of communication, it is broadcasting that has received the most limited First Amendment protection." Federal Communications Commission v. Pacifica Foundation, 438 U.S. 726, 748, 98 S.Ct. 3026, 3040, 57 L.Ed.2d 1073, 1092 (1978).

Although the courts have justified these apparent contradictions on the ground that different media present different first amendment considerations, they do not often explain in any rigorous analytical detail how the differences in media result in constitutional distinctions; and it is even rarer for a court to test the breadth or scope of its holding against the constitutional justification for differences in regulation. For example, the United States Supreme Court in Miami Herald Publishing Co. v. Tornillo, 418 U.S. 241, 94 S.Ct. 2831, 41 L.Ed.2d 730 (1974), struck down a type of political "equal time" legislation imposed by the Florida legislature on Florida newspapers, without ever mentioning or attempting to distinguish the cases which allow precisely such regulation in the broadcast area.

The justification for broadcast regulation has been stated in terms of the "scarcity" of broadcast frequencies. The leading case discussing this point (National Broadcasting Co. v. United

States, 319 U.S. 190, 213, 63 S.Ct. 997, 1008, 87 L.Ed. 1344, 1361 (1943)) set the formulation:

> The plight into which radio fell prior to 1927 was attributable to certain basic facts about radio as a means of communication—its facilities are limited; they are not available to all who may wish to use them; the radio spectrum simply is not large enough to accommodate everybody. There is a fixed natural limitation upon the number of stations that can operate without interfering with one another. Regulation of radio was therefore as vital to its development as traffic control was to the development of the automobile.

But numerical scarcity alone does not justify regulation of other media. As has often been pointed out, there are far more broadcasting stations than daily newspapers in the United States, and it is more difficult (from an economic point of view) to start a newspaper than a radio station. By numerical standards, newspapers are "scarcer".

It is not numerical scarcity, then, that justifies the regulatory difference. Rather, broadcasting imposes a duty upon the government which it does not face in the print media—the duty of making choices as between two or more potential broadcasters wishing to utilize the same broadcast space. Two newspapers can, without governmental intervention, physically operate in the same community at the same time; their survival would depend on competitive market forces. In radio, however, if there is but one frequency available for use in a particular community, then, by the laws of physics, two stations cannot physically operate on it, for to do so would result in neither being heard. And since it has been determined to be important to the society at large that *someone* be heard, at base it is the necessity for governmental choice which distinguishes broadcasting from other types of media, and which requires governmental intervention in order that the choice be made.

Theoretical problems remain, even with the "choice" rationale. The government is not always faced with the necessity of choice. There may be only one applicant for a particular open frequency. The Commission may be considering a proposed sale from A to B so that the only question before it is B's qualifications. The case may involve merely a protest by a citizens' group that a particular broadcaster is not operating "in the public interest" because it fails to give coverage to minority points of view or fails to hire minority or women employees. There is in these cases no requirement of choice between competing applicants. Yet even here the Commission can constitutionally, and indeed does, regulate.

Perhaps the best rationale for governmental regulation is that the legal basis for Commission action is an amalgam. There is a clear public need that some form of broadcasting exist. And to some extent broadcasting must be recognized as a public resource, perhaps analogous to an interstate traffic system, or a national park system, or a national environmental policy. Technical considerations make broadcast frequencies "scarce" resources and impose an obligation on the government to (a) make choices and (b) set standards to make certain that the "resource" is not wasted or misused. The government's traditional "police power" further allows it to impose certain limitations (as, for example, to protect children from "obscene or indecent" material). All governmental regulation of broadcasting can be traced to at least one of these considerations and, although they are not present at all times, together they represent the foundation of broadcast regulation.

This foundation will not support every form of governmental action. The First Amendment places limits even upon government regulation of "scarce" resources. See Columbia Broadcasting System, Inc. v. Democratic National Committee, 412 U.S. 94, 93 S.Ct. 2080, 36 L.Ed.2d 772 (1973). And procedural and substantive due process considerations impose requirements that sometimes outweigh even considerations of necessity. The tension between the necessity for governmental regulation and the common recognition of the dangers posed by such regulation forms the matrix in which broadcast law has developed.

F.   NATURE OF THE BROADCAST RIGHT

Although there may have been other methods of insuring the existence of a nationwide communications system, as, for example, by lottery or by auctioning off frequencies to the highest bidder and granting the winner a right in perpetuity subject to defeasance for misconduct, Congress nevertheless chose to institute a licensing procedure by which broadcasters are granted a limited privilege to broadcast over a particular frequency for a fixed term.   Congress stipulated that the grant of the privilege gives the licensee no vested property interest in the frequency or any guarantee that the license will be renewed.   47 U.S.C.A. § 309(h).   Section 307(d) of the Communications Act limits the license of a radio broadcasting station to a maximum of seven years, with a requirement that the broadcaster file for renewal of that license every seven years if it wishes to continue broadcasting.   Television station licenses are granted for a period of five years, with provisions for renewal every five years (see Omnibus Budget Reconciliation Act of 1981, 95 Stat. 736–37). Licenses will be granted only if the "public convenience, interest, or necessity will be served thereby."   Section 310(b) of the Act states that no license may be transferred to any person or entity, directly or indirectly, without the prior approval of the Commission, and Section 310(a) of the Act mandates that station licenses shall be granted only to citizens and cannot be held by aliens, foreign governments, or corporations of which any officer or director is an alien or of which more than one fifth of the stock is voted by aliens or representatives of foreign governments.

These restrictions have practical implications. Although, as will be seen, a licensee who has given "meritorious service" has a "legitimate renewal expectancy," nevertheless, there is no guarantee that its license will be renewed or, indeed, that there will even be an available frequency over which to operate at the expiration of the license term. Transcontinent Television Corp. v. Federal Communications Commission, 113 U.S. App.D.C. 384, 308 F.2d 339 (1962). Nor is the Commission required to grant a license for the full five or seven year term. It may, and occasionally does, grant a license for a shorter term if it believes that action would be more appropriate or if it has doubts about the qualifications of the licensee sufficient to desire an opportunity to review its operation for an interval shorter than five or seven years. Moreover, the license, pursuant to statute, carries obligations which have been held to be constitutional. Thus, for example, the licensee must make equal time available for political candidates; it must meet the requirements of the Fairness Doctrine; it cannot broadcast material which is "obscene" or indecent; it cannot broadcast lottery information (except for state-run lotteries under certain conditions); and,

in general, it must "operate in the public interest."

On the other hand, the licensee possesses certain constitutional and statutory protections
which derive not from any "right" in the license
itself, but rather from constitutional protections
against arbitrary action of government. Thus, although a license can be revoked during its term,
the Commission can only do so after giving notice
to the licensee and a full opportunity to be heard.
47 U.S.C.A. § 312(c). Moreover, the Commission
carries the burden of proof in such a revocation
proceeding whereas in the initial licensing phase
and in the renewal phase it is the applicant who
must carry the burden of persuading the Commission that it is qualified. Similarly, the Commission cannot act arbitrarily or capriciously and
must explain its decisions through written findings (Saginaw Broadcasting Co. v. Federal Communications Commission, 68 App.D.C. 282, 96
F.2d 554 (1938)) on a public record containing full
explanation of its rationale and actions. Greater
Boston Television Corp. v. Federal Communications Commission, 143 U.S.App.D.C. 383, 444 F.2d
841 (1970). The Commission's decisions are
appealable to the United States Court of Appeals
and the court must be satisfied that the Commission has exercised its decision-making powers in
accordance with constitution and statute.

G. COMMISSION FUNCTIONS IN BROADCASTING REGULATION

Analytically, the Commission exercises three different types of functions in the regulation of broadcasting: (1) licensing, which involves the choice of licensee either initially or at renewal time; (2) operational supervision, which involves oversight as to whether a licensee is meeting the conditions of its license; and (3) planning, by which the Commission attempts to integrate new and emerging technology into the broadcast regulatory scheme. These functions will be discussed in the following chapters.

CHAPTER X

THE LICENSING POLICIES OF THE FCC

The Commission's primary statutory function is licensing. Section 301 of the Communications Act stipulates that no person shall use or operate any apparatus for radio transmission except by virtue of a license to operate granted by the Commission. Section 307(a) requires that licenses be granted to applicants only "if public convenience, interest, or necessity will be served thereby." Section 303 gives the Commission the power to classify different types of stations, to prescribe the nature of the service to be rendered by different types of stations, and to assign the bands of frequencies for each individual station. A license from the Commission is, in essence, an exclusive right to operate a station on a particular frequency at a prescribed power.

Before turning to the intricacies of the licensing process, it is instructive to consider the Commission's frequency allocations policy. The nature of that policy has a profound impact upon the type of communication system that the public possesses.

A. FREQUENCY ALLOCATION

The Commission has designated a portion of the spectrum for "broadcast" use, and has further subdivided the broadcast "band" into distinct portions. One set of frequencies is set aside for standard (or AM) broadcast stations, another group for frequency modulation (FM) stations, and a third for use by television stations. But the manner in which it chooses to assign specific frequencies within these groupings is not the same.

1. AM Allocation

The Commission immediately confronts a fact of physics: because of electrical interference considerations, the number of individual broadcast stations which can operate in a particular bandwidth varies inversely with their power. The higher the power, the smaller the number of stations which can be accommodated. The Commission could have chosen an allocations policy which would have led to a small number of very powerful stations, each being given the task of covering very large distances. This system was rejected on the ground, inter alia, that the nation should have a large rather than a small number of individual voices. Conversely, the Commission could have allowed a very large number of stations, giving each low power. The difficulty here was that the coverage area of such stations might be so small as to preclude financial viabili-

[*337*]

ty. Instead, the Commission opted for a compromise. The present AM allocation policy allows three classes of stations:

(a) The so-called "clear channel" stations, approximately 25 in number, which operate at 50 kilowatts (the highest permissible power for any commercial AM station), and which cover a radius of approximately 80 to 90 miles during daytime hours and which (because of a scientific phenomenon) can be heard during the night at distances which sometimes reach 500 or 600 miles. These few "clear channel" stations are heavily protected from interference by other stations;

(b) Lower power, so-called "regional" stations which operate at a power usually of 5 or 10 kw and which cover a radius of approximately 25 or 30 miles (depending on the terrain); and

(c) So-called "local" stations which operate at a power no greater than 1 kw, cover an area of approximately 8 to 10 miles in radius, and many of which (because of interference considerations) are allowed to operate only during daytime hours. By far the majority of the approximately 4,600 standard broadcast stations in the United States are local stations which operate on a so-called "local" frequency.

See 47 C.F.R. §§ 73.21–73.29 and Regulations of the Commission for a full exposition of the AM broadcast allocations rules.

The second characteristic of the AM allocation system is that, unlike FM or TV, it operates on a "demand" basis. To illustrate, the Commission could have taken all of the available frequencies in the AM band and allocated specific frequencies to specific communities. Thus, New York City, for example, could have been allocated 5 clear channel stations, 6 regional stations and 13 local stations. Chicago could have been allocated a different number of specific classes of stations, Des Moines, Iowa yet a third, and so on throughout all communities in the United States. This type of specific allocation by city has the advantage of ensuring that significant cities have a certain number of broadcast stations, and it also has the virtue of reserving frequencies for future use in areas which are now relatively sparse in population, but which later might become more heavily populated.

Instead, in AM the Commission used an allocation policy which, in effect, allowed maximum scope for a "market type" of demand and which operated with a lesser degree of governmental planning involvement. The Commission first established engineering ground rules stipulating certain power requirements, and also stipulating the amount of allowable interference which a proposed station could cause or accept. Within these ground rules, applicants were entitled to apply for any of the various classes of stations in any community. It was believed (and proved to be the case) that the larger population centers, being able to support the larger number of stations, would attract the largest number of applicants. The Commission desired to put as few restrictions as possible on the number of applicants so that the benefit of radio communication could be realized throughout the country as quickly as applicants could design proposed facilities which would fit within the Commission's overall engineering guidelines.

The "demand" system still governs the allocation of AM stations, although the engineering ground rules have become so stringent that it is virtually impossible to design a new AM station which will fit within them. As a practical matter, the number of AM stations has not significantly increased in the past decade, and (absent a radical policy change) is not likely to do so in the future.

2. Television Allocation

Although the technology of television was virtually fully developed by 1934, a number of factors (including WW II) delayed its entry into the marketplace until the late 1940's. By that time the Commission had considerable experience with the "demand" allocation system and had identified certain shortcomings in it, particularly the fact that it engendered a great deal of complicated, lengthy and difficult litigation. It tended to favor the more populated areas over the less populated, since every time a station is granted to a larger community, by necessity it might preclude use of that frequency in smaller communities which had not as yet stimulated entrepreneurs to view them as places for radio stations. The demand system was essentially an "unplanned" one whereby future growth might not adequately be considered.

The Commission therefore discarded the demand system in television and turned towards a simplified, more specific allocation policy which assigned specific frequencies to specific communities. There are no different *classes* of television stations. All television stations are either on VHF or UHF frequencies. They can all operate day and night, and all have the same maximum power limitations (though, for technical reasons, the power limitations of VHF stations as a group are somewhat different than those of UHF).

Each city only has available to it those specific frequencies which the Commission has chosen to assign. Those allocations are part of the Commission's rules, and any change in them requires a formal request for the Commission to institute a rule making proceeding in accordance with the Administrative Procedure Act. Moreover, certain frequencies are reserved for use only by non-commercial stations, and some of these frequencies, even now, lie fallow, an example of the Commission allowing for future growth. Because there are no interference "ground rules" for television, there is much less engineering litigation in television cases, and there is no need for the Commission to compare in the hearing process (as it does in AM) the relative needs of communities for a particular frequency which is sought by competing applicants. The needs of the various communities have already been evaluated in the rule making process by which the frequencies were assigned.

3. FM Allocation

FM allocation, though originally on a "demand" basis, is now handled in the same manner as television allocation. Specific frequencies are assigned to specific cities according to a table of allocations, which can be changed only through the institution of a formal rule making proceeding. The only essential difference is that in FM there are two classes of stations, higher powered ones (which can operate up to 50 kw) and lower powered ones (which are limited to 3 kw). There are also channels reserved strictly for educational use.

B. THE SHOWING AN APPLICANT MUST MAKE—BASIC QUALIFICATIONS

Having found a frequency which can be used in accordance with the Commission's rules, what type of showing must be made by the applicant in order to convince the Commission that the public interest requires a grant of the license?

We must here make a distinction between so-called "basic" qualifications and "comparative" qualifications. The Commission is not always faced with the necessity of choosing between particular applicants; there may be only one applicant for the particular frequency. But whether or not a choice is required, there are certain qualifications which *all* applicants must meet, some specifically required by the Communications Act itself, and others having been set by the Commission under its policy making authority to determine requirements in the public interest. We will first discuss so-called "basic" qualifications.

1. Citizenship

Section 310 of the Act mandates that a license may not be held by a non-citizen, a foreign government, a foreign corporation, or any corporation of which any officer or director is an alien or of which more than one fifth of the capital stock is owned by non-citizens. The above restrictions are mandatory. They cannot be waived by the Commission and can be changed only by Congress. Other provisions of Section 310 specifically allow licenses to be held by foreign pilots, ships and radio ham operators under certain circumstances.

2. Character

By statute (Section 308(b) of the Act), the Commission must evaluate the applicant to determine whether it possesses the requisite "character" qualifications. But neither the Act nor the Commission's rules spell out the requirements

[*343*]

which constitute "good character" or those which will be deemed "bad character". "Bad character" traits could be as extensive as human experience. The Commission primarily concerns itself with the type of bad character traits which would raise questions as to the honesty of the applicant, its potential performance as a broadcaster, or its proclivity towards violating governmental regulations.

Honesty and candor are essential because the Commission could not function effectively if its licensees were dishonest. The Commission possesses neither the staff nor the budget to check independently every licensee representation. The information with which it deals is almost always information given to it by its licensees; it relies upon their veracity to do its work. Therefore, a licensee or an applicant who has been found to have knowingly misrepresented a fact to the Commission is in serious danger of having its license application denied, even if the misrepresentation is in an area of little significance. The significance of the misrepresentation is far less important than the fact that the misrepresentation occurred. Federal Communications Commission v. WOKO, Inc., 329 U.S. 223, 67 S.Ct. 213, 91 L.Ed. 204 (1946). Where misrepresentation occurs, the Commission need not even take into consideration other positive qualities which the applicant can demonstrate, such as a meritorious past programming service. Immaculate Conception Church v. Federal Communications Commission,

116 U.S.App.D.C. 73, 320 F.2d 795 (1963). A review of the cases where the Commission either denied an initial application or denied renewal of an existing license indicates that, by far, the greatest percentage of denials occurred where the Commission found knowing misrepresentation to have occurred.

Violations of criminal law also raise the risk of denial of an application on character grounds, although here the Commission has adopted a more flexible attitude. Felonious violation of criminal law involving moral turpitude (such as murder, robbery, rape, etc.) almost certainly would result in denial. But disqualification is not automatic. There have been instances of serious violations which have not resulted in outright denial such as, for example, a conviction for gun running to Israel in 1950, a felony. Las Vegas Television, Inc., 14 Pike and Fisher R.R. 1273 (1957). The Commission is likely to be forgiving if the crime occurred years ago and involved a law which had been routinely disregarded, for example, operating a speakeasy during Prohibition at a time and place where such operation was not uncommon. See WGCM Broadcasting Co., 3 Pike and Fisher R.R. 1138 (1947). The Commission attempts to take note of the nature of the felony and its relevance in determining whether or not a particular applicant could be expected to show the proper solicitude for the Commission's Rules and Regulations. The Commission ordinarily will ignore common misdemeanors, traffic violations, and the like. L. B. Wilson, Inc., 3 Pike and Fisher R.R.2d 61 (1964).

Somewhat related are violations of regulatory statutes. An applicant convicted of having repeatedly violated federal regulatory laws in his non-communications related business, has had his application denied on basic character grounds (Bulova and Henshel, 11 F.C.C. 137 (1946), affirmed sub nom. Mester v. United States, 70 F.Supp. 118 (E.D.N.Y.), 332 U.S. 749, 68 S.Ct. 70, 92 L.Ed. 336 (1947), because the nature of the violation showed a knowing disdain for governmental regulations. But an unintentional violation of the Food, Drug, and Cosmetic Act did not result in denial in another case. Brown Radio & Television Co., 5 Pike and Fisher R.R.2d 288 (1965).

Nor are criminal violations of the Federal antitrust laws necessarily grounds for disqualification. A number of nationwide companies (among them General Electric and Westinghouse) were found to have violated the Sherman Act through price fixing in their non-communications related businesses. In considering whether to take away their broadcast licenses, the Commission found that the communications sections of these companies were separate from the other areas, were not handled by any of the persons involved in the price fixing, and were characterized by a history of meritorious programming and pioneering broadcast efforts. Weighing these factors (which, as noted above, it is not required to do in misrepresentation cases) led the Commission to renew the licenses. Westinghouse Broadcasting Co., Inc., 22 Pike and Fisher R.R. 1023 (1962); General Electric Co., 2 Pike and Fisher R.R.2d 1038 (1964).

On the other hand, violations of the Sherman Act by a newspaper which engaged in predatory competitive tactics, and with no past broadcasting history against which to weigh them, could be grounds for refusal (see, e.g., Mansfield Journal Co. v. Federal Communication Commission, 86 U.S.App.D.C. 102, 180 F.2d 28 (1950)). Although the Commission does not enforce the antitrust laws, it will consider adjudicated violations of those acts as relevant to a character determination, and in at least one case (Wometco Enterprises, Inc., 22 Pike and Fisher R.R.2d 89 (1971)), it has itself acted as trier of fact in determining whether an antitrust violation occurred. Ordinarily, however, the Commission will not adjudicate non-broadcast controversies which are the subject of other court proceedings. In such cases the Commission will generally grant the application conditioned upon the outcome of the adjudication in the courts. See, e.g., RKO General, Inc., 15 Pike and Fisher R.R.2d 943 (1969).

One final point should be emphasized. We have discussed character defects as they relate to basic qualifications, i.e., those qualifications which must exist regardless of whether a choice must be made between applicants. But even if a past transgression does not rise to the level of a basic disqualification, nevertheless it still may be significant in a comparative sense. When faced with a choice between an applicant against whom no character question is raised and one who has in the past violated a law, but not in a manner which absolutely disqualifies it, the Commission is most likely, all other things being equal, to choose the non-lawbreaker. Thus, character qualifications can be considered both as basic and comparative in nature.

3. Financial Qualifications

The Communications Act and the Commission's policies require that an applicant demonstrate its financial capability to construct and operate its proposed facility. The theory behind this requirement is that a "scarce" public resource should not be wasted in the hands of an operator which does not have the financial capability to run it. Thus, the Commission has established a minimum standard which applicants must meet. Applicants for new stations (AM, FM or television) must demonstrate financial capability to construct and operate the station for 90 days, even assuming that the station earns no revenue. Financial Qualifications, 43 Pike and Fisher R.R.2d 1101 (1978); 45 Pike and Fisher R.R.2d 925 (1979). If the applicant must rely upon anticipated revenues, then it is obligated to file evidence that these revenues will, in fact, be earned such as, for example, affidavits from prospective advertisers indicating a willingness and desire to advertise over the facility. Swanee Broadcasting

Co., 7 Pike and Fisher R.R.2d 405 (1966). In certain cases as, for example, when payments to equipment suppliers or lending institutions will be deferred, the Commission may require a showing of financial capability even beyond the 90-day period. See Sampson Broadcasting Co., Inc., 33 Pike and Fisher R.R.2d 923 (1975).

A similar policy applies to the purchase of a broadcast station. Purchasers must have sufficient capital to consummate the transaction and to meet expenses for a three month period. See Financial Qualifications, 49 Pike and Fisher R.R.2d 1291 (1981). The Commission's concern in this area rests primarily with those stations which are being sold because they are already in financial difficulty. Here the Commission will require proof that the purchaser has the financial capability to overcome the seller's deficits.

Significantly, financial qualifications are *not* considered on a comparative basis. The fact that one applicant may have more finances available than a competing applicant will not result in a preference for the former, because to do so would reward wealth alone, a result which the Commission does not desire. Scripps-Howard Radio, Inc. v. Federal Communications Commission, 89 U.S. App.D.C. 13, 189 F.2d 677 (1951). Every applicant need only show sufficient capital to meet minimum qualifications. Once it has done so, additional financial capability per se is ignored.

4. Technical Showing

All applicants, of course, must demonstrate that they will meet all of the technical requirements set forth in the Commission's rules such as, for example, utilizing transmitting equipment which has been appropriately "type approved" by the Commission, proposing to operate within the height and power limitations for the various classes of stations, operating during the hours appropriate for the frequency sought and causing or receiving no more than the allowed amount of interference. This showing of technical qualifications, moreover, has extremely important procedural ramifications because although normally the Commission cannot deny an application without giving the applicant a hearing, the Commission may, under certain circumstances, properly refuse even to consider an application if it fails to meet certain technical requirements. As a matter of practice, an application is not "filed" with the Commission; it is only "tendered" for filing and must first be "accepted" for filing even before the processing stage is reached. If an application, on its face, patently fails to meet certain technical minimum requirements, it will not even be "accepted" for filing, much less processed. For example, as noted above, in AM radio the Commission has established a set of engineering "ground rules" which every applicant must meet. In FM and television allocations, the Commission has allocated specific frequencies to specific cities. If an AM application fails to meet the ground rules, or if an FM or TV applicant specifies a frequency other than one already assigned to the particular community involved, the Commission will not accept these applications for filing. United States v. Storer Broadcasting Co., 351 U.S. 192, 76 S.Ct. 763, 100 L.Ed. 1081 (1956); Ranger v. Federal Communications Commission, 111 U.S.App.D.C. 44, 294 F.2d 240 (1961).

But the courts have ruled that the Commission cannot refuse to accept an application failing to meet minimum technical requirements where the applicant makes a strong prima facie showing in the application that because of its particular situation, the requirements should not be applied. See Storer Broadcasting Co., supra. Thus, for example, where the Commission's rules did not permit AM applications for nighttime operation of local stations on "clear channels," an applicant which sought such operation argued that its application should be considered because it was a unique "good music" station which would directionalize its antenna to protect the clear channel station. The Commission's refusal even to accept the application for filing was reversed by the Court of Appeals on the grounds that the applicant had at least made a prima facie showing that the rule should be waived in its case, and the Commission was required to give the application "reflective consideration." WAIT Radio v. Federal Communications Commission, 135 U.S.App. D.C. 317, 418 F.2d 1153 (1969). But such a holding is unusual. Absent special circumstances, an application which does not meet fundamental technical standards need not be processed through the hearing phase.

5. Diversity of Media Ownership

One premise upon which the First Amendment is based is the existence of a flourishing marketplace of ideas, with truth emerging not from governmental regulation but, rather, from the clash of many voices. Associated Press v. United States, 326 U.S. 1, 65 S.Ct. 1416, 89 L.Ed. 2013 (1945). Where no government regulation is constitutionally permitted, the economic marketplace determines the number of voices to be heard; the government's role is limited to ensuring (through appropriate antitrust involvement and legislation) that the economic model succeeds. Where, as in broadcasting, government regulation is allowed, and where inherently it creates market monopolies, the question arises as to in what manner the Commission should act to ensure hoped-for multiplicity and diversity.

The Commission has attempted to respond to the problem by enacting so-called "multiple ownership rules" which restrict persons or entities from acquiring excessive power through ownership of radio and television facilities. Congress (or the Commission) might, of course, have attempted to limit each applicant to only one radio facility, either AM, FM or television, so that no one could own more than one station anywhere in the United States; neither has chosen to do so.

Conversely, the absence of any limitation posed the threat that radio economics might well follow the path of newspaper economics whereby a relatively small number of entities control a large number of daily newspapers throughout the country, and sometimes control all of the daily newspapers in a particular community. The Commission's multiple ownership rules attempt to strike a balance between these extremes, allowing multiple ownership of commercial media by a single entity in certain instances, and forbidding it in others. Non-commercial stations are exempt from the operation of these rules. The multiple ownership rules operate in much the same way as its technical rules. If an applicant attempts to apply for more radio facilities than the rules allow, its application will not be accepted for filing, again excepting special circumstances requiring waiver.

There are basically three types of multiple ownership rules: (a) those forbidding multiple ownership of facilities in the same community or area; (b) those limiting ownership of broadcast facilities by single entities no matter where located; and (c) those forbidding newspapers from owning television stations in the same community in which they publish. These rules operate as follows:

(1) Ownership in a single community. The Commission's present multiple ownership rules (47 C.F.R. §§ 73.35 (AM), 73.240 (FM), and 73.636 (TV)) forbid a single entity from

[*353*]

owning more than one station in the *same* service in the same community, or even in nearby communities if their signals would overlap to a proscribed degree. Thus, no single entity could own two AM stations or two FM stations, or two television stations in the same community, the only exception being if the stations are non-commercial. The reasons are obvious. The Commission desires as much competition as possible, at least among stations in the same service area, and will act to stimulate that competition even to the extent of disallowing cross interests of any type, be they directorships, officerships, or ownership even of minority shareholdings.

But what about commercial ownership of stations in *different* services in the same community? Here the matter becomes more complex. It is not prohibited for a single entity to possess an AM and an FM station in the same community. It is prohibited, however, for a single owner to have both an AM and a television station in the same community, or in nearby communities if their signals overlap to a proscribed degree. Moreover, it is forbidden for a single entity to own a TV and an FM station in the same community or in nearby communities if their contours improperly overlap. The rules also prohibit common ownership of a broadcast station and a cable television system which lies within the station's local service area. 47 C.F.R. § 76.501 (1981). The reader recognizes, of course, that there exist today a number of instances where a single entity owns an AM, FM and television station in the same community in apparent violation of the rules. The explanation is that these combinations grew up prior to the passage of the present multiple ownership rules, and were "grandfathered" so that divestiture was not required. However, these rules will not be waived for these "grandfathered" stations in case of a future sale, so that, in practical effect, combinations in contravention of the now existing multiple ownership rules cannot be sold as a package, absent a waiver of the rules.

(2) The second aspect of the multiple owner-ship rules is an absolute limit on the num-ber of commercial AM, FM or television stations which a single entity can own, no matter where located. A single entity can own no more than seven AM, seven FM and seven television stations anywhere in the United States—a total of 21 stations. And, with respect to television, only five of those seven stations may be VHF televi-sion stations. Ownership of more than the maximum is considered, on its face, to be inconsistent with the public interest and an application therefor will not be accepted for filing. In counting the number of per-missible stations, the Commission will in-

clude in the total any station in which the same person is an officer, director or voting shareholder. If the corporation has more than 50 shareholders, then the Commission will consider, for purposes of the rules, only stockholders who are either officers, directors, or own more than one percent of the voting stock. If the stockholder is a mutual fund, it is considered only if it holds more than three percent of the stock of the company or if its representatives are officers or directors of the company.

For example, if A is a director of three AM stations in different cities, a five percent stockholder in three other AM stations in three other cities, and an officer in a seventh AM station in a seventh city, none of these seven licensees can apply for another AM station, no matter where located, because to do so would allow common ownership of a number of stations in excess of those allowed. This "cumulative effect" can cause quite complex problems which cannot be adequately covered in this work. The reader is referred to 47 C.F.R. §§ 73.35, 73.240 and 73.636 for a more detailed exposition. The key point to remember, however, is that there is an absolute limit to the number of commercial broadcast facilities which can be held under common ownership.

(3) A third aspect of the rules is the prohibition of so-called "regional concentration." The rules prohibit common ownership, operation or control of three broadcast stations where any two are within 100 miles of the third if there is primary service contour overlap of any of the stations. Commonly owned AM and FM stations licensed to communities within 15 miles of each other are treated as one station for purposes of these rule.

(4) Broadcasting/Newspaper Combinations. Until 1975, there was no prohibition against ownership of a broadcast station by a newspaper in the same community. Although the Commission acknowledged as early as 1944 that such ownership might lead, at least in certain circumstances, to a monopoly both in the economic and the informational senses, nevertheless, it was not persuaded that the feared results were inevitable nor that the problem could not be handled in ways other than outright prohibition. In 1975, though still finding no specific evidence of monopoly abuse, the Commission nevertheless concluded on policy grounds that the public interest would be best served, and the twin goals of economic competition and competition in the marketplace of ideas furthered, if fu-

ture newspaper-broadcasting combinations were prohibited by rule. Therefore, it prohibited the ownership of either AM, FM, or TV stations by daily newspapers in communities over which the AM, FM or TV stations place a signal of a particular strength. See Second Report and Order, Docket No. 18110, 50 F.C.C.2d 1046 (1975). Existing combinations were almost all grandfathered with the proviso that they could not be sold as a unit to a third party. In 16 instances, the Commission actually ordered divestiture by newspaper-broadcaster owners. These were instances where the newspapers and radio stations represented the only media of their kind in the particular community, thus constituting an effective monopoly. See FCC v. National Citizens Committee for Broadcasting, et al., 436 U.S. 775, 98 S.Ct. 2096, 56 L.Ed.2d 697 (1978).

The above discussion relates to the showing which must be made to meet basic qualifications, i.e., they represent multiple ownership standards which must be met even to have an application considered by the Commission. But, as was the case with character qualifications, the Commission also considers multiple ownership characteristics on a comparative basis. Thus, if applicant A for an FM license already holds an AM license for the same community, and applicant B holds no other broadcast interests, applicant B will, all other things being equal, be preferred. Applicant B may be preferred even if in another area of comparison, for example past broadcast experience, A would be found slightly superior. Industrial Business, 30 Pike and Fisher R.R.2d 1123 (1974). The fact that A's application complies with the multiple ownership rules allows A to be considered. It does not foreclose the issue if a choice must be made.

6. Community Ascertainment Studies

The Commission has evolved a policy requiring broadcasters to demonstrate, a familiarity with the community to be served, and particularly a familiarity with the needs and problems of that community. Although the broadcaster has by statute (47 U.S.C.A. § 326) discretion to choose the programming it wishes to present, it nevertheless must do so in light of the particular problems and needs of its community if it is to operate "in the public interest."

Although the Commission had erected a highly formularized ascertainment process which at one time applied to all types of broadcasting stations, its recent "deregulation" thrust has drawn a distinction between radio and television broadcasting. Radio broadcasters (AM or FM) are no longer required to follow formal and specific ascertainment procedures. The radio broadcaster has discretion to utilize whatever ascertainment methodology seems appropriate. There are no specific interview procedures which must be followed. The only paperwork required is a listing in the station's public file of the five to ten public issues which the broadcaster believes to be most pressing, and a brief description of the programs broadcast to meet these needs. For radio broadcasters, the manner of ascertainment of public issues is neither a basic nor a comparative criterion. Persons dissatisfied with a station's performance have the burden of demonstrating, at renewal time, the manner in which the station has failed its programming obligations.

Television broadcasters, on the other hand, are still required to follow a highly formal interview-survey process, which is outlined in detail in two Primers—a Primer to be used by applicants for new or improved facilities (27 F.C.C.2d 650 (1971)) and a Primer covering ascertainment studies by applicants for renewal of license, 57 F.C.C.2d 418 (1976). Although these Primers differ somewhat, the essential requirement of both is that the applicant undertake two separate interview studies: (a) a series of interviews with community leaders representing a diverse cross section of the community; and (b) a survey of the general public undertaken on a random sampling basis.

The community leader survey must be undertaken by the applicant's senior staff, although 50% of the inquiries can be undertaken by lower level employees, provided that they report their findings to a senior official. It is essential that the community leaders represent a cross section;

[*360*]

representatives of the poor, minority groups, youth, ethnic groups, and even loosely organized elements of the population should be represented.

The general public survey must be carried out on a random sample basis, following procedures designed to develop a statistically valid cross section of the general population. As a check, the Commission will consult the demographic breakdown of the community as represented in the decennial census.

The surveys are not (indeed they are forbidden to be) merely program preference surveys. The applicant's purpose is not to determine the programming desires of the interviewees, but rather to ask them what, in their opinion, are the most pressing "problems and needs of the community." What the Commission seeks is an indication that, in the non-entertainment area, the applicant has made an attempt to devise programs to meet the needs as discerned in the surveys. Television broadcast stations, for example, are also required to place in their public files a list of the five to ten most pressing needs in the community, and a description of the programs broadcast to meet those needs.

Significantly, although the ascertainment process remains as a basic qualification for television applicants, it no longer will be used as a basis for comparative evaluation between two television applicants. See Second Report and Order, Docket 79–137, 50 Pike and Fisher R.R.2d 381 (1981).

7. Programming

Contrary to a widely held misconception, the Commission has never established official minimum norms or requirements for any programming category. There is, for example, no requirement that a station broadcast a specific minimum percentage of "public affairs" programs, or "news." Station licenses (usually FM) have been granted even though the applicant proposed no public affairs or news programming. Although frequently asked to set minimum norms, the Commission has never done so, primarily on First Amendment grounds. Section 326 of the Act forbids the Commission to act as a "censor." Setting up required minimums would, in the Commission's view, be tantamount to censorship. See Hubbard Broadcasting, Inc., 48 F.C.C.2d 517 (1974); Report and Order, 66 F.C.C.2d 419, 428–29 (1977); National Black Media Coalition v. FCC, 589 F.2d 578, 581 (D.C.Cir. 1978).

Despite the absence of specific programming minimums, the Commission had evolved a series of unofficial "guidelines" which, prior to 1981, were used as application processing criteria. The industry was made aware of those program proposals which the Commission granted as a matter of routine (i.e. by staff action alone, without the necessity of action by the Commissioners), and those which were at least delayed in processing while the Commission requests additional information from the applicant to determine why it believes the particular proposal would serve "the public interest." The Commission's staff used a rule of thumb to separate the unquestionably acceptable from the troublesome, and that rule of thumb became the standard which most applicants for renewal of license in fact used.

As part of its "deregulation" effort, the Commission in 1981 abandoned use of the "programming guidelines" for radio stations (AM or FM). Programming for radio stations is now regulated essentially by the marketplace, subject to the right of listeners to attack a station's performance at renewal time. This policy is grounded upon a belief that there are a sufficient number of broadcast stations to insure a broad range of radio coverage which will cover minority as well as majority taste. See Deregulation of Radio, 46 Fed.Reg.13888 (1981). The only programming information required from radio applicants for new stations or for the transfer of existing stations is a short narrative description of the proposed programming. Applicants for renewal of license need not file programming information, unless there is contemplated a substantial change in the programming as originally proposed.

Programming "guidelines" still exist for commercial television stations (except UHF stations not affiliated with major networks). For VHF and UHF network affiliated stations, the Commission uses the following guideline: routine approval is limited to those which show 5% or more local programming and 5% or more "informational programming" (i.e., news plus public affairs) during the hours of 6:00 a. m. to midnight. See FCC Report No. 14173, issued May 12, 1976, revising 47 C.F.R. § 0.281(a)(8)(i) of the Rules.

Nor has the Commission ever enacted a formal limitation on the amount or type of commercial time which can be broadcast in a program hour. Here again, however, a rule of thumb had developed whereby stations whose commercial proposals meet a particular norm will pass muster unquestioned, whereas those exceeding that norm must explain further. These norms were originally derived from standards self-imposed by the National Association of Broadcasters. The norms for radio were deleted in 1981 as part of the deregulation effort. Guidelines still exist, however, for commercial television stations. Generally speaking, if television stations propose to exceed 16 minutes of commercial matter per hour, the application cannot be routinely granted. (See 47 C.F.R. § 0.281(a)(7)(i)(1981)). But the 16 minutes standard, self-imposed by the National Association of Broadcasters, was attacked by the Justice Department as a violation of the anti-trust laws and has been voluntarily withdrawn by the Association in settlement of the antitrust action. See United States v. National Association of Broadcasters, 536 F.Supp. 149 (D.D.C.1982).

Commercial television advertising during children's programs has been a source of Commission concern. The Commission has refused, even here, to adopt specific limitations on commercial advertising, although repeatedly requested to do so. Nevertheless, the Commission has emphasized the need for industry self-regulation in this field, and the National Association of Broadcasters has imposed some norms upon its members with respect to children's programs. See *Action for Children's Television v. FCC,* 564 F.2d 458, 464 (D.C. Cir. 1977). Such programs should contain no more than 9 minutes and thirty seconds per hour of commercial matter on weekends and 12 minutes during the week.

8. Equal Employment Showing

Since 1969 the Commission has required all applicants to adopt and file an affirmative action equal opportunity program to ensure non-discrimination against minority groups such as Blacks, Chicanos, American Indians, Spanish surnamed and women. See 47 C.F.R. §§ 73.125, 73.301, 73.599, 73.680 and 73.793. In essence, this program obligates the applicant to take specific and affirmative action in recruiting, advancement, and training to ensure equality of opportunity. The program must be positive in terms of recruitment and training; merely refraining from overt discrimination is insufficient. The representations in the application then become the standard against which the applicant's performance is tested. *Report and Order,* 18 F.C.C.2d 240 (1969). There are stringent reporting requirements imposed upon stations whose programs appear to be

in less than full compliance with the Rules. Bob
Jones University, Inc., 42 F.C.C.2d 522 (1973).

The Commission has not, as of the date of this
writing, adopted a required system of quotas,
goals and time tables with respect to hiring and
advancement. There is no requirement, for example, that a station's minority employment be
specifically consistent with the percentage of minority or female population in the particular community. There is no case in which the Commission has denied an application because of
imbalance in the work force. But the Court of
Appeals has indicated the possibility that a renewal application might be denied where the licensee indicates the percentage of minority or female employment to be "outside the zone of
reasonableness" when compared with the
demographics of the community as a whole.
Stone v. Federal Communications Commission,
151 U.S.App.D.C. 145, 466 F.2d 316, rehearing denied, 466 F.2d 331 (1972). It has also indicated
that this "zone of reasonableness" is not a constant and may change over time—what is reasonable for a station merely beginning its affirmative action program might not be reasonable
three years later. The Commission has further
held that although it did not impose any goals or
quotas, applicants were required to take affirmative action to insure that its pool of prospective
employees generally reflected the demographics
of the work force in the area. Notice of Inquiry,
July 16, 1975, Docket No. 20550, 40 Fed.Reg.

31625 (1975). Here again, the Commission utilizes a series of "guidelines" in determining whether a station's employment profiles merit routine approval of their renewal applications. Under current guidelines, stations employing from five to ten employees must have a profile for ethnic and racial employment in lower paying jobs that reflects, in percentage terms, at least fifty percent of the racial and ethnic mix in the local employment market generally. In the top four job categories (i.e., officers and managers, professionals, technicians and sales persons), the personnel profile must reflect twenty-five percent or more of the local employment mix. Stations with more than ten employees must reach the fifty percent figure for overall employment and for the top four job categories as well. Stations with 50 or more employees receive a complete review of their equal employment programs regardless of their employment profile. The Commission continually monitors equal employment opportunity performance by requiring stations with five or more full-time employees to file yearly employment profiles. See FCC Public Notice, EEO Processing Guidelines, 45 Fed.Reg. 16335 (March 3, 1980).

C.   PROCESSING THE APPLICATION

Section 307 of the Act states that the Commission "shall grant to any applicant therefor" a license if the public convenience, interest or necessity will be served thereby. Sections 307(a) and

309(d)(2) of the Act indicate that the Commission may grant an application making the proper showing without evidentiary hearing, but Section 309(e) states that if (a) a substantial and material question of fact is presented or (b) the Commission "for any reason" is unable to make a finding that the grant would be in the public interest, then the application must be designated for "full hearing" with the "burden of proof" upon the applicant. The key with respect to factual disputes is that they must be material and substantial. Factual ambiguity which would not be significant even if resolved does not require hearing. See Stone v. Federal Communications Commission, 151 U.S.App.D.C. 145, 466 F.2d 316 (1972). The importance of the second condition is that the Commission may be required to hold a hearing even if there are no factual disputes, if there are policy or public interest questions which can only be resolved after public evidentiary hearing. See Citizens Committee to save WEFM v. Federal Communications Commission, 165 U.S.App.D.C. 185, 506 F.2d 246 (D.C.Cir. 1973); Citizens Committee to Preserve Voice of the Arts in Atlanta v. Federal Communications Commission, 141 U.S. App.D.C. 109, 436 F.2d 263 (D.C.Cir. 1970).

D. PARTICIPATION BY NON–APPLICANTS IN THE PROCESSING OF APPLICATIONS

The broadcast application process is not merely a duet between the Commission and the applicant. Other participants may have a significant role in the process, even if they are not themselves applicants. Generally, these non-applicant participants are either (1) other broadcast stations which may be affected by a grant of the application, or (2) representatives of the public who may be affected.

1. Participation by Other Broadcast Stations

There are essentially two reasons why another broadcast station might be allowed to intervene in the application process:

(a) because a grant would itself act as a "modification" of the intervening station's license, thus requiring a hearing by statute; or

(b) because the intervening station might be a party economically "adversely aggrieved or affected" by a grant, thus being accorded intervenor's status.

An example of the first would exist where the grant of the application to station A would cause objectionable electrical interference (as defined in the FCC Rules) within the normally protected contours of station B. All AM stations have an area in which they are protected from interference by the Commission's engineering rules. The normally protected contours of station B as defined in the rules at the time of the grant to B become part of B's license. Because Section 316(a) of the Act forbids a "modification" of B's

[*369*]

license without a "public hearing," B is entitled to protest the grant to A and to be accorded a hearing on its protest. It should be noted, however, that the "modification" would occur only if the grant becomes effective during B's three-year license term.

Aside from a Section 316 modification, however, an existing station might also intervene in Commission proceedings if it can demonstrate that grant of a pending application would have an adverse economic effect on it. The Supreme Court has held that the regulatory system has been established so as to allow other broadcasters to act as "private attorneys general," bringing to the Commission's attention shortcomings in applications by other applicants. Naturally, such action would not be altruistic, but would be spurred by potential economic injury to the intervening station. Because such intervention might bring to the Commission's attention matters which it otherwise might miss, such intervention is allowed, so long as the prima facie fact of adverse economic impact is demonstrated. Importantly, however, the intervening station cannot urge economic injury to itself as a ground upon which to deny the pending application. The Commission is not required to shield stations from competition. The economic injury to the station only acts to allow it entry into the proceeding. Once in the proceeding, however, it must base its objection on public, not private, interest factors. See Federal Communications Commission v.

Sanders Bros. Radio Station, 309 U.S. 470, 60
S.Ct. 693, 84 L.Ed. 869 (1940).

2. Participation by the Public

Until the landmark decision by the United
States Court of Appeals for the District of Columbia in Office of Communications of the United
Church of Christ v. Federal Communications
Commission, 123 U.S.App.D.C. 328, 359 F.2d 994
(1966), the public played virtually no part in the
licensing process. Standing to participate in that
process was limited to persons who were "parties
in interest," a classification limited by Commission practice and interpretation to other stations
complaining of electrical interference or to those
persons or stations claiming specific adverse economic injury. These were the only groups which
the Commission recognized as being parties aggrieved. The interests of the listening public at
large were to be represented by the Commission
itself, which, by statute, was required to act only
in the public interest.

United Church of Christ acted to open up the
Commission's forum to public participation. Rejecting the notion that only economic injury or
electrical interference conferred participatory
rights and recognizing that the Commission may
not always be able to reflect public sentiment as
well as those persons actually affected, the court
held that representatives of the public could participate in the licensing process upon a showing
that a grant of the application sought would have

a particular effect upon them. Examples of such representatives might be a Black group in a southern community protesting a renewal grant to a licensee who, in the past, had repeatedly manifested disregard of the needs or interests of the Black members of that community. The Commission can, of course, properly protect the orderly character of its proceeding by refusing to allow the public to participate en masse, and by requiring that they do so through representative groups. The Court did not hold that a citizen could gain entry merely by asserting a bare general listenership interest without specific injury to himself or herself. But a representative citizens group which can demonstrate a particular injury which a member might suffer as a result of the grant would have sufficient statutory "standing" to participate.

Since United Church of Christ, citizens' groups have participated with respect to hundreds of applications. Public interest law firms have been organized specializing in the representation of minority group interests in application proceedings. Women's groups have been effective in attacking applicants as being unresponsive to women as listeners and employees. Ethnic groups have been allowed to participate on the grounds that particular applicants did not evidence sufficient awareness of their needs.

The form which such participation ordinarily takes is the filing of a "Petition to Deny" the application. If the Petition raises a substantial or material question of fact or a policy issue which the Commission cannot resolve on the basis of the information in the application alone, the application will be designated for hearing. The burden of proceeding with the evidence on the issue or issues raised in the Petition will be placed by the Commission upon the party best suited to do so. The ultimate burden of proof, however, remains with the broadcast applicant as to the grant of its application for license.

E. COMPARATIVE QUALIFICATIONS— THE NEED FOR CHOICE

How does the Commission choose between applicants when it can grant but one of a number of competing applications? This question arises in a number of different situations. The first concerns applicants for a new frequency which has never been used before. The second concerns an existing station seeking renewal of its license and a challenge by new competitors who desire to take the license away. The situations differ and we will discuss each separately.

1. The Non-renewal Situation

The Commission must often choose between applicants for the same new facility, and the choice may depend not only upon the nature of the applicants but also upon the nature of the facility sought.

This can best be illustrated as follows. In allocating the AM spectrum, the Commission did not follow the policy of allocating specific frequencies for use in specific cities. Thus, often two applicants would file for the same frequency in different communities and, under the Commission's engineering rules, the frequency could only be used in one of them. Thus, the choice was not only between applicants, but between communities. Should the Commission choose the best qualified applicant? Or should it award the station to the applicant who seeks to serve the community with the greatest need?

The answer can be found in Section 307(b) of the Communications Act which specifies that the Commission shall make such distribution of licenses "among the several States and communities as to provide a fair, efficient, and equitable distribution of radio service to each of the same." This statutory mandate, as interpreted by the Supreme Court (Federal Communications Commission v. Allentown Broadcasting Corp., 349 U.S. 358, 75 S.Ct. 855, 99 L.Ed. 1147 (1955)), requires the Commission to determine first which community has the greatest need for the frequency and to award the station to the applicant seeking to serve that community, without making any comparison between the nature of the applicants with respect to their background, history, multiple ownership characteristics, and other considerations. So long as the applicant for the community of greatest need possesses basic qualifications its application will be granted without considering comparative qualifications.

This mandate requires, of course, that the Commission establish criteria for determining relative need as among different communities. Generally speaking, the criteria are as follows:

(a) every community of substantial size is entitled to its own local transmission facility and, if it does not have one, will be presumed to have a greater need than another community which already has one or more local stations;

(b) the Commission desires to maximize competition and, given a choice, will prefer competition to its absence. Thus, regardless of the size of the communities, the Commission will prefer to add a second station to a community in preference to adding a third or fourth to another community since, by so doing, it would create competition where none exists; and

(c) if the contesting communities already have multiple broadcast stations, the Commission will then look to the applicant which will make more effective use of the frequency; this usually means the applicant applying for the community with the larger population, but may also involve other complex engineering valuations.

These criteria have introduced certain problems of their own, particularly with respect to suburban communities. Applicants seeking to take advantage of the priority given to applicants for the *first* station in a particular community

have applied for facilities in small suburban
towns or communities which do not have their
"own" station, but from which they could also
cover a large metropolitan area, including the
central city which already has a number of stations. Had the applicant applied for the central
city, it would have lost its comparative advantage, although in fact the intent of the applicant
really is to serve the larger community, using its
designation of the suburban community merely
as a method of obtaining a comparative preference. Recognizing this problem, the Commission
in 1965 adopted a so-called "Suburban Policy,"
which states that an applicant for a small community which nevertheless places a primary signal
of strength over an adjacent larger community
will be presumed to be applying for the larger adjacent community no matter what its application
may designate. Policy Statement on Section
307(b) Considerations for Standard Broadcast Facilities Involving Suburban Communities, 30 Fed.
Reg. 17077 (1965). Although this policy has not
completely eliminated the so-called "suburban
problem," it has lessened its impact. It should be
noted, however, that the "presumption does not
apply in uncontested cases."

But sometimes the Commission simply cannot
make the choice based upon a comparison of communities either because the communities demonstrate an equal need or because the applicants
seek to serve the same community. How then
does the Commission choose between applicants?
Until 1965, the criteria used to compare appli-

cants were less than clear, and the relative weight accorded the criteria by the Commission was so inconsistently applied at times as to raise serious charges that the purported criteria were used merely to mask preconceived results. In 1965, to clarify and simplify the comparative process, the Commission set forth its present policy on comparative broadcast hearings. Policy Statement on Comparative Broadcast Hearings, 1 F.C.C.2d 393 (1965). Asserting its primary objectives to be (a) the "best practicable service" to the public and (b) a maximum diffusion of control of the media of mass communications, the Commission indicated the material comparative criteria to be the following:

(a) Diversification of Control of Mass Communications.

This has become, in practice, the most important non-engineering criteria. All other things being equal (and even when all other things are not necessarily equal) the applicant who possesses no other broadcast interests will be preferred to the one who has other commercial media interests in the same area. Of course, the nature of the applicant's interests is itself important. The less the degree of interest in other stations or media, the less will be the significance of the multiple ownership factor. The Commission's policy is to consider the applicant's interests in existing media to the degree that they are larger, are in or are close to the community being applied for, are significant in terms of size and are significant with respect to other media in their respective locality. But there is no doubt that an applicant with significant holdings in other mass media is at a comparative disadvantage.

(b) Full-Time Participation in Station Operation by Owners and Local Residence of Applicants.

This factor is considered to be of "substantial" importance since the Commission believes that "it is inherently desirable that local responsibility and day-to-day performance be closely associated" and that "there is a likelihood of greater sensitivity to an area's changing needs" to the extent that the proprietors participate in day-to-day operation. 1 F.C.C.2d at 395. Thus, the applicant who proposes to participate actively in the station's operation will be preferred to one who will rely solely upon a hired staff. But the Commission is interested in *full-time* participation. To the extent that the owner proposes only part-time participation, the credit given drops sharply, and no credit will be given to participation of any person who will not devote "substantial amounts of time on a daily basis" in such positions as General Manager, Station Manager, Program Director or Business Manager. Ibid.

The credit given will increase in the case of applicants who are women or members of minority groups, who are also local residents and who will participate in the operation of the station. But an applicant's past broadcast experience is generally deemed of minor significance.

(c) Proposed Program Service.

Although seemingly anomalous, the Commission will not ordinarily use as a comparative criteria the proposed program services of competing applicants unless there are material and substantial differences between them of a magnitude such as is demonstrated by one applicant proposing an all foreign language station and another proposing a contemporary music format. The reason derives from the Commission's experience which indicates that applicants generally propose similar program formats, and even if they differ somewhat, the "minor differences among applicants are apt to prove to be of no significance." 1 F.C.C.2d at 397. Moreover, comparing program proposals might turn the application process into a type of "bidding" auction with applicants vying to outpromise each other and with little likelihood that their programming would, in fact, be significantly different from the bulk of the programming presented by other stations. The Commission is also concerned with keeping hearing records free of immaterial clutter (1 F.C.C.2d at 394) in the form of fulsome expositions more suited to advertising agency prose. The Commission is always concerned that forcing it to compare different program formats would cast it in the role of censor, and might involve subjective qualitative judgments of the type which the Commission would prefer not to make. Thus, as part of its recent "deregulation" effort, the Commission adopted a policy of ignoring changes in radio entertainment programs on the ground that there are a sufficient number of radio stations to allow that issue to be determined by the economic marketplace. This policy was affirmed by the Supreme Court in FCC v. WNCN Listeners Guild, 450 U.S. 582, 101 S.Ct. 1266, 67 L.Ed.2d 521 (1981).

(d) Past Broadcast Record.

The Commission uses an applicant's past broadcast record as a significant comparative factor only if the past record is either "unusually good or unusually poor," since such factors give some indication of performance in the future. A past record which is "within the bounds of average performance will be disregarded." 1 F.C.C.2d at 398.

(e) Efficient Use of the Frequency.

Where one or more competing applicants propose an operation which, for one or more engineering reasons, would be more efficient, this fact will be considered of significance in determining the preference.

(f) Character.

As noted in our discussion of basic qualifications, the character of applicants may also be considered not only on an absolute, but also on a comparative basis; character deficiencies may be such as to doom applicants on a comparative basis, even if they do not disqualify them. However, for character to be placed in issue, the Commission must so specify in the designated hearing issues, and the Commission has made clear that it will not allow the hearing to be converted "into a search for opponents' minor blemishes, no matter how remote in the past or how insignificant." 1 F.C.C.2d at 399.

(g) Other Factors.

The above framework does not exhaust the possibilities. Since the comparisons take place on a case by case basis, it would be impossible to list all situations which might arise. But it does indicate the nature of the pertinent criteria which the Commission generally considers. If an applicant desires consideration of another factor not specifically enumerated above, it must make a special request that the matter be considered. Unless the Commission specifically designates the requested issue for hearing, it will not be considered.

Obviously, in the real world, comparisons between applicants do not fall neatly into place. One applicant may deserve a preference on diversification grounds, whereas its opponent may show a superior past broadcast record. The precise manner in which the Commission weighs the various preferences can only be discerned by reviewing the many cases in which the preferences have been applied.

2. The Renewal Situation

What are the comparative factors when one of the applicants is not a newcomer, but instead, seeks a renewal of its license in competition with a newcomer which seeks to replace it? Will the Commission apply the same criteria as it does when the applicants are applying for a new facility, or will it give a preference to an applicant who has demonstrated its ability by actually running the station sought? This is a particularly vexing question because, on the one hand, giving preference to the existing licensee would tend to freeze out newcomers. On the other, ignoring past performance would be unfair to a licensee who has spent considerable sums in building up its station, which might not be recovered if its license were to be denied. Moreover, such a policy might introduce an element of instability in the broadcast industry which ultimately would not serve the public interest. But if credit is to be given for past performance, how much and in what way is it to be given?

The Commission first resolved this problem (Hearst Radio, Inc. (WBAL), 15 F.C.C. 1149 (1951)) by giving a decisive preference to the renewal applicant. The Commission reasoned that it was weighing a proven past record against a mere proposal, and feared a challenger might easily outpromise but not necessarily outperform an existing station. This policy, of course, virtually ruled out successful challenges at renewal time.

[*382*]

Although the Commission later became dissatisfied with the stringency of the Hearst policy, its attempts to change that policy (at one point to liberalize it and at another to tighten it) came to nought. See, e.g., Greater Boston Television Corp. v. Federal Communications Commission, 143 U.S.App.D.C. 383, 444 F.2d 841 (1970); Citizens Communications Center v. Federal Communications Commission, 145 U.S.App.D.C. 32, 447 F.2d 1201 (1971). The present posture of renewal comparisons is essentially that embodied in Hearst, with this gloss: the Administrative Law Judge will determine whether the incumbent was providing "minimal" or "substantial" service. If "minimal," the incumbent will not receive a comparative plus and, if the challenger's proposal appears viable and likely to be effectuated, the challenger would receive a programming plus. However, if the incumbent is found to have rendered "substantial" service, it will be given a comparative preference of major, and probably decisive, significance. See Deregulation of Radio, 46 Fed.Reg. 13888, 13896 (1981). This may be true even where the challenger is entitled to a significant preference in the area of ownership of mass media and would ordinarily have been preferred if both applicants had sought a new facility. See Central Florida Enterprises, Inc. v. FCC, 683 F.2d 503 (D.C.Cir. 1982). Here again, only broad principles can be outlined. The resolution of individual cases must depend upon the facts of each case.

F. RANDOM SELECTION AS A LICENSING MECHANISM

Congress and the Commission have expressed dissatisfaction with the traditional comparative hearing process as a mechanism to choose between competing applicants. It has been estimated that the average delay caused by a comparative hearing is three years; some have taken as long as ten years. There is an enormous economic and social loss associated with the process. The frequency lies fallow during the hearing, thereby depriving the public of a needed service. There are high tangible costs to the applicants not only through out-of-pocket and legal and engineering fees, but also through unrealized profits. There are extensive costs to the Commission (and ultimately, of course, to taxpayers) in terms of engineering and legal manpower drains. See Notice of Inquiry, 45 Fed.Reg. 29335 (May 2, 1980).

Prior to 1982, the comparative hearing mechanism was mandated by statute. In 1981, Congress amended Section 309(i) of the Communications Act (47 U.S.C.A. § 309(i)) to allow the Commission the discretion to utilize a random selection (i.e., lottery) licensing mechanism, but only after the Commission first determined the basic qualifications of applicants. Congress further mandated that the Commission (if it wished to use a random selection method) must establish rules and procedures to ensure that members of groups or organizations "which are underrepresented in the ownership of telecommunications facilities will be granted significant preferences." (Omnibus Reconciliation Act of 1981, 95 Stat. 736–37).

After studying the possibilities of instituting such a mechanism, the Commission, in 1982, declined to adopt a random selection methodology, primarily because it believed that requiring the Commission to determine basic qualifications of all applicants prior to holding a lottery "would not produce the operating economies which Congress sought to provide" (Report and Order, February 25, 1982, General Docket No. 81–768, 47 Fed.Reg. 11886 (Mar. 19, 1982)). The Commission also identified a number of problems under the 1981 legislation:

1. The key to expeditious processing is the reduction in the number and rigidity of the criteria used to establish "basic qualifications." Paradoxically, however, the easier it becomes to meet these criteria, the more applicants will apply, thus increasing the Commission's processing burdens. Expedition may have to be purchased at the expense of foregoing close scrutiny of potential applicants. Is this in the public interest?

2. The statutory provisions requiring "significant preferences" to groups or organizations, or their members, which are "underrepresented" in the ownership of telecommunications facilities pose particularly vexing problems. The statute and its legislative his-

[*385*]

tory are quite vague as to the meaning and definition of these terms. The statutory class could conceivably include virtually everyone in the general population except, perhaps, unaffiliated white males. The difficulty is exacerbated by the undefined relationship that a "member" of an underrepresented group must have to the group in order to qualify for a preference. There may be serious constitutional challenge to the statutory language as being overbroad and overinclusive, violating First Amendment and equal protection requirements.

3.   Even if the class could be narrowly defined as to avoid overbreadth (to include, for example, the same types of women and minority groups as are protected by the civil rights statutes) the preference provisions are subject to the attack that they establish a quota system without any finding of specific *past* Commission discrimination, and thus violate the Supreme Court's Bakke holding (Regents of the University of California v. Bakke, 438 U.S. 265, 98 S.Ct. 2733, 57 L.Ed.2d 750 (1978)).

4.   How can the Commission determine which groups are underrepresented? What documentation should be required? Should the findings be made on a national, regional, or market basis?

5.   How should the Commission evaluate an applicant's ownership to determine whether it is eligible for a preference? For example, if

less than 50% of the applicant is owned by persons in the preference class, should the entire applicant entity be given the "significant preference"?

6. How should the preference be weighed as against other criteria, or should it be weighed at all?

The resolution of these issues in specific cases can generate as much litigation time and effort as the comparative hearing process it was intended to replace, thus defeating the very purpose of the random selection system.

Congress responded to certain (although not all) of these points by revising Section 309(i) of the Act in 1982, in a manner which gave the Commission more flexibility in establishing a lottery mechanism for licensee selection. The new legislation, however, (Public Law 97–259, § 115) continues to require that the Commission, if it chooses to institute a lottery system, must grant "significant preferences" to applicants who would increase "diversification of ownership of mass media" and to any applicant "controlled by members of a minority group."

Despite these difficulties, however, the Commission appears to favor a lottery system, and this may very well be the wave of the future in broadcast licensing, particularly for emerging technologies such as low power television stations, where the number of applicants will be large.

CHAPTER XI

FCC CONTROL OF BROADCAST OPERATIONS

Although the Commission's primary function is and has been the licensing of broadcast stations, it has been involved from its inception, and increasingly in the past two decades, with the supervision of the manner in which stations are operated. Section 326 of the Act specifically forbids the Commission to "censor" material broadcast by a radio facility, and an overly broad reading of this restriction might make it appear that the Commission plays no part in the content of program material. Such is not the case; there are some areas in which, Section 326 notwithstanding, the Commission can and does control program content. These areas include: (1) political broadcasting; (2) programming under the so-called "Fairness Doctrine"; (3) obscenity and lottery programming; (4) so-called network "prime time" programming; (5) "anti-payola" and "anti-plugola" statutes; and (6) nebulous regulation by "raised eyebrow" in such areas as "family viewing time," drug lyrics and sexually stimulating radio programming.

A. POLITICAL BROADCASTING

From the inception of broadcast legislation, Congress has recognized the enormous potential of radio as a political tool. A major concern of the lawmakers is that a broadcasting facility might improperly influence an election by affording only one candidate access to its audience. To prevent this possibility, Congress enacted what is now Section 315 of the Communications Act which provides that "If any licensee shall permit any person who is a legally qualified candidate for any public office to use a broadcasting station, he shall afford equal opportunities to all other such candidates for that office in the use of such broadcasting station," (47 U.S.C.A. § 315) subject to certain specific exceptions which will be discussed below. The section, as amended, also provides that the rates charged each candidate must be equal and, moreover, that during election campaigns candidates must be given the "lowest unit charge" which is offered by the station to commercial advertisers for comparable time. Although rarely invoked, there are civil and criminal penalties for willful and knowing violations of the statute.

The political broadcasting statute is quite precise in its application, leaves virtually no room for broadcaster discretion except in the area of news coverage and operates with a type of mathematical certainty not usually found in broadcasting regulation. Nevertheless, despite Congress' attempt at clarity, Section 315 law is often misunderstood because of its ad hoc application.

1. "Use"

Although it is generally thought that the "equal opportunities" provision of Section 315 applies to all election broadcasts, the provision is limited to those circumstances where the candidate himself or herself appears on (i.e. "uses") the broadcast. Section 315 thus does not apply to a broadcast or advertisement on behalf of the candidate in which the candidate does not appear. This is a critical distinction. Unless the candidate appears, Section 315 simply does not apply.

The candidate's appearance is considered a "use" whenever (a) his or her identity can reasonably be presumed to be known to the audience and (b) when the appearance is of sufficient magnitude to be considered an integral part of the program. Thus, for example, there have been instances where a station staff person is also a candidate for a local office. The voice of the staff person might be used, for example, as an unidentified voice in a radio station commercial. If the voice is not distinctive or well known enough to be immediately identifiable, the use of the voice would not be considered an "appearance." See, e.g., National Urban Coalition, 23 F.C.C.2d 123 (1970); Letter to WNEP–TV, 40 F.C.C. 431 (1965). If, however, the voice is so familiar as to be reasonably identified with the staff person-candidate, then the appearance would be a "use." Station WBAX, 17 F.C.C.2d 316 (1969). Similarly, a five second introduction by a candidate to a one half hour program devoted to appearances by supporters of the candidate and on which a candidate appears at no other time, would not be so integral to the program as to make the entire one half hour program a "use" by the candidate entitling an opponent to one half hour of time. The opponent would, of course, be entitled to a five second appearance under the "equal time" doctrine because all appearances, no matter how brief, are uses. See Letter to KUGN, 40 F.C.C. 293 (1958). The problem becomes much more complicated when the candidate appears for one minute on a five minute program. In this latter case the Commission would probably consider the one minute appearance to be of sufficient magnitude to entitle an opponent to equal time for the entire five minute program.

The above discussion also illustrates another aspect of the "use" doctrine: a candidate's appearance will be considered a "use" even if the candidate is appearing for a completely unrelated purpose and never mentions his or her candidacy. Letter to United Community Campaigns of America, 40 F.C.C. 390 (1964). The classic example would be a station weatherperson or announcer who is also a candidate for local office. An appearance by either in their normal roles, in which they present the news or the weather, would, nevertheless (assuming they can be identified) be considered a "use" entitling their opponent to equal time, even if they never mention their candidacy. See Newscaster Candidacy, 40 F.C.C. 433 (1965); Station WBAX, 17 F.C.C.2d

316 (1969). When Ronald Reagan sought the Republican Presidential nomination in 1976, stations which presented his 20 year old movies during the campaign incurred equal time obligations. Adrian Weiss Productions, 36 Pike and Fisher R.R.2d 292 (1976). The reason is simply that candidates' appearances would, if nothing else, be to their benefit merely because of the so-called "identification factor" in politics, i.e. people are more likely to vote for persons whose names they can remember or identify. As a practical matter, on-air staff personnel who become candidates are usually taken off the air by the station so as to avoid equal time problems.

2. Exemptions from Equal Time Requirement

The stringency of the "use" doctrine led Congress in 1959 to create certain specific exemptions to the "equal time" doctrine. Thus, the equal time doctrine is not applicable where the appearance by the candidate takes place on any:

(1) bona fide newscast,

(2) bona fide news interview,

(3) bona fide news documentary (if the appearance of the candidate is incidental to the presentation of the subject or subjects covered by the news documentary), or

(4) on-the-spot coverage of bona fide news events (including but not limited to political conventions and activities incidental thereto). 47 U.S.C.A. § 315(a).

The exemptions were enacted in 1959 so as to avoid the situation where an appearance by an incumbent at a routine affair such as a ribbon cutting ceremony or a greeting of visiting dignitaries on a newscast could trigger demands for equal time by all of his or her opponents. See Columbia Broadcasting System, Inc., 18 Pike and Fisher R.R. 238, recon. den. 26 F.C.C. 715 (1959). It was believed that applying the "use" doctrine in all its rigor would, in practice, force stations to ignore such events in their news programming even though, in the exercise of their editorial judgment, they would otherwise have presented such material because of its interest or importance to the public or both.

The first three exemptions, i.e., newscasts, news interviews and news documentaries are rather straight-forward and have been further defined by rather extensive legislative history indicating their scope. Underlying them is the notion that such programs are essentially under the control of the station (and not the candidate) so that the candidate cannot misuse his or her appearance to gain an improper advantage. The inclusion of the concept "bona fide" in the exemption represents a restriction on the station. If the appearance on the news program is intended by the station to be aimed at favoring one candidate over another, the appearance would not be "bona fide" under the statute and thus would not be exempt.

The fourth exemption, however, "on-the-spot coverage of a bona fide news event" is less well defined in the legislative history and raises the question whether the definition of bona fide news event should be based upon the subjective determination of the broadcaster or upon an objective determination by the Commission. For example, two gubernatorial candidates have been invited by a local professional group to debate important issues. The debate is considered a "bona fide news event" by a local station which desires to carry it live as a matter of interest to its audience. Would the debate be an exempt program so that the station need not offer equal time to other candidates for the same office who are not invited to the debate? Similarly, if a station believed a presidential press conference to be a newsworthy item to be presented in its entirety, would the station's belief in the program's newsworthiness render it an exempt "bona fide news event"? The Commission first held in 1964 that the mere subjective judgment of the station was not alone dispositive and that the Commission would ultimately determine exemptions based on objective criteria such as whether the fact of candidacy was an integral part of the appearance or merely incidental thereto. Columbia Broadcasting System, Inc., 40 F.C.C. 395 (1964). The Commission later changed its mind. Now, at least with respect to debates and press conferences by candidates, it is the bona fide subjective judgment of the station which determines the exemption.

If the station, in good faith, believes the debate or news conference to be newsworthy, it can cover these items without invoking the equal time rules for opposing candidates. Petitions of the Aspen Institute, 55 F.C.C.2d 697 (1975), affirmed Chisholm v. Federal Communications Commission, 538 F.2d 349 (D.C.Cir. 1976), cert. denied 429 U.S. 890, 97 S.Ct. 247, 50 L.Ed.2d 173. This interpretation, however, has been explicitly limited to debates and press conferences. Whether or not the same theory will in the future apply to other types of appearances by candidates is unclear.

It should be emphasized that the "equal time" doctrine is not the sole determinant of a candidate's ability to obtain air time. Even if a particular program would be considered "exempt" from the equal time requirements of Section 315, or the broadcast is not a "use" invoking equal time requirements, nevertheless there are other doctrines which could be used to gain access to the media. These include the "Fairness Doctrine" (a different clause of Section 315), the "reasonable access" doctrine of Section 312 of the Act, and the "personal attack rule" discussed below.

3. Reasonable Access (Section 312(a)(7))

The equal opportunities statute requires fairness, not access. Indeed, Section 315(a) specifically states that "No obligation is imposed under this subsection upon any licensee to allow the use of its station by any such [legally qualified] candidate." Technically, a station could avoid Section 315 entirely simply by refusing to allow any candidate to appear. But in so doing it would violate other sections of the Communications Act. Thus, with respect to federal candidates, Section 312(a) (7) of the Act specifically includes, as a ground for revocation of license, "willful or repeated failure to allow reasonable access to or to permit purchase of reasonable amounts of time for the use of a broadcasting station by a legally qualified candidate for Federal elective office on behalf of his candidacy." CBS, Inc. v. FCC, 453 U.S. 367, 101 S.Ct. 2813, 69 L.Ed.2d 706 (1981). And although state and local candidates are not specifically mentioned under the access provisions of Section 312(a), the Commission has interpreted the general "public interest" standard of Section 307 of the Act to forbid any station from simply refusing to allow political candidates to use the station's facility in any way simply to avoid equal time obligations. Some access must be given to certain state and local candidates, although the rules in this respect are imprecise.

What represents "reasonable access" for federal and state candidates has not been precisely defined—the concept necessarily varies with the circumstances. But the Commission has set forth certain guidelines. If, for example, there are dozens of state or local candidates for state or local elective offices, the FCC has never required that every candidate for every office must be given access. A broadcast station is not a common carrier and access cannot be achieved on demand. A station can prune out election campaigns for minor offices and allocate time only for the major offices on the state and local level. This flexibility with respect to state offices arises because there is no specific requirement in the Act that all state or local candidates must be given access. See Use of Broadcast and Cablecast Facilities, Candidates for Public Office, 37 Fed. Reg. 5796, 5804, Q&A 1 (1972).

A station's discretion is much more limited with respect to federal offices. All federal candidates, under the strictures of the statute, must be given "reasonable access." But even here the station retains some discretion to determine the manner of access. Thus, even under Section 312, a station is not required to *sell* programming or advertising time to candidates. Stations can, and some do, take the position that they will sell no program time to candidates, but instead will meet their "access" obligations by presenting, for example, a forum-type debate, inviting all of the candidates to participate on an equal basis, and doing so twice or three times in the campaign. Use of Broadcast and Cablecast Facilities, 37 Fed. Reg. 5796, 5805, Q&A 4, 5 (1972).

But, if a station does choose to sell time, its discretion is further limited by (a) the provisions of Section 315 which require that the time be sold on a basis at least comparable to that offered to commercial clients, and (b) the provisions of the Federal Election Campaign Act of 1971 which require that during a period of 45 days before a primary election and 60 days before a general election, the station may only charge a candidate the "lowest unit rate." The "comparability" requirement means, with respect to federal candidates, that if a station sells 60 or 30 or 5 second announcements during prime time to commercial advertisers, it cannot refuse to sell such announcements during prime time to federal candidates. Public Notice, 47 F.C.C.2d 516 (1974). Thus, it would be illegal for a station to take the position that political issues do not lend themselves to proper discussion in a spot announcement format and should be handled only in programs of five minutes or more. Similarly, a station could not legally relegate all of its advertising for federal candidates to non-prime time periods—this would violate "reasonable access" on a "comparable basis." Summa Corp., 43 F.C.C.2d 602 (1973). The Commission has held it improper for a station to limit political programs for candidates for President to no more than five minutes during prime time. Such a limitation was held not to constitute "reasonable access." And stations must attempt to respond to the individualized situation of a particular candidate rather than adopt "across-the-board" policies. CBS, Inc. v. FCC, 453 U.S. 367, 101 S.Ct. 2813, 69 L.Ed.2d 706 (1981).

4. Lowest Unit Charge

Prior to 1971, Congress required only that stations treat political candidates in ways comparable to commercial advertisers. Thus, no station could charge a political candidate whether federal or state a greater amount than was charged for a comparable announcement presented on behalf of a commercial advertiser. The obvious intent was to prevent stations from taking advantage of the necessity for political candidates to obtain advertising time during election campaigns. For most of the year, the comparability criteria still holds true. However, in 1971, Congress amended Section 315 to require that during a specific election period (45 days preceding the date of a primary election and 60 days preceding the date of a federal or special election) a station may charge a political candidate no more than the lowest unit charge for the same class and amount of time for the same period. 47 U.S.C.A. § 315(b) (Cum. Supp.1976). The station must, during this period, treat the candidate in a manner comparable to its most favored commercial advertiser. The difference between "comparability" and "lowest unit charge" may be illustrated in this way: if a station has an advertiser willing to commit itself to purchasing an advertising schedule which will run an entire year, the station might be willing to give that advertiser a quantity discount so that instead of paying a normal rate of, for example, $10 per announcement, the advertiser need only pay $6 per announcement. Under the comparability standard in effect during most of the year, the station need only give political candidates the $6 rate if the candidate also agreed to purchase a schedule of announcements for the entire year. Since both are being treated in a comparable manner, the terms of the Act have been met. However, under the lowest unit charge concept, enforced during the 45 or 60 day period prior to a primary or general election, a station would be required to offer the $6 rate, even if the candidate bought only one announcement, since this would be the "lowest unit charge" being made for the time in question. In other words, lowest unit charge requires a station to give a political candidate a quantity discount even if the candidate does not purchase the same quantity as would a commercial advertiser receiving the discount.

Even under the lowest unit rate the station still retains some flexibility. It may make distinctions between classes of time so that a candidate seeking, for instance, to purchase prime time advertisements would be required to pay the lowest unit charge for prime time advertisements. Nevertheless, the lowest unit charge rule has given political candidates a significant price advantage in using broadcast facilities. But it must be emphasized that the lowest unit charge criteria is applicable only to a "use" by a legally qualified candidate. Appearances by spokespersons on behalf of a particular candidate would not fall within the lowest unit charge concept because, as discussed above, it would not involve an appearance by the candidate and thus technically would not be a "use." Use of Broadcast and Cablecast Facilities, 37 Fed.Reg. 5796, 5802, Q&A 14 (1972).

5. Legally Qualified Candidates

"Equal time" obligations come into play only upon "uses" followed by demands by "legally qualified candidates for public office." The determination of whether or not a user (or demander) is a legally qualified candidate for public office is made by reference to the law of the state in which the election is being held. Use of Broadcast Facilities By Candidates for Public Office, 35 Fed.Reg. 13048, 13057, Q&A 1 (1970). All elections are not for "public office." For example, the position of delegate to a party convention is not a "public office," even though the name of that person may appear on an election ballot. Russell H. Morgan, 36 Pike and Fisher R.R.2d 890 (1976). Conversely, a candidate can be legally qualified even if his or her name is not on the ballot if such a person, under state law, is making a bona fide "write-in" campaign. Use of Broadcast and Cablecast Facilities, 35 Fed.Reg. 13057, Q&A 2 (1970). But in order to be a legally qualified candidate the person must publicly announce his or her candidacy, even if everyone expects the person to be a candidate. Thus, an incumbent president, for example, cannot be presumed to be a candidate for reelection until such candidacy is announced. Until that time, appearances by the incumbent president would not be considered a "use" triggering equal time requirements. Id. at p. 13059, Q&A 18. And if a purported candidate is too young to serve even if elected, he or she could not demand equal time to respond to an op-

[*401*]

ponent. Socialist Workers Party, 39 F.C.C.2d 89
(1972). The question of whether a person is "legally qualified" can be quite complex, and the
Commission will follow the laws of the particular
state wherever possible. In cases of ambiguity,
the Commission will be the ultimate arbiter of
whether the person is a candidate. CBS, Inc. v.
FCC, 453 U.S. 367, 101 S.Ct. 2813, 69 L.Ed.2d 706
(1981).

6. Censorship

Section 315(a) specifically provides that no licensee can have any "power of censorship over
the material broadcast under the provisions of
this section." Thus, a legally qualified candidate
for public office is free to say anything, whether
or not it relates to the candidacy, and whether or
not the material is scandalous, obscene or in any
other manner unsuitable for broadcast. The obvious intent behind this subsection is to allow candidates to use radio or television time free from
the fetters of any other person or entity. As a
quid pro quo for such freedom, the Supreme
Court has held that no station can be sued for libel or slander arising from such use by a candidate, nor can it be acted against in any manner
by a private person or by the government. Farmers Educational and Cooperative Union v. WDAY,
Inc., 360 U.S. 525, 79 S.Ct. 1302, 3 L.Ed.2d 1407
(1959). This immunity from suit is, the Court declared, constitutionally required to insure free
speech by candidates. The "no censorship" provi-

sion is so stringently interpreted that it would be considered improper for a station to request that a candidate provide it with a copy of the candidate's speech or other materials prior to broadcast, the Commission holding that such a condition might inhibit the candidate in his or her use of the facility. Western Connecticut Broadcasting Co., 28 Pike & Fisher R.R.2d 1091 (1973).

But is must be stressed that the "no censorship" provision applies only to a use by a candidate. It does not apply to a use by a spokesman on behalf of a candidate, and (as will be discussed below) it does not apply to appearances by noncandidates under the "Fairness Doctrine."

7. Necessity for Timely Demand

Equal time rights, though available, can be lost through inactivity or delay. A candidate must make a request of a station for equal time within one week of the day of the first use giving rise to the right to equal opportunity in the use of the broadcast facility. 47 C.F.R. § 73.1940(e) (1981). If the person was not a candidate at the time of the first prior use, he is entitled to equal opportunity with respect to uses made during the week prior to his announcement of his candidacy. Letter to Joseph H. Clark, 40 F.C.C. 332 (1962). Moreover, there is no obligation on the part of the station to inform all other candidates that a particular candidate is appearing on the station. It is assumed, and in essence required, that candidates will be vigilant on their own behalf. The only exception to this rule would be where the candidate—or user—is the licensee of the station involved. Under these circumstances, the Commission has held that the licensee is under an obligation to inform his opponent of the specific days that the licensee would be using the station for his candidacy. Letter to Emerson Stone, Jr., 40 F.C.C. 385 (1964). Absent such special circumstances, however, a licensee is under no obligation to inform candidates of uses by other candidates.

8. Political Editorializing

The Commission's Rules (47 C.F.R. § 73.1930 (1981)) contain special provisions relating to editorializing by licensees. These rules provide that where a licensee in an editorial either endorses or opposes a legally qualified candidate, the licensee must transmit to the other candidates within 24 hours notification of the date and time of the editorial, a script or a tape and an offer of reasonable opportunity for the candidate or his spokesperson to respond. Where such editorials are broadcast within 72 hours of the election, the licensee shall transmit the material sufficiently far in advance of the broadcast to enable candidates to have a reasonable opportunity to present a reply. This obligation, however, only arises with respect to endorsements of candidates. It does not apply to editorials on issues not involving candidates such as, for example, municipal bond issues and referenda. In the latter case, the Fairness Doctrine applies, but the Fairness Doctrine operates in a different manner, as will be discussed below.

9. The "Zapple Doctrine"

Although the "equal time" rule applies only to uses by candidates, the Commission has created what has been termed a "quasi-equal opportunity doctrine," which relates specifically to appearances by spokespersons for candidates. As noted above, appearances by such spokespersons on behalf of candidate A are not "uses" and therefore do not vest any "equal time" rights in A's legally qualified opponents. However, under the "Quasi-Equal Opportunities Doctrine" (known as the "Zapple Doctrine") when a station sells time to supporters or spokespersons of a candidate during an election campaign, the licensee must afford comparable time to the spokesperson for an opponent. Letter to Nicholas Zapple, 23 F.C.C.2d 707 (1970). If the first group of spokespersons purchases time, then the opposing group can also purchase time if it wishes to respond. If the first group is given free time, then the second group must also be given free time. The Zapple Doctrine is, in essence, a type of hybrid between the "Equal Time Doctrine" and the "Fairness Doctrine." But although it contains elements of the "Equal Time Doctrine," there are, nevertheless, important distinctions. Thus, the Zapple Doctrine does not apply to all parties and all candidates. A station may choose not to provide "fringe candidates or minor parties" with broadcast time under "quasi-equal opportunity." First Report, Docket No. 19260, 36 F.C.C.2d 40 (1972). The Zapple Doctrine does not apply outside of campaign periods. And the Equal Opportunities Doctrine is mutually exclusive with the Zapple Doctrine. If a legally qualified candidate appears in the broadcast with his supporters, then the broadcast is a use under the Equal Time Doctrine and the Zapple Doctrine does not apply.

For further elaboration of the now quite complex evolution of political broadcasting, see "The Law of Political Broadcasting and Cablecasting: A Political Primer," 43 Fed.Reg. 36342 (Aug. 16, 1978).

B. THE "FAIRNESS DOCTRINE"

The Fairness Doctrine arose first out of a series of FCC rulings which were later codified by Congress in its 1959 Amendments to Section 315(a) of the Communications Act. P.L. 86–274, 73 Stat. 557. These amendments specifically make reference to the obligation of a broadcaster "to operate in the public interest and to afford reasonable opportunity for the discussion of conflicting views on issues of public importance." This language has been traditionally construed as a type of legislative shorthand which, based upon Commission interpretation and elaboration, enacts into positive law a dual licensee obligation: (a) to devote a reasonable amount of broadcast time to the discussion of controversial issues, and

(b) to do so fairly, i.e., to afford reasonable opportunity for the presentation of opposing viewpoints. Red Lion Broadcasting Co. v. Federal Communications Commission, 395 U.S. 367, 377, 89 S.Ct. 1794, 1799, 23 L.Ed.2d 371, 381 (1969).

1. What Constitutes "Fairness"

The basic notion of "fairness," simply stated, is the obligation to afford reasonable opportunity for the presentation of opposing viewpoints on matters of public controversy. On its simplest level, it means that the broadcaster cannot use its facilities to promulgate only one particular point of view on a major issue. In practice, however, the doctrine becomes quite complex and involves a mixture of government pressure and licensee discretion.

The first criterion is that a station need be fair only with respect to issues of public controversy. There is no fairness obligation with respect to matters which, though of interest to a particular listener, is not a matter of important public controversy in the community. For example, a particular viewer may be quite firm in his or her conviction that there is no God. The viewer may also be quite upset with a station that presents substantial religious programming affirming the existence of God. Yet the presentation of such religious programming would not impose upon the station a Fairness Doctrine obligation to present an agnostic or atheistic point of view, unless the existence of God was at that time a matter of major public controversy. See David S. Tillson, 24 F.C.C.2d 297 (1970). On the other hand, the fact that a religious issue is involved does not necessarily mean that the controversy is one of private morality alone. Presentation of an anti-abortion viewpoint, held for the most devout religious reasons, would nevertheless trigger an equal opportunities obligation if the abortion issue were a matter of local controversy involving, for example, the passage of pro or anti-abortion legislation. The question of whether or not a particular matter is one of public controversy is, as the Commission admits, susceptible to no easy determination. It involves such matters as the level of public debate, the appearance of the issue in local news media, the existence of an election question on the point, and the like. Fairness Report, Docket No. 19260, 48 F.C.C.2d 1, 11–12 (1974).

Assuming that a matter of local public controversy has been covered on the station, what, specifically, are the obligations of the licensee? Is he obligated, for example, to devote "equal time" to the coverage of both sides of the issue? The answer is no. The "Fairness Doctrine" does not operate with the precision of the "equal time" rule for political broadcasting. Indeed, this is one of the basic differences between the two doctrines. The licensee need merely demonstrate that he has afforded a reasonable amount of time (not necessarily equal) to proponents of varying points of view. "Applicability of the Fairness

Doctrine in the Handling of Controversial Issues of Public Importance," 29 Fed.Reg. 10415, 10419 ¶ 12 (1964) (hereafter referred to as "1964 Fairness Primer").

Moreover, the Fairness Doctrine vests a broad discretion in the licensee not only as to the amount of time to be devoted to the controversy, but to the issues to be covered, the viewpoints to be presented, the appropriate spokespersons, the format of the programming, and other similar programming decisions. With the exception of the personal attack aspect of the Fairness Doctrine (discussed below), the "reasonable access" rights of Federal candidates, and the specialized rules covering political editorials, no particular person or group has a constitutional or legislative right of access to the facilities of a broadcast station. The Supreme Court in Columbia Broadcasting System, Inc. v. Democratic National Committee, 412 U.S. 94, 111, 93 S.Ct. 2080, 2090–2091, 36 L.Ed.2d 772, 788–789 (1973) rejected the "right of access" theory and reaffirmed the rule that a broadcast station is not a common carrier which must open its facilities on demand, even if the demand is made on behalf of a worthwhile cause. And the United States Court of Appeals has held that the Commission's role in reviewing Fairness Doctrine judgments of a licensee is akin to the role played by the courts in reviewing the actions of an administrative agency. The Commission cannot substitute its judgment for that of the broadcaster and penalize it because the Commission disagrees with the broadcaster's exercise of judgment. Only when the broadcaster's judgment is of such an egregious nature that no reasonable person could doubt that it is an abuse of discretion can the Commission step in and order a particular course of action by the broadcaster. Straus Communications, Inc., v. Federal Communications Commission, 530 F.2d 1001 (D.C.Cir. 1976).

Nevertheless, there are certain imposed limits to licensee discretion, even in Fairness Doctrine situations. Thus, as part of its public interest obligation, a broadcaster must affirmatively encourage the presentation of opposing views even to the point of itself seeking them out. 1964 Fairness Primer, 29 Fed.Reg. 10415, 10418, ¶ 9. A broadcaster cannot defend its refusal to present varying points of view on the basis that no one asked to reply. If the licensee has reason to believe that there is an identifiable group or person which would speak out on an issue had it been informed of the broadcast, the licensee must seek that group out. Columbia Broadcasting System, Inc., 34 F.C.C.2d 773 (1972). And the licensee is required to present contrasting viewpoints even if it receives no consideration. Thus, under the doctrine enunciated in Cullman Broadcasting Co., 40 F.C.C. 576 (1963), if one side of a controversial issue is broadcast on a sponsored basis, the licensee must broadcast contrasting viewpoints even if those with contrasting viewpoints cannot afford to purchase the time. But there is no required ratio of time to be given to the various sides. The Commission has rejected as inappropriate such a "mechanical" approach. Fairness Report, 48 F.C.C.2d 1, 17 (1974).

It must be emphasized that the Commission's role in Fairness Doctrine situations is not that of a continuing monitor to insure that licensees adhere to the tenets of the doctrine. Rather, the Commission's role essentially is to enforce the doctrine upon the filing of appropriate complaints by members of the public. This is critical because the Commission has listed certain prerequisites to an appropriate Fairness complaint which, in fact, limit the practical impact of the Fairness Doctrine upon broadcasters. In its 1964 Fairness Doctrine Primer the Commission stipulated that it will act only where a complainant includes in his or her complaint to the Commission:

> . . . specific information indicating (1) the particular station involved; (2) the particular issue of a controversial nature discussed over the air; (3) the date and time when the program was carried; (4) the basis for the claim that the station has presented only one side of the question; and (5) whether the station had afforded or has plans to afford, an opportunity for the presentation of contrasting viewpoints. 29 Fed.Reg. 10415, 10416.

The last of these elements is particularly significant because it places upon the complainant the burden of prima facie demonstrating that the licensee has failed to present varying viewpoints

on the point at issue. Unless such a prima facie
case is made, the station need not even respond
because, in the Commission's view, forcing stations to respond to less than prima facie showings would place too great a burden upon licensees and might force them to eschew coverage of
controversial issues entirely. Wilderness Society,
41 F.C.C.2d 103 (1973).

The burden imposed on complainants of making such a prima facie showing may be one explanation for the fact that while the Commission receives thousands of Fairness Doctrine complaints
(4417 in 1979 alone), only a very few of these are
ever followed up with demands upon licensees for
further information (approximately 45 in 1979).
And an even smaller number of complaints ever
becomes the basis for a Commission decision. In
only a minuscule number of cases has the Commission ever reached the determination that the
broadcaster in fact breached his responsibilities
under the Fairness Doctrine. Some commenta-
tors have even suggested that the Doctrine exists
only because of the infrequency of its use by the
Commission. A more vigorous enforcement
might well doom the Doctrine as having an improper "chilling effect" on freedom of licensee
speech. See Robinson dissent to Opinion and Order on Reconsideration of Fairness Report, 58
F.C.C.2d 691, 703 (1974); Bazelon dissent in Bran-
dywine-Main Line Radio, Inc. v. Federal Communications Commission, 153 U.S.App.D.C. 305, 473
F.2d 16, 63 (1972).

The Doctrine has raised some interesting problems with respect to the presentation of commercial spot announcements and news programs. When the question of whether cigarette smoking was dangerous was under investigation by, among others, the Surgeon General of the United States, cigarette companies continued to advertise their product over radio and television. In response to a complaint, the Commission, rather surprisingly, held that the mere presentation of product advertising was itself a statement of a "point of view" on the "controversial issue" of whether cigarettes were damaging (even if, as was invariably the case, the product advertising never mentioned the controversy). Thus, stations which presented cigarette advertising were under an obligation to present "anti cigarette advertising" in some reasonable proportion to the amount of cigarette ads presented. WCBS–TV, 8 F.C.C.2d 381 (1967). This ruling, affirmed by the Court of Appeals (Banzhaf v. Federal Communications Commission, 132 U.S.App.D.C. 14, 405 F.2d 1082 (1968), cert. denied 396 U.S. 842, 90 S.Ct. 50, 24 L.Ed.2d 93 (1969)), ultimately led to demands by environmentalists and others to respond to product advertisements for, among others, automobiles, gasoline engines, and public utilities on the grounds that advertisements of these products and companies were statements on the controversial issue of pollution, whether or not the controversy was mentioned in the commercial announcement. After some confusion

[*413*]

and litigation the Commission ultimately ruled that its earlier cigarette holding was erroneously based. Fairness Report, 48 F.C.C.2d at 26 (1974). The present rule is that product advertising per se is not a statement on a controversial issue so long as the advertising merely extols the virtues of the product and takes no explicit position on matters of public controversy. Ibid.

With respect to news programs, the charge is often made that a particular news program is "slanted" or "biased." The Commission has recognized that direct intervention into the thought processes of broadcast newspersons could well have an extremely "chilling effect" in an area explicitly protected by the First Amendment. Thus, the Commission has held that absent some extrinsic evidence of deliberate news slanting, the Commission will not entertain complaints concerning the "fairness" of news presentations. Hunger in America, 20 F.C.C.2d 143 (1969).

2. Personal Attack Rule

The Personal Attack Rule is an aspect of the Fairness Doctrine relating to the right of a person attacked to gain access to the broadcast facility to defend himself or herself. The Personal Attack Rule is quite precise and specific. It holds that when, during the presentation of views on a controversial issue of public importance, an attack is made upon the honesty, character, integrity or like personal qualities of an identified person or group, the licensee shall, within a reasonable time and in no event later than one week after the attack, transmit to the person or group attacked (1) notification of the date, time and identification of the broadcast; (2) a script or tape of the attack; and (3) an offer of a reasonable opportunity to respond over the licensee's facilities. The rule does not apply to:

1. attacks on foreign groups or foreign public figures;

2. personal attacks made by legally qualified candidates, their authorized spokesmen, or persons associated with them; and

3. bona fide newscasts, bona fide news interviews or on-the-spot coverage of bona fide news events.

The key features of the rule are that the rule does not apply to every personal attack carried on the station, but only to a personal attack broadcast during the presentation of views on a controversial issue of public importance. A person attacked at some other time will have no redress from the Commission but must look to the law of defamation for remedy. Straus Communications, Inc. v. Federal Communications Commission, 530 F.2d 1001 (D.C.Cir. 1976). Moreover, the attack must be as to the person's honesty, character, integrity or like personal qualities if the rule is to be invoked. An attack, for example, upon a person alleging that a person's ideas are "stupid" would not be considered a personal attack for the purposes of the rule. Mrs. Frank Diesz, 27

F.C.C.2d 859 (1971). Finally, if the Personal Attack Rule applies, the person attacked has an absolute right to appear in his or her own defense. The station has no discretion to require that the defense be made by another person. This is in contrast to practice under the Fairness Doctrine generally by which the licensee is not required to choose any particular person or group to present the contrasting point of view.

C.   OBSCENITY AND INDECENCY

Although not contained in the Communications Act of 1934, the Criminal Code of the United States (18 U.S.C.A. § 1464) contains a specific prohibition against broadcast stations presenting any material which is "obscene" or "indecent." Although rarely invoked, the "obscenity" section of the statute has been held constitutional under the prevailing theory that obscenity is not protected by the First Amendment. Illinois Citizens Committee for Broadcasting v. Federal Communications Commission, 515 F.2d 397 (D.C.Cir.), rehearing denied 515 F.2d 407 (D.C.Cir. 1975).

With respect to "obscenity," the general standard is that followed in the normal "obscenity" case, i.e., whether or not the material taken as a whole appeals to an average person's prurient interest without any redeeming social value when considered in connection with contemporary community standards. Miller v. California, 413 U.S. 15, 93 S.Ct. 2607, 37 L.Ed.2d 419 (1973). In practice, however, the courts have applied a more expansive concept of prurience than that applied to other forms of media. But there are few reported cases and the outlines of such standards for broadcasting have not yet been fully delineated. The courts have approved Commission prohibition of explicitly sexual programming where, during daytime hours, listeners freely discuss their sexual practices, in a normal "disc jockey" format readily accessible to children. See Illinois Citizens Committee v. Federal Communications Commission, supra. Beyond this, however, the line between protected programming and "obscenity" is far from clear.

The "indecency" standard has also been upheld as a constitutionally proper exercise (under certain circumstances) of the state's police power. FCC v. Pacifica Foundation, 438 U.S. 726, 98 S.Ct. 3026, 57 L.Ed.2d 1073 (1978). Significantly, however, the Supreme Court has allowed the Commission to give the concept of "indecency" a broader definition than that of "obscenity." Material which is "patently offensive," "sexual" and "excretory" may, if broadcast during times when children are presumed to be in the audience, be punishable even if not "obscene." Pacifica, supra. The case is instructive because the Court had previously defined the concept of "indecency" to be coextensive with "obscenity" if presented in books and films. Pacifica is an excellent example of the court applying different statutory and constitutional standards to broadcasting, primarily because of broadcaster's ease of access to children and the difficulty of parental supervision.

D. LOTTERIES

The federal criminal code generally prohibits any station from broadcasting any information concerning a lottery. 18 U.S.C.A. § 1304. A lottery is any game or contest which contains the elements of prize, chance and "consideration." These elements are construed in terms of a type of federal common law of lotteries followed by the Federal Communications Commission, the Post Office Department and the Department of Justice. Because of the varying state law definitions of these terms, it would be impossible to rely upon often conflicting state definitions to control radio, which is, by statute, an interstate activity. See Federal Communications Commission v. American Broadcasting Co., 347 U.S. 284, 74 S.Ct. 593, 98 L.Ed. 699 (1954). This area of the law can become quite complex particularly in determining whether "consideration" is present. The federal common law of "consideration" has been established to mean a monetary detriment to the participant in the contest rather than merely a benefit to the contest operator. For example, the requirement of the listener mailing in a post card to a station would not be considered "consideration," even though the station may thereby "benefit" by obtaining a list of members of its audience or by the contest enlarging the station's audience. Federal Communications

[*418*]

Commission v. American Broadcasting Co., supra;
cf. Caples Co. v. Federal Communications Commission, 100 U.S.App.D.C. 126, 243 F.2d 232
(1957).

There is one exception to the general lottery
ban. A station is now allowed to broadcast any
information it wishes about a state authorized lottery in its own or adjacent state so long as the
station is located in a state which has its own official lottery. 18 U.S.C.A. § 1307 (Cum.Supp.1976).

E.   PRIME TIME ACCESS RULE

The Commission, over the years, has evolved a
series of policies which have specific impact upon
the material presented by a network affiliated
broadcast station. Networks are, generally
speaking, organizations which have been created
for the purpose of producing and distributing programming to individual stations and also to act as
advertising clearance centers for all network affiliated stations. Although networks can (and do)
act as licensees of individual stations, the networks themselves are not regulated by the Commission and the Commission has no power directly to regulate their operations. But the
Commission can and does indirectly regulate the
networks through its power over the licenses of
individual stations. This regulation is apparent
in the so-called "Network Rules" which prohibit
any individual station from entering into contracts with networks which contain certain provisions that the Commission finds offensive to the

public interest. See, e.g., 47 C.F.R. §§ 73.132, 73.658 (1981). These prohibitions forbid network contract clauses which would prevent the licensee from broadcasting the programs of any other network, or which would prevent another station in the affiliate's area from broadcasting a network program if the affiliate declines to broadcast it. The Rules also require that television network affiliation terms be no longer than 2 years, and that the television affiliate be granted the right to reject network programs which it believes unsatisfactory. Among the most important of these rules are provisions covering television prime time programming. These rules, referred to as the "Prime Time Access Rules," reflect a concern with the lack of local programming activity among network affiliates. They provide (47 C.F.R. § 73.658(k)) that television stations owned by or affiliated with a national television network in the 50 largest television markets shall devote during the four hours of prime time (7–11 p. m. Eastern Time and Pacific Time and 6–10 p. m. Central Time and Mountain Time) no more than three hours to the presentation of programs from a national network, including programs which formerly had been presented on national networks. The only exception is that certain categories of programs need not be counted toward the three hour limitation such as (1) programs designed for children, public affairs programs or documentary programs; (2) special news programs and political broadcasts; (3) regular network news broadcasts up to one-half hour when immediately adjacent to a full hour of locally produced news programming; and (4) run-overs of sporting events and network broadcasts of national sports events or other programs of a special nature. In practical effect, the Prime Time Access Rule means that only three hours of the four hour prime time period will be devoted to network produced or distributed entertainment programs, one-half hour will be devoted to network news programming and the remaining one-half hour will consist of either non-network produced entertainment programs or special documentary or public affairs features. The Prime Time Access Rule represents as definite a restriction on program content as the courts have countenanced. It has been justified as appropriate regulation in the public interest and not program censorship otherwise prohibited by Section 326 of the Act. Mt. Mansfield Television, Inc. v. Federal Communications Commission, 442 F.2d 470 (2d Cir. 1971).

Other rules prohibit television networks from engaging in "syndicating" non-network programming, or from having an ownership interest in broadcast programming produced by others. 47 C.F.R. § 73.658(i) (1981).

F. SPONSORSHIP IDENTIFICATION RULES: "ANTI–PAYOLA" AND "ANTI–PLUGOLA" REQUIREMENTS

Congress and the Commission have expressed concern that broadcast frequencies not be used by "hidden persuaders." Although most sponsors purchase time specifically to identify themselves and/or their products, there are occasions when persons wish to use programming time anonymously to further their own purposes. Such use can occur in a number of ways. Record promoters may offer money to disc jockeys to induce them to play their records ("payola") or to advertise certain activities ("plugola") without the public being aware that such material is being broadcast for pay. Other examples include broadcasting paid political matter or material concerning controversial issues without identifying the person or group presenting the material.

Because it is believed important that the audience be aware of the person paying the piper, Section 508 of the Communications Act and Section 73.1212 of the Commission's Rules stipulate that any person who pays or receives money or other valuable consideration for including any material as part of programming to be broadcast over a station must report that transaction to the licensee or licensees over whose facilities the program is aired. In turn, under Section 317 of the Act and Section 73.1212 of the Rules, the licensee is required to identify over the air, clearly and concisely, the person making the payment, and the fact that payment was made.

Further, Section 73.1212(d) of the Rules require that if any material or service is given to a station as an inducement to use such material or service in the broadcast of political matters or during the discussion of controversial issues of public importance, an announcement must be made indicating the material or service that was received by the station and identifying the person or entity which provided that material or service.

G. CONTESTS

Both Congress and the Commission have adopted standards of conduct governing broadcast contests. Section 73.1216 of the Rules mandates that a station must fully and accurately disclose the material terms of any contest which the station presents and the contest must be conducted in the manner advertised. The material terms include entry qualifications, eligibility restrictions, deadline dates, prize information, basis for valuation of prizes and tie-breaking procedures.

Section 509 of the Communications Act provides that, in contests of "intellectual knowledge, intellectual skill or chance," it is illegal to supply any contestant with any special or secret assistance, to persuade or intimidate a contestant from refraining from using his knowledge or skill or to engage in any prearrangement or predetermination of the outcome.

CHAPTER XII

EMERGING TECHNOLOGIES

A.   TELEVISION BY CABLE

CATV (cable television) arose because of inherent limitations in commercial television. Television is merely the wireless transmission of visual and aural material over the air. Because of physical peculiarities, the distance which the television signal can travel over the air is limited. This fact, together with the Commission's television allocation policy whereby only a limited number of frequencies were assigned to designated cities throughout the country, posed significant reception problems for many residents of outlying areas, or areas on the fringe of larger cities. The problem was exacerbated by the fact that even some of the larger cities to which frequencies were assigned were only assigned three VHF channels, and some only two; thus there were large areas of the country which could receive no more than two or, at most, three signals. There were some communities located in mountainous terrain which could not even obtain adequate reception from the two or three stations which they theoretically should have been able to receive over the air.

The solution to the problem for many of these communities was to erect extremely tall receiving towers at the highest point in the area to pick up the off-the-air signals and then retransmit the signals over wires run from the tower to various homes (subscribers). Typically, the home subscriber would pay a one-time installation fee for the wiring and a monthly fee for the service.

Although the original CATV systems were intended mainly to fill in the blanks within stations' normal coverage areas, it soon became apparent that CATV could also bring in service from distant cities which, under the Commission's allocation plan, were never intended to render service to that particular cable community. Thus, for example, a city such as Kingston, New York, located 90 miles from New York City, was never intended by the Commission to receive off-the-air service from the New York City television stations; the Commission intended Kingston to be served by the closer Albany, New York, facilities. However, cable television could bring in all of the New York stations, an obvious benefit to the residents of Kingston, but also a possible economic detriment to the Albany station, which could have its "natural audience" in Kingston fragmented. Morever, CATV system operators could offer other communications services, including programming services such as sports events and feature films. This latter capability caused many to begin referring to CATV as "cable television," implying that the new service was much more than merely a community antenna.

Cable television also posed legal problems:

(a) Was cable television subject to FCC jurisdiction? It was not in existence when the Communications Act was passed, and might be considered merely a receiving rather than a transmitting unit, thus not "broadcasting".

(b) If the Commission did have jurisdiction, did the federal government preempt the field of regulation so that state or local governmental bodies were deprived of jurisdiction over such systems? This question was particularly important since cable television systems required local construction of wire lines and thus had a significant effect on the local citizenry;

(c) If jurisdiction was to be shared between a federal and local agency, how should the power to regulate cable be allocated?

(d) How was the Commission to reconcile the new technology of cable and its potential for carrying distant signals over the entire country with the existing Commission policy of station allocation?

(e) How did cable television comport with the copyright laws?

At first, the Commission refused to take jurisdiction over cable on the grounds that its power to do so was in question and that it did not feel the impact of cable television at the time was sufficient to invoke discretionary jurisdiction. Frontier Broadcasting Co. v. Collier, 24 F.C.C. 251 (1958). In 1966, the Commission changed course and adopted the first general federal regulation of cable systems, asserting that some overall comprehensive federal regulation was necessary to meet the Commission's responsibility to promote, maintain, and supervise an effective television service throughout the country. Second Report and Order, 2 F.C.C.2d 725 (1966). The Commission's power to assert jurisdiction under its general grant of power from Congress and in the absence of specific legislation concerning cable television was affirmed by the Supreme Court in United States v. Southwestern Cable Co., 392 U.S. 157, 88 S.Ct. 1994, 20 L.Ed.2d 1001 (1968).

Since 1966 Commission regulation of cablevision, although changing in its details, has mainly concerned five areas: (1) jurisdictional division of regulatory power between the Commission, on the one hand, and local authorities on the other; (2) regulation of cable importation of distant signals and imposition of requirements for mandatory signal carriage; (3) regulations requiring cable systems to render so-called "non-duplication" programming protection to local television stations; (4) regulations imposing affirmative obligations on cablevision systems to initiate their own programming and to make available to the public so-called "access" channels on which anyone has the right to purchase time; and (5) imposition of regulatory strictures upon cable systems similar to those placed upon radio stations, such as rules limiting concentration of ownership and control, equal employment reporting requirements and, for cable origination programming, political and fairness requirements and anti-obscenity provisions. Some Commission restrictions initially imposed upon cable systems have been overturned by the courts; others have been voluntarily rescinded by the Commission. We will discuss these matters briefly below. It should be emphasized, however, that they are quite detailed and reference should be made to Part 76 of the Commission Rules for a full understanding of their extent.

1. Jurisdictional Division

The Commission has accepted a bifurcated jurisdictional basis for the regulation of cable systems. State or local government agencies issue the franchise or license for the specific cable operator and impose whatever obligations they think necessary, subject to certain FCC standards. These Commission standards are that, with respect to systems serving 1000 or more subscribers, franchise fees must be no more than 3% of gross revenues; if the fee is 3–5% of such revenues, the Commission will approve it upon a showing by the system that the fee will not interfere with federal or local regulatory goals. In addition, the Commission recommends, but does not require, that the local body (1) hold public proceedings prior to the issuance of franchises;

(2) consider the legal, character, financial, technical and other qualifications of the applicant, (3)
limit the duration of the franchise to 15 years, (4)
require early implementation and completion of
construction and (5) regulate subscriber charges
and reasonable franchise fees. 47 C.F.R. § 76.31
(1981).

Before commencing operations or adding a
new signal, each cable system must file with the
Commission a registration statement in which it
demonstrates that it will comply with the signal
carriage and the equal employment rules of the
Commission.

One further point should be noted. A number
of cities and localities throughout the country
have attempted to exercise control over cablevision franchising through the cable franchise contract it negotiates with the cable system operator.
In one instance, the Supreme Court has held that
when a city attempted to regulate cablevision in a
manner that went beyond its home rule authority,
its activity fell outside the normal "state action"
exemption from antitrust liability and, if the franchise contract is deemed to be anti-competitive,
the city may be held to have violated the Sherman
Antitrust Act. See Community Communications
Co. v. City of Boulder, Colorado, ___ U.S. ___,
102 S.Ct. 835, 70 L.Ed.2d 810 (1982). As a result
of the decision in the Community Communications case, a number of state legislatures have
amended their cities' home rule charters to give

the local jurisdictions broad authority to restrict the cable franchises which they award.

2. Signal Carriage Rules

The potential impact of cable television upon the Commission's television allocation scheme has two aspects: first, the importation of distant signals might fragment the audience of the local television station since the local station would now be required to compete with "outside" signals not originally anticipated in the Commission's allocations policy. This is the so-called "distant signal" problem. Second, unless the local cable system is required to carry the signals of the local stations, viewers who choose to subscribe to the system usually would not be able to receive the signal of the local station because they would probably disconnect their regular antennae.

To complicate matters further, the cablevision impact upon independent, non-network and UHF television stations is paradoxical. To the extent cablevision systems carried local, non-network, UHF stations, the cablevision system helped them since it eliminated most of the technical advantages which off-the-air VHF reception possessed over UHF reception. On the other hand, to the extent these systems carried distant signals, they tended to fragment the audience and, therefore, harmed local non-network UHF facilities.

The Commission, in 1972, attempted to resolve these issues and integrate cablevision in the television scheme by enacting a series of rules aimed at protecting local stations, while at the same time allowing cablevision to reach a mature development. With respect to the "distant signal" problem, the Commission limited the number of signals from distant stations that a cable system could transmit, the limit varying according to market size and the number of available over-the-air signals within the market. For example, in the top 50 markets, cable systems under the 1972 "distant signal" rules could only carry three network stations, three independent and (under certain circumstances) two additional independent signals. Limits were also imposed on cablevision systems in the second 50 largest markets and in the smaller markets.

These limitations (although a relaxation of more stringent rules enacted in 1966) nevertheless, were very restrictive. In 1979, the Commission ultimately rescinded all of its distant signal rules so that cablevision systems are now free to carry any distant signals without restriction. See Malrite TV v. Federal Communications Commission, 652 F.2d 1140 (2d Cir. 1981).

With respect to mandatory carriage, the Commission's Rules (Sections 76.57(a), 76.59(a), 76.61(a), 76.63(a)), require that, upon request, the cablevision system must carry what would normally be considered the "local" television stations in the cablevision communities. For example, a cable system located in a community either wholly or even partially within a 35-mile radius of one of the top-50 television markets must carry, on demand, all television broadcast stations licensed to communities within the television market, all non-commercial educational stations which place a Grade B signal over the cable community, and all stations which are "significantly viewed" in the cable community, based on a level of viewership defined in the rules. There is one exception: cable systems are not required to carry "local" pay television programs. 47 C.F.R. § 76.64 (1981).

In sum, the balance has been struck by allowing cablevision systems to carry as many signals as they wish, from wherever they wish, subject only to the requirement that they must also carry so-called "local" non-pay-TV stations.

3. Non–duplication Protection

Another problem caused by the importation of distant signals arises when the same cable systems carry "local" and "distant" stations which may both be broadcasting the same network program. Because such duplication through the use of cable television could have a detrimental economic effect on the local station that had obtained exclusivity for the program under its network agreement, the Commission has enacted rules which require that cable systems with more than 1000 subscribers delete the network programs of duplicating distant stations under certain circumstances. See 47 C.F.R. §§ 76.92–76.99 (1981). The deletion is made in accordance with certain priorities set forth in the Commission's Rules; a "local" television station has the right to require the deletion of a duplicating network program from the signal of a lower priority station. See 47 C.F.R. § 76.92. In order to invoke such protection the station requesting deletion must formally notify the cable system.

A closely related problem concerns the carriage of distant non-network programs. Typically, non-network programs are "syndicated" on a market-by-market basis. Importation of distant signals could upset these commercial arrangements to the detriment of the copyright holder or the stations which purchase license rights from these copyright holders. The Commission in 1972 enacted certain exclusivity rules which, in essence, required cable systems in major markets to black out a distant syndicated program when a commercial television station in the market has exclusive rights to the broadcast of that program or, in certain cases, to black out the distant program even prior to the sale of such rights in the cable system's market. In 1980, as part of its cable deregulation effort, the Commission abolished these exclusivity rules so that there is no longer any restriction on carriage of distant syndicated programs. See Malrite T.V. v. FCC, 652 F.2d 1140 (2d Cir. 1981).

4. Other Operating Regulations

In addition to the so-called carriage and nonduplication rules discussed above, the Commission has imposed upon cable systems certain operating requirements similar to those imposed upon broadcast stations. Thus, despite the fact that cable may not be considered "broadcasting" in the usual sense, nonetheless, to the extent cable systems originate their own programs, the Commission's Rules require that these systems follow all of the "equal time" and "lowest unit rate" political broadcast regulations promulgated pursuant to Section 315 of the Communications Act, adhere to the rules concerning the Fairness Doctrine, personal attack and political editorial rules, forego broadcasting lottery information except that concerning a state-run lottery and only then under certain conditions, not transmit obscenity or "indecency", even on the so-called "access" channels, identify all material which is sponsored, and maintain certain records. Finally, the Rules require that all cable systems follow an affirmative action equal employment plan. See 47 C.F.R. §§ 76.205 thru 76.221; 76.305; 76.311 (1981).

5. Initiation and Origination of Programming

Up to this point, we have been viewing cable television as a service which does nothing more than receive signals originated by television stations and re-transmit them, by wire, to subscribers. Cable systems, however, are not limited merely to re-transmission. Once the wiring to the various homes has been hooked up, cable systems have the capability of offering various other communications services, such as originating programming in a studio and transmitting such programming through the already connected wires to its subscribers. Moreover, although the laws of physics limit the number of off-the-air signals which can be received, modern technology allows a far greater number of signals to be transmitted by wire. Some cable systems can carry more than 100 separate channels.

The Commission has been concerned that the unused capability not be wasted. In 1969, therefore, the Commission required that all cable systems having a total of 3500 or more subscribers must engage to a significant extent in locally oriented original programming. Such a requirement forces the cable owner to become a program producer and not merely a conduit for the distribution of programming presented by television stations. The validity of such a requirement, forcing cable systems to originate local programming, was sustained by a five to four vote of the Supreme Court in United States v. Midwest Video Corp., 406 U.S. 649, 92 S.Ct. 1860, 32 L.Ed.2d 390 (1972). But the Chief Justice (who voted with the majority) took pains to point out that in making such a requirement the Commission appeared to be reaching the limits of its authority under the Communications Act. Actually, the Commission had voluntarily stepped back from its position during the course of the Midwest litigation. It suspended the mandatory program origination rule and never reinstated it.

The Chief Justice's remarks were prophetic. The mandatory program origination rules appear to have been the high water mark of Commission cable regulation. Not long thereafter, the Court of Appeals struck down Commission rules restricting the ability of cablevision systems to present certain feature films and sports programs, holding that such regulation was beyond the power of the Commission because it was not "reasonably ancillary" to the Commission's long-term regulatory goals and responsibilities. See Home Box Office, Inc. v. FCC, 567 F.2d 9 (D.C.Cir. 1977), cert. denied, 434 U.S. 829, 98 S.Ct. 111, 54 L.Ed.2d 89. And in 1979, the Supreme Court struck down the Commission's rules requiring that cablevision systems offer channels to the public on a lease basis (so-called "access" channels) on the grounds that these provisions also went beyond the Commission's regulatory powers. See Federal Communications Commission v. Midwest Video Corp., 440 U.S. 689, 99 S.Ct. 1435, 59 L.Ed.2d 692 (1979).

6. Access Programming

Perhaps the most intriguing aspect of the Commission's original cable rules was that portion which in 1976 created so-called "access" channels for use by persons other than the cable operator to originate programming on the system. Under these rules, all new cable systems with 3500 or more subscribers were required to maintain at least one specifically designated non-commercial public access channel available to anyone who wished to use it on a first-come, non-discriminatory basis, a second channel available for use by local educational authorities, a third channel available for local government authorities and a fourth channel available for lease to the general public. The systems had to maintain equipment and facilities necessary for the production of programming for these channels. The public access channel was to be made available without charge, except that production costs could be assessed for live studio presentations exceeding five minutes. Advertising designed to promote the sale of commercial products or services, candidacies for public office, lottery information and obscene material was not permitted on the public access channel. Channel capacity was to be made available on a first-come, non-discriminatory basis under certain conditions.

A key element in the concept of "access" channels was the prohibition against the cablevision systems determining or influencing the content of "access" programming in any way. The Commission's purpose was to force cablevision systems to offer a vehicle by which non-broadcasters could reach a mass audience free of cablevision operator censorship. This feature, however, proved to be the concept's Achilles Heel. The Supreme Court held that requiring access under these conditions imposed "common carrier" obligations on cable operators in derogation of Section 3(h) of the Communications Act,

(47 U.S.C.A. § 153(h)). Congress, in the Court's view, intended persons engaged in broadcasting to retain journalistic and editorial discretion. Commission regulation which acted to deny that discretion could not be viewed as "reasonably ancillary" to the Commission's statutory responsibilities and thus, went beyond its statutory powers. Federal Communications Commission v. Midwest Video Corp., 440 U.S. 689, 99 S.Ct. 1435, 59 L.Ed.2d 692 (1979).

The fact that the Commission (absent a change in the law) cannot require "access" programming does not mean that such programming is non-existent. Prior to the Supreme Court's *Midwest* holding, a number ôf cablevision systems, in fact, leased channels on an "access" basis, and they continue to do so. And using the broad franchising power given them by their state legislatures, many local jurisdictions are requiring prospective franchisees to dedicate certain of their channels for public access in any new cable franchise contracts which may be signed. This has caused cable trade association organizations to complain to Congress, and legislation that would eliminate the local power to require access channels has been proposed. This movement to limit local and states rights has been resisted by the National League of Cities.

7. Copyright Problems

One of the earliest legal problems to be faced with the advent of cable television was whether a cable system, by the act of receiving a program broadcast over the air and then sending the program by wire to various subscribers, was undertaking a "performance for profit," thereupon subjecting itself to liability either to the television station whose program it was re-transmitting, or to the copyright holders of the work being presented on the station. It was argued by the cable interests that cable systems were not "performing" in the sense contemplated by the copyright laws since they were merely receiving material sent out over the air by stations which had already paid a copyright fee. Imposing liability on the cable system would, the argument ran, result in double payment to the copyright holder. Others argued that whether or not copyright fees should be paid depended upon whether the cable system merely filled in the blanks within a station's normal service contour or whether the cable system extended the range of a station's service beyond the normal service contour.

The Supreme Court dealt with the issue in two landmark cases absolving cable systems of copyright liability for material picked up over the air and then sent through wire, on the ground that this was not a "performance" but merely a mechanical, passive act no different in quality than the erecting by a single person of an extremely tall receiving antenna to improve his or her own reception. Because such an act did not subject the individual to copyright liability, the provision of such a service for profit did not

[*439*]

change the quality of the act for copyright purposes under the then existing copyright act. Fortnightly Corp. v. United Artists Television, Inc., 392 U.S. 390, 88 S.Ct. 2084, 20 L.Ed.2d 1176 (1968); Teleprompter Corp. v. Columbia Broadcasting System, Inc., 415 U.S. 394, 94 S.Ct. 1129, 39 L.Ed.2d 415 (1974).

The Fortnightly and Teleprompter decisions led Congress to enact significant revisions of the copyright statute. Under the Copyright Act as it now reads, cablevision systems are free to retransmit television signals containing copyrighted materials without obtaining permission of the copyright holder, but the systems must pay a compulsory license fee. The amount of that fee, and the manner in which the fee is to be disbursed, are determined by the Copyright Royalty Tribunal, a statutory body created by Congress for this purpose. See 17 U.S.C.A. § 111.

8. Cable Programming Regulation

One of the areas open to cable operators is the presentation for a separate fee of feature films and sports events on the unused channel capacity of the system. Because the potential return to the film producer and sport producer from cable exhibition might be larger than the amounts which could be paid by television stations or networks, depending upon the number of subscribers to the cable system, it was feared that film or sport producers would withhold their product from commercial television and make it available only to cable television subscribers. To prevent the feared "siphoning" of products from commercial television to pay cable television, the Commission enacted a series of regulations which prohibited cable systems from presenting certain film or sports presentations which were available on "off the air" or on "free" television. Essentially, these Rules attempted to prohibit pay cablecasting of feature films or sports events which traditionally had been broadcast on commercial television.

Significantly, the so-called "siphoning" restrictions arose prior to the 1976 Copyright Act revisions which established a compulsory license arrangement for cablevision. At least part of the impetus for the adoption of these rules was a belief that cablevision was getting a "free ride" by obtaining, at no cost, program material for which television stations had paid significant amounts in copyright fees. The adoption of the compulsory license system influenced the Commission to reevaluate its film and sports programming restrictions. In 1979, the Commission repealed all of these restrictions. See Malrite T.V. v. Federal Communications Commission, 652 F.2d 1140 (2d Cir. 1981).

In sum, the only programming restrictions which still remain upon the type of material which can be presented on cablevision systems relate to the non-duplication protection afforded network programs (47 C.F.R. §§ 76.92 thru 76.99 (1981)), and those portions of the Commission's rules placing a blackout upon the cablecasting of sports events taking place locally (See 47 C.F.R. § 76.67) (1981).

B. OVER THE AIR PAY TELEVISION

Over-the-air pay television (termed "subscription television" by the Commission) is a mechanism by which television programs are broadcast over the air via a scrambled signal, which can be decoded by a device attached for a fee to the subscriber's television set. The material is intended to be received only by those persons who pay a fee or charge. Although not a "new" technology (the first application to establish such a service was filed with the Commission in 1952), nevertheless, for a variety of reasons, regular pay television broadcasting began on a significant scale only in the late 1970's, and as of mid-1982, there were only 27 over-the-air pay television stations in operation in 18 markets.

The critical difference between over-the-air pay television and cablevision, is that pay television uses channels and frequencies which otherwise would be used by the so-called "free" service; pay television and free television thus compete for scarce frequency space. Cablevision, on the other hand, does not use the radio spectrum and thus does not compete for frequency space with the free service. Pay television was vigorously opposed on two grounds: (a) since frequencies are scarce, they should be used only for conventional programming which would be "free"

[*442*]

to all viewers; (b) even if authorized, the Commission should place programming restrictions upon the pay service to prevent the "siphoning" of popular programming from free to pay stations. Although the Commission refused to prohibit over-the-air pay television, it nevertheless placed certain restrictions on the presentation of feature films and sports programming over pay television, the effect of which was to severely restrict the ability of such stations to present certain of these features. The Commission's authority to enact such restrictions (which were virtually identical to restrictions which the Commission initially placed on cable television) was affirmed by the court as a valid exercise of the Commission's power to supervise broadcasting. National Association of Theatre Owners v. FCC, 420 F.2d 194 (D.C.Cir. 1969), cert. denied, 397 U.S. 922, 90 S.Ct. 914, 25 L.Ed.2d 102 (1970).

Despite the affirmance, however, pay television programming restrictions were anomalous. The Court of Appeals had refused to allow the Commission to place the same type of program restrictions upon cablevision systems (see Home Box Office, Inc. v. FCC, 567 F.2d 9 (D.C.Cir. 1977), cert. denied, 434 U.S. 829, 98 S.Ct. 111, 54 L.Ed.2d 89). This left pay television in the vulnerable position of being the only type of "pay" service with program restrictions. Therefore, to treat both services equally, the Commission voluntarily repealed all program content restrictions. 43 Fed.Reg. 15322 (April 12, 1978).

In June, 1982, the Commission removed the last major restrictions to open competition for pay television by repealing the rule whereby pay television stations were prohibited in communities with four or fewer non-subscription ("free") stations. It also repealed the rules which had required pay television licensees to broadcast a minimum of 28 hours per week of "free" programming. The Commission also deleted its ascertainment requirements for pay television stations and its rules requiring pay television licensees to lease (rather than sell) decoders to subscribers. Whether leased or sold, however, charges to subscribers for decoders must be applied on a non-discriminatory basis (47 Fed.Reg. 30069 (July 12, 1982)).

The Commission's rules still prohibit pay television stations from entering into any arrangement which compromises its ability to make a free choice of subscription programs to present. The station can, however, (subject to Commission approval) agree to schedule a specific program at a specific time, or a specific number of hours during the broadcast day, and, upon making a satisfactory showing to the Commission, such a facility may enter into an agreement whereby it agrees to obtain all or a specified portion of its programming from one source.

In sum, pay television stations are now merely a somewhat specialized type of regular television facility, generally subject to the same rules and policies applicable to all television stations (Fairness Doctrine, Political Equal Time and Access

Rules, Lowest Unit Charge Rules, Obscenity Statutes).

C. LOW POWER TELEVISION BROADCASTING

In 1982, the Commission inaugurated low power television (LPTV), the first new broad scale broadcast service authorized in more than twenty years. The LPTV service allows low power stations (maximum power of 100 watts VHF and 1000 watts UHF, encompassing a coverage area of approximately 10–15 miles) to operate on any available channel, on a secondary (i.e., non-interference) basis to regular full service stations. "Secondary basis" means that any low power station creating interference to a full service station must either eliminate the interference or cease operations. See Final Rule, LPTV General Docket No. 82–107, 47 Fed.Reg. 21468, May 18, 1982.

In order to facilitate entry, such stations would be subject to minimal programming rules, i.e., the fairness doctrine, the prohibitions against obscenity and lotteries, the equal time and access rules for political candidates, the anti-payola and anti-plugola statutes, the copyright laws and the personal attack rule. Beyond this, however, the service is virtually unregulated. There are no restrictions on ownership; existing full service stations, networks and cable systems can own and operate LPTV's anywhere in the country with no limitation on the total number which any single entity may own. LPTV stations have no community ascertainment obligations or program log requirements (maintenance logs are required); they may carry pay television programming whether or not there are any "free" television stations in the community, and the Commission has not reserved or set aside any specific channels or frequencies for educational stations. Significantly, LPTV's can carry satellite-originated programming. Therefore, even though each individual station may reach only a limited coverage area, the availability of satellite broadcasting might facilitate the creation of LPTV networks. The minimal regulatory posture adopted by the Commission is grounded on its belief that market forces, rather than regulatory planning, should be allowed to dictate operational and structural aspects of the new service.

The perceived benefits of LPTV include not only a significant increase in new broadcasting outlets (as many as 1,000 new stations in a few years) but also the opening up of new opportunities for ownership by minority groups. The relatively inexpensive nature of these facilities will, it is believed, facilitate entry into the market by minority groups who, for a variety of reasons, came late to the table with respect to the ownership of full service radio and television facilities.

The mere prospect of this new service generated an impressive response. There were 5,000 applications on file for such facilities even before the LPTV service was officially authorized.

Paradoxically, the ease of entry into the service is the factor which most threatens its early implementation. The huge number of applications already on file has strained the Commission's processing resources. The delays and expenses inherent in the comparative hearing process (many of the LPTV applications will be mutually exclusive) threaten to delay full implementation of the service for years. The low power television service is, thus, an excellent candidate for "random selection" (lottery). The Commission initially declined to adopt a lottery system (Report and Order, General Docket No. 81–768, 47 Fed.Reg. 11886 (March 19, 1982). Because Section 309 of the Communications Act has now been revised along the lines sought by the Commission, the agency has now proposed to use a lottery system for this service. See Second Notice of Proposed Rule Making, Gen. Docket No. 81–768, FCC 82–420, Oct. 7, 1982.

D. MULTIPOINT DISTRIBUTION
SERVICE (MDS)

Despite the emergence of cablevision and pay television, and despite the nationwide saturation of television sets, there are still approximately 1.2 million households which have no access to television service and there are approximately 4 million households which receive only one or two channels (see 47 Fed.Reg. at 1967, Jan. 13, 1982). There are additional millions of households which receive only three or four channels. Technologies have been developing to attempt to alleviate the shortage.

The multipoint distribution service (MDS) is one such technological alternative. A multipoint distribution service typically consists of a microwave transmitter and antenna at the transmitting site broadcasting over a microwave frequency omnidirectionally covering a line of sight area of approximately 10 to 20 miles. The signal is then received by a receiving antenna at a particular site. The signal is converted from the microwave frequency to a lower frequency compatible with the customer's television set. The signal is passed from the downconverter through a cable to the customer's set on a VHF channel which is vacant in the community (see 45 Fed.Reg. 29350 at ¶ 24 (May 2, 1980)).

Economically, the arrangement is as follows: the transmitting equipment is licensed to an entity which acts as a common carrier. The licensee as a common carrier does not have control over the programming presented on the channel. Persons wishing to present programming over the system (called "subscribers") lease air time on the transmitter and make the programming available for transmission. Time is usually sold to a programmer on a block basis. The subscriber also typically owns the receiving antenna and the downconverter. The subscriber then contracts with the customer for delivery of the program to the customer's set. In essence, the transaction is very close to a point-to-point transmission, using the air waves rather than a wire.

At present, there are only one or two channels available in most communities for the service, and in many cases there are multiple applicants for the few channels. These channels are being allocated via the comparative hearing method, with all of its attendant delays and expenses. The Commission is holding an inquiry as to a more efficient method and MDS is a prime candidate for selection by lottery. (See CC Docket No. 80–116). Another Commission inquiry seeks to allocate additional MDS channels in the top 50 markets (CC Docket No. 80–112).

Because the service is called a "common carrier" service, neither licensees nor subscribers (i.e., programmers) are subject to the equal time or fairness rules, the access rules for political candidates, ascertainment requirements, program logs or the other doctrines which control broadcast operations. Although the service was first authorized in 1970, there are at present only approximately 185 MDS systems. Most of these systems came into operation in the very late 1970s. Typically, the program fare consists of movies.

E.   DIRECT BROADCAST SATELLITES (DBS)

Satellite communications offers the possibility of program distribution via satellite directly to small, inexpensive receiving dishes located at individual homes, or to larger, more complex commu-

[*449*]

nity antenna systems. Individual applicants would construct and launch satellites, which offer channels available for use by programmers. The final contours of this service are not yet clear. Some programming could be paid for by individual customers (i.e., pay television), some could be advertiser supported. DBS could provide programming to some cable stations and even to some television broadcast stations, thereby perhaps replacing coaxial cable as the nationwide distribution system. Some of the questions which remain to be resolved are: the total number of satellites to be utilized, the number of channels on each, whether satellite time should be bought or leased, the frequencies over which they will operate (this depends on frequency allocation), and the most efficient manner in which to use the available spectrum. The Commission is conducting inquiries on these matters. See Notice of Inquiry, 45 Fed.Reg. 72719 (Nov. 3, 1980).

The advantages of direct satellite broadcasting are obvious. It will add additional programming channels. Perhaps most important, this service can effectively serve inner-city and rural areas where cable television may not be profitable because of the high installation cost. Direct satellite broadcasting is less expensive to offer than cablevision and would clearly increase the number of voices in the marketplace.

Permanent rules will be promulgated in 1983, after an international conference allotting frequencies and orbital slots to the Western Hemisphere nations. In the meantime, the FCC has established interim guidelines for DBS operators. Licenses would be granted for five years, and licensees would be required to meet international guidelines. DBS services with broadcast characteristics would be subject to the broadcast statutes of the Communications Act, but not subject to Commission policies not codified in the Act. The only exception to this requirement is equal employment opportunity, a rule not contained in the Communications Act, but one with which DBS operators must comply. DBS operators offering common carrier-type services are subject only to the common carrier statutes of the Communications Act. The FCC is not requiring DBS licensees to conduct ascertainments and will not restrict the number of stations or channels a licensee may control. 47 Fed.Reg. 31555 (July 21, 1982). Operators have been allocated space on the broadcast spectrum currently occupied by approximately 900 microwave operators who will have to be relocated elsewhere on the spectrum. It is estimated, however, that DBS systems will not come on line until late 1985.

*

INDEX

References are to Pages

[*453*]

.

ADVERTISING
See Commercial Speech

CABLE TELEVISION
As a threat to commercial broadcasting, 440–441
Cable television programming regulations, 440–442
    Nature of pay cable television, 440–441
    Reasons for regulations, 440–441
    Repeal of "siphoning" and other restrictions, 441
Copyright, 426–437
    Compulsory license payment under 1976 Revision Act, 440
    Problems posed by cable transmission of copyrighted materials, 426, 438–440
    Retransmission of programs not a performance for profit under 1909 Act, 439–440
Distinguished from over the air pay television, 442–443
FCC regulation, 424–442
    Areas of, 427–428
    Bifurcated jurisdiction, 428–429
        Commission regulatory authority, 428–429
        Local and state regulatory authority, 429–430
    History and background, 424–438
    Program duplication rules, 432–433
        Commercial network programs, 432–433
        Non-network syndicated programs, 433
        Protection for copyright holders, 432
        Reasons for, 432
        Requirements of, 432–433
    Program origination rules, 434–436
        Original rule, 435
        Present rule, 435
        Reason for, 434–435
        Validity of, 435–436
    Public access rules, 436–438
        Access channels, 436–437
        Cable companies affected, 436, 438
        Prohibition of advertising on public access channels, 437
        Reason for, 437
        Requirements, 436–437
        Voiding of, 437–438
Legal problems posed by Cable Television, 426
    Allocation of regulatory power ("shared jurisdiction"), 426

[*456*]

INDEX
References are to Pages

INDEX
References are to Pages

[*469*]

†